Rethinking Marketing

Rethinking Marketing

Developing a new understanding of markets

Håkan Håkansson
Norwegian School of Management

Debbie Harrison
Norwegian School of Management BI

Alexandra Waluszewski
Uppsala University

John Wiley & Sons, Ltd

Other Wiley Editorial Offices

John Wiley & Sons, Inc., 111 River Street, Hoboken, NJ 07030, USA

Jossey-Bass, 989 Market Street, San Francisco, CA 94103-1741, USA

Wiley-VCH Verlag GmbH, Boschstr. 12, D-69469 Weinheim, Germany

John Wiley & Sons Australia Ltd, 33 Park Road, Milton, Queensland 4064, Australia

John Wiley & Sons (Asia) Pte Ltd, 2 Clementi Loop #02-01, Jin Xing Distripark, Singapore 129809

John Wiley & Sons Canada Ltd, 22 Worcester Road, Etobicoke, Ontario, Canada M9W 1L1

Wiley also publishes its books in a variety of electronic formats. Some content that appears
in print may not be available in electronic books.

Library of Congress Cataloging-in-Publication Data

Håkansson, Håkan, 1947–
Rethinking marketing : developing a new understanding of markets / Håkan Håkansson
with Debbie Harrison, Alexandra Waluszewski.
    p. cm.
"This book is the result of the seminar that was held in May 2003 in Oslo."
Includes bibliographical references and index.
ISBN 0-470-02147-0 (cloth : alk. paper)
1. Marketing—Congresses. I. Harrison, Debbie. II. Waluszewski, Alexandra III. Title.
HF5411.H35 2004
658.8—dc22   2004007923

British Library Cataloguing in Publication Data

A catalogue record for this book is available from the British Library

ISBN 0–470–02147–0

Project-managed by Originator, Gt Yarmouth, Norfolk (typeset in 10/12pt Garamond)
Printed and bound in Great Britain by TJ International Ltd, Padstow, Cornwall
This book is printed on acid-free paper responsibly manufactured from sustainable forestry
in which at least two trees are planted for each one used for paper production.

Contents

Contributors

James C. Anderson is the William L. Ford Distinguished Professor of Marketing and Wholesale Distribution and Professor of Behavioral Science in Management, Kellogg School of Management, Northwestern University in Chicago, USA. He is also the Irwin Gross Distinguished ISBM Research Fellow at the Institute for the Study of Business Markets (ISBM), located at Penn State University in State College, USA and a Visiting Research Professor at the School of Technology & Management, University of Twente, The Netherlands.

Luis Araujo is a Reader in Industrial Marketing at Lancaster University Management School, UK. His research and interests focus on inter-organizational relationships and networks.

Keith Blois is a Fellow in Industrial Marketing at Templeton College, University of Oxford, UK. His research interests include business-to-business marketing, marketing of services, and industrial economics. He has an extensive list of publications including papers in *Strategic Management Journal, Quarterly Journal of Economics, Journal of Industrial Economics, Journal of Management Studies, Long Range Planning, Journal of Business Ethics* and *Industrial Marketing Management*. He is the Editor of *The Oxford Textbook of Marketing*.

Anna Dubois is Associate Professor at the Department of Industrial Marketing, Chalmers University of Technology in Gothenburg, Sweden. She is the author of *Organising Industrial Activities Across Firm Boundaries* published by Routledge in 1998 and has recently published articles on industrial purchasing and networks in the *European Journal of Purchasing and Supply Management, Construction Management & Economics, Industrial Marketing Management, Journal of Management Studies* and *Journal of Customer Behaviour*.

Geoff Easton is Professor of Marketing in the Management School at Lancaster University, UK. He has a DBA from Manchester Business School and a PhD from London Business School. He worked for Rank Xerox, the National Coal Board and DRG before becoming an academic. His research has been mainly in the area of inter-organizational exchange relationships and industrial networks. He also has an interest in the creation and dissemination of marketing knowledge and has written papers and chapters on the sociology of marketing knowledge, critical realism, case research methods and complexity theory simulation. Currently, he is focusing on issues of the everyday behaviour of marketing managers in organizational markets.

David Ford is Professor of Marketing at the University of Bath, School of Management, UK. He is a founder member of the IMP Group of researchers. His current books, written with other members of the IMP group, are *Managing Business Relationships* (2nd edn, John Wiley & Sons, 2003, now also available in Japanese), *Understanding Business Marketing and Purchasing* (3rd edn, International Thomson, 2001), *Managing and Marketing Technology* (2nd edn, International Thomson, 2001, now available in Chinese) and *The Business Marketing Course* (John Wiley & Sons, 2002).

Lars-Erik Gadde is Professor of Industrial Marketing at Chalmers University of Technology in Gothenburg, Sweden and is an Associate of the Faculty of the Norwegian School of Management in Sandvika, Norway. His publications include contributions in the areas of purchasing and distribution in industrial networks. His most recent book is *Managing Business Relationships* (John Wiley & Sons, 2003), co-authored with David Ford, Håkan Håkansson and Ivan Snehota.

Geir Gripsrud is Professor of Marketing and Dean of Bachelor Studies at the Norwegian School of Management, BI, Oslo, Norway. Prior to joining the faculty he worked for several years at the Norwegian Fund for Market and Distribution Research on research projects dealing with the structure of distribution systems and competition in retailing. He has also worked for the Norwegian Trade Council on international marketing, which constitutes his other main area of interest. He has published in a number of academic journals including *Journal of Industrial Economics, Journal of International Business, Journal of Physical Distribution and Materials Management, International Journal of Research in Marketing* and *Journal of Business Research.*

Håkan Håkansson is the NEMI Professor of International Management at the Norwegian School of Management, BI, Oslo, Norway. He is one of the founder members of the international IMP Group. His publications include a number of articles in international journals as well as a number of books. Research interests include the way industrial markets work, especially marketing, technological development and/or purchasing issues.

Debbie Harrison is an Associate Professor in the Department of Strategy and Logistics at the Norwegian School of Management, BI, Oslo, Norway. She has published articles in the *Journal of Business Research, Technology Analysis and Strategic Management* and the *Journal of Management Studies* in the areas of network change, path dependence and relationship dissolution. Her current research interests focus on resource development in user networks and inter-organizational routines.

Inge Jan Henjesand is Associate Professor of Marketing and Executive Vice President for Research and Academic Faculty at the Norwegian School of Management, BI, Oslo, Norway. He earned his PhD at the Norwegian School for Economics and Business Administration, Bergen, Norway. His current research interests include services marketing, generic marketing and the role of the consumer in creating value in the value chain.

Roy Howell is currently the J.B. Hoskins Professor of Marketing at Texas Tech University, Lubbock, Texas, USA, a position he has held since 1982. He served as Chairman of the Marketing Department from 1993 to 1996 and as Dean of the College from 1996 to 2001. He previously served on the faculty at the University of Illinois at Urbana-Champaign. He has served on the Editorial Review Board of the *Journal of Marketing Research*, the *Journal of Marketing* and the *Journal of the Academy of Marketing Science*, among others. His research interests are in the areas of marketing strategy and research methods.

Michael Johnson teaches in Michigan Business School's MBA and PhD programmes as well as at a variety of the School's executive educations seminars. He is one of the founding members of Michigan's National Quality Research Center where he has been instrumental in the development of the American Customer Satisfaction Index. He has published over 100 articles and industry reports throughout his academic career and authored five books including the recently published *Competing in a Service Economy: How to Create a Competitive Advantage through Service Development and Innovation* (Jossey-Bass, 2003). As an industry consultant he works with a variety of companies and public agencies on issues pertaining to managing customer relationships, product and service quality improvement, product and service development, and customer satisfaction measurement and management.

Gøran Persson is Professor of Business Logistics at the Norwegian School of Management in Oslo. He received his MSc and Tech.lic. from the University of Lund in Sweden. His current research interests include logistics alliances and partnership sourcing, logistics strategy and supply chain management. He has written or edited several books on business logistics and supply management and has published in several journals including the *International Journal of Logistics Management, Transportation Review* and *Journal of Chain and Network Science*. He was the first Norwegian to receive the Logistics Management Award in 1990 (the LOGMA Award), and in 1993 he received the Norwegian Purchasing Award by the Norwegian Purchasing Association.

Frans Prenkert holds a PhD in Industrial Marketing from Uppsala University, Sweden. He is currently serving as Assistant Professor and Researcher at the Department of Economics, Business Administration, Statistics and Informatics at Örebro University, Sweden. His research interests include theoretical modelling of markets and business exchange activity, the study of exchange relations, networks and firms as organized human activity systems and the use of information technology in such systems.

Thomas Ritter joined the Copenhagen Business School as an Associate Professor in January 2001 after holding academic positions in Germany and the UK. His main research interests are in business relationship and inter-firm network management, collaborative value creation and the impact of modern information technology on networking. His work has been published in journals including the *International Journal of Research in Marketing, Journal of Business Research, Industrial Marketing Management* and *Journal of Business and Industrial Marketing.* He has also written a book on network competence and edited a volume on international relationships and networks. He has taught various courses on bachelor, MBA and executive-level courses and consults with firms on business network issues.

Fred Selnes is Professor in Marketing at the Norwegian School of Management, BI, Oslo, Norway. He holds a doctoral degree from the Norwegian School of Economics and Business Administration, a master degree in marketing from Northwestern University and became a Bachelor in Business Administration at the Norwegian School of Management. He has published a number of articles related to managing customer relationships, both business-to-business and business-to-consumer. His consulting is primarily related to managing customer relationships, but also covers more general marketing-strategic issues.

Ivan Snehota is Professor of Marketing at the University of Lugano in Switzerland and at the Department of Business Studies at Uppsala University in Sweden. He is the author and co-author of several books and articles on various topics of business-to-business marketing and business development and is a founding member of the IMP research programme on international industrial marketing, or IMP Group.

Sigurd Villads Troye is Professor of Marketing at the Norwegian School of Economics and Business Administration, Bergen, Norway. He earned his PhD at the University of Illinois at Urbana-Champaign. His current research interests include the theory of science and its intersection with methodology and statistics, services marketing, generic marketing and prosumption (i.e., the role of the consumer in the value chain).

Alexandra Waluszewski is Associate Professor at the Department for Business Studies and the STS Centre, Uppsala University, Sweden. Her research interest is industrial and technological development, especially in terms of processes that take place across the borders of both companies and relationships. She has published several studies within both the IMP and STS research traditions and is also a freelance writer.

Preface

In 2002 the Norwegian School of Management received a grant from the Research Council of Norway for a 4-year project entitled "Towards a new understanding of marketing". One of the main activities for the first year was to ask an international group of researchers what they saw as important challenges for contemporary marketing. This book is the result of the seminar that was held in May 2003 in Oslo. We managed to mobilize a number of leading European and American researchers and had a very fruitful seminar. We hope that this book will contribute to the prevailing discussion of what marketing is and should be both in practice and in theory.

For us it has been a very rewarding process. We are grateful to all the contributing authors. We are also grateful to all the participants in the seminar and those who were involved in reviewing different contributions. Especially, we would like to thank the following: Lars-Gunnar Mattsson from Stockholm School of Economics; Ajah Kohli from Emory; Torger Reve, Sophie Cantillon, Nina Veflen Olsen, Atle Følgesfold, Ann Karin Refsland Fougner, Thomas Hoholm, Lars Huemer and Svanhild Haugnes from the Norwegian School of Management; and Ann-Charlott Pedersen and Elsebeth Holmen from the Norwegian School of Technology.

This book should be seen not only as an attempt to create a solid starting point for further research within the project but also for further discussions about marketing.

Håkan Håkansson
Debbie Harrison
Alexandra Waluszewski
Oslo, February, 2004

Introduction: rethinking marketing

1

Håkan Håkansson, Inge-Jan Henjesand and Alexandra Waluszewski

---

Marketing management takes place when at least one party to a potential exchange gives thought to objectives and means of achieving desired response from other parties. (Philip Kotler, 1991)

Marketing is the process of planning and executing the conception, pricing, promotion, and distribution of ideas, goods, and services to create exchanges that satisfy individual and organizational objectives. (AMA, 2004)

Classical marketing thinking and contemporary market exchange

In 1967, when Philip Kotler presented his now widely famous book *Marketing Management*, neither academic nor business audiences were spoiled with approaches offering serious analyses of the concept of marketing. Since then we have witnessed a dramatic increase in academic involvement in this field. When, in the mid-1960s, the American Marketing Association (AMA) launched the *Journal of Marketing Research*, a research journal devoted specifically to marketing issues, the association's membership numbered about 3,000. By the end of the century this figure had increased tenfold. Meanwhile, the successive ten editions of Philip Kotler's work were developed and adapted to more current trends in marketing. They were accompanied by an extensive supply of marketing literature, encompassing everything from basic textbooks to research publications and covering issues ranging from how to handle CRM (customer relationship management) to e-trade.

As marketing research and literature expanded dramatically during the last four decades of the 20th century, so did the issues that a marketing business organization had to manage. For example, in the mid-1960s when one of America's market leaders of pulp production equipment was approached by one of its Scandinavian paper-producing customers to engage in a product development project, the project was primarily carried out between these two parties. Later, however, some German customers got involved to test the new product. Thirty years later,

when the same American equipment supplier was approached by the same Scandinavian customer to engage in a similar product development project, the change
of scenery was fundamental. The American pulp producers had gone through
several mergers to end up as a highly specialized unit within a company that
supplied the paper industry with a wide variety of process technologies.
Moreover, its in-house production had decreased radically. Only certain key
components and assembly were left internally, while the main production
activities were outsourced. The Scandinavian paper producer had become one
unit within a network of suppliers delivering high-quality graphic paper to a
number of large German publishing houses, initiated by the latter to create a co-
ordinated development of certain quality and production volume. These big
German publishing houses had in their turn to cope with consumers who now
could choose between buying a "traditional" paper magazine or an electronic one.
Furthermore, consumers were not only supplied with alternative technological
solutions they also had a strong awareness of environmental issues. Organized
in non-governmental environmental groups these consumers selected publishing
houses with "green" demands on anything from input material and production
processes to the environmental effects of the post-consumption end product. (For
a further description of this case see Håkansson and Waluszewski, 2002.)

Although this short empirical illustration concerns specific companies and how
their marketing endeavours over the last three decades have expanded, both in
terms of issues and interfaces the pattern is typical. From scholars in the history of
technology we know that industrial buying and selling has always been an issue of
more or less deep interaction, whether it concerns steam engines in the 18th
century (Lindqvist, 1984) or electricity consumption in the 19th and 20th
centuries (Hughes, 1983). However, if business organizations in the 1960s and
1970s could still manage marketing as interaction processes including mainly
one counterpart, the complexity in terms of the number of involved actors and
their interconnections increased tenfold during the last decades of the 20th
century. From being an issue of interaction taking place between easily
identified business partners, marketing emerged to become an intricate process
involving a group of somewhat clearly outlined companies and organizations on
both the supply and user sides – each with its special interest in the creation of
supply and demand. Thus, while the academic world engaged in expanding the
theoretical toolbox of economic theory to include analytical models for exploring
the content and function of marketing, the marketing organizations themselves
were struggling with fundamental changes in the market exchange process. This
development confronts the marketing researcher with a challenging issue: To what
extent is there a fit between classical marketing thinking and contemporary
marketing acting?

The issue of how well classical marketing thinking, supplied by the state of the
art of marketing which encompasses analytical tools as well as normative recommendations, fits contemporary marketing activity is far from trivial. It forces us to
consider the underlying assumptions of marketing theory and to confront them

with the empirical characteristics of market exchange. It articulates questions about the suitability of the present analytical tools, when marketing tends to be characterized by diffuse roles and borders between sellers and buyers and when institutional actors, other than the traditional producers and users, start to intervene in the process. Furthermore, it raises questions concerning the suitability of current analytical tools, when efficiency and innovation issues take place in a context characterized by blurred or overlapping borders between production and consumption. To investigate these questions, the state of the art of marketing and its underlying assumptions of the constitution of markets has to be confronted with empirical observations of the main characteristics of contemporary marketing.

Dynamic markets versus a static model world

Any attempt to give an account of the state of the art of marketing is linked with the risk of making oversimplifications and unfair treatment of a very rich range of complex research tools. Despite these risks an elaboration of this view may be useful for several purposes. First, it can increase our awareness of the underlying assumptions on economic exchange that the state of the art of marketing rests on, including how they colour both research analyses and normative advice. Second, it can increase our awareness of the fit or misfit between empirical indications on fundamental market changes and mainstream research tools. Third, a characterization of the state of the art of contemporary marketing theory can expose both recent theoretical contributions in this field and the changing empirical phenomenon they address.

What almost all marketing models have in common, whether dealing with consumers, service or B2B marketing, is the influential heritage from traditional economic theory. Concepts like "markets", "need satisfaction", "market segmentation", "goal formulation", "planning", "implementation" and "control" reveal a rather specific and detailed understanding of how a market and its exchange activities are constituted as well as of how it can be managed. Once developed to simplify and translate the operations of the empirical world to mathematical representations, a main characteristic of the stylized market of economic theory is that it is a non-dynamic arena. But, as Wilk (1996, p. 51) underlines, this successful simplification had a price – it meant "taking away the random, complicating or unique variables", or all the dynamic features that characterize exchange.

A first characteristic of the stylized marketplace is that economic agents that are independent and rational, acting to reach goals that are absolute and consistent, over time populate it and do not influence each other. Second, the resources exchanged in order to reach these goals are considered *homogeneous* (i.e., their value is independent of how they are combined: Pasinetti, 1981). These assumptions fit like a glove with the AMA's (1985) definition of marketing's core activities as being a "process of planning and executing". What appears to be trickier, however, is to match this view with empirical observations of how the market and its exchange activities are constituted and with the new directions in which they are developing. Table 1.1 gives a brief overview of some basic assumptions of the state of the art of marketing theory in contrast with some fundamental empirical observations of markets and their exchange activities, articulated both by academic scholars and the business world (Håkansson and Snehota, 1995; Achrol and Kotler, 1999; Kinnear, 1999; Håkansson and Waluszewski, 2002; Sheth and Parvatiyar, 2000; and Ford et al., 2003).

Let us now discuss these differences in a more detailed way.

Marketing actors according to state-of-the-art versus empirical observations

The role of the marketing actor is, according to Kotler (2001), to strive for "organizational goals of the company being more effective than its competitors in creating, delivering, and communicating customer value to its chosen target markets." Dibb et al. (2001) add attention to the context and claim that the main activity of the marketing actor is to "facilitate and expedite satisfying exchange relationships in a dynamic environment through the creation, distribution, promotion and pricing of goods, services and ideas." Anderson and Narus (1999) focus on the delivered value and the main task of the marketing actor becomes to manage "the process of understanding, creating and delivering value to targeted business markets and customers."

Whether reflected in Kotler's classic work or in some more recent contributions, the view of the *marketing actor* exhibits a high fidelity to the economic actor, once developed within economic theory. As both the table opposite and the quotations above reveal, the typical marketing actor is assumed to be independent from other actors, including the buyers. Marketing actors are believed to have different or even conflicting interests compared with their buyers, the boundaries between them being clear and distinct. Furthermore, marketers and their customers are thought to act in a context characterized by exchange processes allowing optimal resource allocation, where price is the most important exchange mechanism. With this understanding, the role of the marketing actor becomes obvious: to identify targets and to compete. What is left to the customer is to make passive choices between given offers.

When economic actors are understood as independent, separate units with clear boundaries that either provide or receive objects of value, the exchanges that take place may well be described as transactions. The nature of the transaction is such that an object of value (e.g., a good) is exchanged for another (payment). Transactions have no history, and patterns of inter-organizational interchange only reflect the degree to which the conditions for separate transactions have continued to be satisfied. These strict simplifications, combined with "the idea that complications

Table 1.1—Comparing existing theoretical assumptions with empirical observations

	Theoretical assumptions in used models	**Empirical observations**
View of actors and the relationships between them	• Actors are independent • The anonymous, static market exchange is the norm • Business/Organizational units have distinct boundaries	• Actors are interdependent • Dynamic interaction between well-known counterparts is the norm • Business/Organizational units' boundaries blurred due to alliances, joint ventures, logistics partnerships, technical partnership, co-operative development and network-type organization
	• Actors search for information that corresponds to their goals	• Actors do not search and exploit all available information. There is interaction between goals and means
	• Each market transaction has a separate exchange episode as the norm	• Each market transaction has one episode interaction over time due to technical adaptations, commercial adaptations, financial adaptations, social adaptations including customer programmes
View on value creation and innovation	• Value creation and innovation are the supplier's responsibility	• Value creation and innovation are the responsibility of directly and indirectly related companies. Value creation and innovation are increasing due to IKEA-type organizations, value shops, product development on behalf of client companies, outsourcing, alliances and joint ventures

continued

Table 1.1—(*cont.*)

	Theoretical assumptions in used models	**Empirical observations**
	• Distributors and other intermediaries do not engage in value creation and innovation, except in time and space utility	• Distributors and other intermediaries highly involved in innovation and value creation
	• End-users do not engage in value creation and innovation. They just consume what others have provided	• End-users do not just consume they also change the nature of the offering and actively take part in value creation
View on the exchange object	• Easy to identify and separate out (mostly tangible objects that can be transported and inspected prior to delivery)	• Important aspects of the offering are embedded in the exchange process. They are intangible and difficult to separate out (e.g., brand, reputation, service, interactions)

can be introduced once the basic relationships become clear" (Wilk, 1996, p. 51), have certainly contributed to the emergence of a common marketing language, which is both rich and precise. However, the gap between classical marketing thinking and empirical impressions of contemporary marketing is impressive. What appears as particularly restricting is when we, as McCloskey (1990, 1998) argues, treat "economic poetry" as "empirical observations", "stylized facts" or "approximations of the good".

If we, consciously or not, consider the state of the art's marketing actors and their relationship with customers and competitors as the norm, the following empirical observations (among others), described in Håkansson (1982), Håkansson and Snehota (1995) and many business magazines, appear as rather anomalous:

• The average industrial customer–supplier relationship is more than ten years old.
• Both from the supplier and user side there are several functions, such as production, technological development, administration and distribution, which engage in the exchange process.
• Several of these exchange processes are informal and difficult to observe (e.g., direct or indirect co-operative activities among suppliers, customers, end-users, NGOs and institutional actors).
• Several customer–supplier exchange processes become more formalized: "competitors" co-operate in alliances; suppliers and customers engage in joint

ventures; "competing" suppliers create networks in order to engage in logistic partnerships; and customers initiate technical co-operation among "competing" suppliers.

Thus, there is a definite clash between how the nature of transactions is depicted in economic theory, which is central to the state of the art of marketing, and how it presents itself in empirical observations of contemporary marketing. While short-term transactions are the norm of economic theory, repeated interaction or long-term relationships appear as the empirical norm. Even in situations where buyer and seller remain independent in a legal and formal sense and where the interaction is not as deep as within business-to-business exchange, such phenomena as loyalty and customer retention programmes, customer satisfaction surveys, customer hot lines and bonus programmes for preferred customers indicate that firms try to replace transactions by long-term relationships that encompass a much wider range of buyer–seller interfaces and activities than ordering and invoicing.

While "playing the market" is how the buyer behaves according to economic theory and the state of the art of marketing, the empirical norm, whether the purchaser is a professional or a consumer, appears as staying loyal to both companies and products. Both buying companies and buying consumers rely more often on their own experience or the experience of others in their social network as a guideline for future action, rather than efficiently utilizing all available sources of information; for example, when e-trade on the Internet was developed, many professional marketers thought that this arena would facilitate the search for price information and contribute to a frictionless exchange. Empirical experiences draw attention to how the Internet is used to strengthen and renew established interaction patterns, rather than breaking existing relationships. And while passive consumption of a given object is the norm of economic theory, empirical observation draws attention to active purchasing and consumption. Both professional buyers and consumers typically are actively involved in using and changing the nature of the consumption object in different ways.

There are certainly a number of researchers and managers who have observed the same changes and there are a large number of books supporting, for example, the importance of relationships (e.g., Sheth and Parvatiyar, 2000). But, and this is our main argument, the recent attention to the existence of relationships has not changed the basic thinking concerning the constitution of marketing. From a theoretical point of view, relationships are treated as just another aspect to consider beside the "four Ps".

Value creation and innovation according to state-of-the-art versus empirical observations

In the state of the art of marketing, value creation is the task of the marketing actor. Kotler (2001, p. 35) interprets the phenomenon of value creation as follows:

"Customers are value-maximizers. They will buy from the firm they perceive to offer the highest customer delivered value." Building value is, according to Anderson and Narus (2004, p. 86), the process of "what a supplier is doing, or could do, for defined market segments and customer firms." The ability to deliver such value is, according to Best (2000, p. 24), "directly related to its ability to develop market-based strategies that deliver high levels of customer satisfaction." Porter's (1985) widely adopted value chain concept suggests that the marketing firm's ability to create value can be improved through *identifying competitors' costs and performance as benchmarks* to compare and compete against.

Thus, the state of the art of marketing also reveals a great conformity with the basic assumptions of economic theory when it comes to the interpretation of how resources are created and used. Product innovation and value creation are primarily the endeavour of a manufacturing plant, supplemented by the efforts of intermediaries that create time and place utility. Neither professional purchasers nor consumers are regarded as having an active role in the process of product development and value creation. Their function is more that of destruction than production: they consume and digest what others have created.

In the empirical world of marketing this perspective appears as far too narrow. If interaction with professional purchasers has always included innovation and value creation issues, they have been both more evident and more complicated when companies organize in network-like structures. While the model world underlines the importance of a value chain, the empirical world also organizes their interactive development activities in value shops and value networks (Stabel and Fjeldstad, 1998). Companies like IKEA and Dell Computers provide examples of how such interactive development can be organized – despite having limited or no production capacity. Instead of managing the value creation process these companies co-ordinate development interaction over several organizational borders, including issues like product and process development and design.

However, it is not only professional buyers who participate in the innovation and value creation process. IKEA also draws our attention to the role of the consumer in the value creation process: customers can be directly involved in the production of the final product. Furthermore, new production principles, such as just-in-time which is implemented in the computer and automotive industries, and new information systems, which make it possible for the end-customer to specify product requirements prior to the actual point of pro-duction, are both changing the way production and consumption are related.

Key issues in contemporary markets

If it is rather easy to observe certain aspects of the contemporary, fundamental changes in the market exchange process, such as alliances, joint ventures, logistic co-operation and technical partnerships, yet others are more hidden. However, underneath the tip of the iceberg a substantial body of informal co-operation is evolving. If the traditional marketing situation once included an interaction between a buyer and seller with all traditional business activities in-house, today exchange between such counterparts is becoming increasingly rare. Instead, marketing tends to be an issue between exchange partners who are organized in network-like structures. Thus, relationships have become a key phenomenon and an indication of an exchange pattern within the markets far from the one described in Table 1.1.

In contemporary economic literature, attention is increasing toward these network-like structures. There is also an increasing number of approaches that not only pay attention to the emerging network-like structures but also encourage companies to develop them, from cluster schools (Porter, 1985, 1990) to social networks (Powell, 1998). Also, in state-of-the-art marketing the issue of relationships and networks is treated as a positive phenomenon that can be used to create benefits. According to Kotler (2001, p. 7), "long-term mutually satisfying relations with key partners – customers, suppliers, distributors" can be achieved by "promising and delivering high-quality products and services at fair prices to the other parties over time." Building long-term relationships, argue Dibb et al. (2001, p. 153), "encourages a match between the seller's competitive advantage and the buyer's requirements over the life cycle of the items being purchased."

However, as the quotations above indicate, the problem of how to handle the empirical phenomenon of network structures has generally been solved through the method described by Wilk (1996): by hanging on to the underlying assumptions of economic theory and introducing complications once the basic relationships are set clear. Thus, most approaches that pay attention to network-like structures still rest heavily on assumptions made in traditional economic theory. As a consequence, interaction and relationships are treated as some kind of exceptions, occurring within certain geographical or technological areas or certain commercial systems. Inside these structures there are relationships – outside there is a traditional market.

However, if we rethink markets and base our analytical tools on the empirical and theoretical experience of interaction and relationships, the issue of networks and their consequences is grasped differently. If we, as Edith Penrose (1959) suggests, accept that the outcome of exchange activities is a result of the way a resource is activated (which creates some "services"), then the core of any marketing process is to create combinations of resources – within organizations, within relationships between organizations or even due to indirect interaction over the borders of visible relationships. Thus, in order to analyse such processes we need research tools that allow us to capture the interaction between any kind of business or organizational actors engaged in exchanging heterogeneous resources. One possible starting point for such a development is suggested by the industrial network or industrial marketing and purchasing (IMP) network approach and its underlying assumption that a company's technological, social and economic features are the result of its interaction with other companies (for more recent work see www.impgroup.org).

Resting heavily on empirical observations and, among others, the heterogeneity assumption made by Wroe Alderson, Edith Penrose and others, market exchange in the IMP interpretation is a process of handling interdependency and incompleteness – and, therefore, development possibilities and dynamics. If any seller's or buyer's knowledge about each activated resource is never complete and this, especially regards the effects of how the exchanged resource functions in combination with other resources used by the two counterparts, market exchange becomes a process that is truly dynamic. Furthermore, it becomes a process that by definition goes beyond the borders of companies, organizations and individuals – and beyond their visible relationships. In addition, it becomes a process that includes the active involvement of exchanging actors on both the selling and purchasing, or consuming, side.

There are at least three economic arguments that underline the benefits that can be created by a conscious development of a network-like market exchange.

The first argument is that through relationships it is possible to reduce production and other handling costs since activities can be linked to each other across firm boundaries. The relationship makes it possible to reach scale effects even when designing adapted solutions, as the two parties can develop a solution where standardized parts (modulation) are combined with unique ones. In the same way, relationships can be used to reduce the costs for stocks and capital through linking companies to each other. Both these types of efficient relationship solutions are documented within electronics as well as within the automotive and other engineering industries. A similar pattern is also emerging in consumer markets where consumers increasingly enter long-term relationships in order to obtain relational benefits. This can explain why retail bank customers remain loyal to one supplier even if the short-term gain of "playing the market" would be beneficial. The long-term gain of having efficient relationships is affecting consumers' short-term behaviour. A new emerging pattern is that customers will take part in value creation (i.e., production) through increased involvement within the context of relationships. This has become even more so with the emerging communication technologies.

A second argument is that relationships can be used to increase innovation or technical development. Co-operation with customers has become focused, and much interest has been devoted to lead users. Relationships are important as they provide a framework for the resources from the two units to systematically relate to each other. Resources can be combined and confronted, and new features and uses can be found. The development of co-operative relationships in technical development has especially been focused in all developments where the investments in research and development are high. In consumer markets, successful companies also use their customers to guide innovation in both product and process innovation. Continuous monitoring of customer satisfaction has, for example, become common in most companies working with consumers.

A third argument is that relationships can be used to influence others. Such influence can be used to develop the two aspects above, but it can also be a negative factor creating inefficient solutions. A significant finding in studies of consumer behaviour is that most consumers actually do not seek market information in most decision making. Rather, they seem to rely on others' experiences and recommendations, often referred to as word of mouth. The sources are usually their social network and their commercial friendships.

A rethinking seminar and this book

The picture sketched above concerning the gap between classical scientific marketing models and empirical observations of contemporary marketing was the starting point for a seminar in Oslo in May 2003, where a group of researchers came together to discuss these and related issues. The main objective of the seminar was to address fundamental marketing issues based on empirical experiences – relevant both for B2C and B2B. Thus, the seminar questioned the large difference that is expected to exist between these two fields. Still, both the seminar and this book were biased toward investigating the constitution of market exchange, with less attention devoted to the interesting question of whether the differences between B2C (business to consumer) and B2B (business to business) are more a result of analytical thinking than of empirical observations.

The main content of the seminar and this book was a discussion of classical marketing thinking versus empirical interpretations of market exchange: what kind of theoretical tools are we using, what kind of assumptions are they built on and how well does this thinking fit with the empirical problems and opportunities faced by today's marketing actors?

In the following chapters we will look at 11 contributions, each reflecting different aspects of market exchange – with the common denominator that they all challenge the classical way of framing marketing issues. There are three chapters on the way the market is assumed to function in general; five chapters penetrate the basic process of interaction between market actors; three look at scientific approaches to studies of marketing; and the final chapter is an attempt to summarize the contributions in relation to one specific issue: the need for a rethinking of marketing. In other words the need for new scientific approaches that, compared with the existing and dominant marketing mix model, better fit contemporary marketing activities.

References

Achrol, R.S. and Kotler, P. (1999). Marketing in the network economy. *Journal of Marketing*, **63**(Special issue): 146–163.
AMA (2004). American Marketing Association's webpage www.marketingpower.com

Anderson, J.C. and Narus, J.A. (2004). *Business Market Management. Understanding, Creating and Delivering Value.* Upper Saddle River, NJ: Prentice Hall.

Best, R.J. (2000). *Market-based Management: Strategies for Growing Value and Profitability.* Englewood Cliffs, NJ: Prentice Hall.

Dibb, S., Simkin, L., Pride, W.M. and Ferell, O.C. (2001). *Marketing: Concepts and Strategies.* Boston: Houghton-Mifflin.

Ford, D., Gadde, L-E., Håkansson, H. and Snehota, I. (2003). *Managing Business Relationships.* Chichester, UK: John Wiley & Sons.

Håkansson, H. (ed.) (1982). *International Marketing and Purchasing of Industrial Goods.* Chichester, UK: John Wiley & Sons.

Håkansson, H. and Snehota, I. (1995). *Developing Relationships in Business Networks.* London: Routledge.

Håkansson, H. and Waluszewski, A. (2002). *Managing Technological Development: IKEA, the Environment and Technology.* London: Routledge.

Hughes, T. (1983). *Networks of Power: Electrification in Western Society (1880–1930).* Baltimore: Johns Hopkins University Press.

Kinnear, T.C. (1999). Introduction: A perspective on how firms relate to their markets. *Journal of Marketing,* **63**(Special issue): 112–114.

Kotler, P. (1991). *Marketing Management: Analysis, Planning, Implementation and Control* (7th edn). Englewood Cliffs, NJ: Prentice Hall.

Kotler, P. (2001). *A Framework for Marketing Management.* Englewood Cliffs, NJ: Prentice Hall.

Lindqvist, S. (1984). *Technology on Trial: The Introduction of Steam Power Technology into Sweden, 1715–1736.* Stockholm: Almkvist and Wiksell.

McCloskey, D.N. (1990). *If You're So Smart: The Narrative of Economic Expertise.* Chicago: University of Chicago Press.

McCloskey, D.N. (1998). *The Rhetoric of Economics* (2nd edn). Madison, WI: University of Wisconsin Press.

Pasinetti, L. (1981). *Structural Change and Economic Growth: A Theoretical Essay on the Dynamics of the Wealth of Nations.* Cambridge, UK: Cambridge University Press.

Penrose, E.T. (1959). *The Theory of the Growth of the Firm.* Oxford, UK: Basil Blackwell.

Porter, M.E. (1985). *Competitive Advantage.* New York: Free Press.

Porter, M.E. (1990). *The Competitive Advantage of Nations.* London: Macmillan.

Stabel, C. and Fjeldstad, Ø. (1998). Configuring value for competitive advantage: On chains, shops and networks. *Strategic Management Journal,* **19**: 413–437.

Sheth, J.N. and Parvatiyar, A. (eds). (2000). *Handbook of Relationship Marketing.* Thousand Oak, CA: Sage.

Wilk, R.R. (1996). *Economics and Cultures. Foundation of Economic Anthropology.* Oxford, UK: Westview Press.

Powell, W.W. (1998). Learning from collaboration: Knowledge and networks in the biotechnology and pharmaceutical industries. *California Management Review,* **40**(3): 228–240.

Part One
Market forms

One prerequisite when investigating the role of marketing is to examine the constitution of the market when exchange is characterized by interaction between heterogeneous resources. The term "market" is far from neutral in either the academic or the empirical world. It has been and still is used in a wide variety of contexts. It can be related to anything from a market for money, for shares, for products or for marriages. A conceptualization of a market can be highly abstract, such as the international market for currencies, or represent a concrete phenomenon, like a local market for fresh foods. The term is used to identify something that we all have a view of and can relate to – even if we might disagree about how a market works. However, when discussing a topic like "market mechanisms", "market" has a more precise meaning in an economic context. Although this word is often used, as McCloskey (1990) argues, as a description of an empirical phenomenon, it is coloured by its heritage from price theory and interlinked with a specific understanding of other concepts, such as supply, demand, competition, substitutes, and equilibrium. Thus, used in an economic context the word "market" brings with it not just some descriptive dimensions but also a certain logic: there is a specific and clear way in which markets are supposed to function.

In this part of the book, three chapters look at the multidimensionality of the word and how it can be related to the ways in which markets function in the real world. The authors use three rather different approaches, however. Ivan Snehota (Chapter 2) uses a deductive approach and describes how the term attained meaning within the classical models. The author examines some of the key assumptions underpinning the classical understanding of markets and uses research carried out within the IMP (industrial marketing and purchasing) tradition to identify some of the challenges to this view. A central theme is that the pure economic dimension of the classical market model should be complemented with social and technical dimensions. More importantly, due to the interplay with these other dimensions the economic dimension will take new forms. By identifying some "weak" points within the classical view, Snehota argues for the need to develop an alternative theoretical model. This can be used to identify new problems, to reformulate earlier identified problems and to propose alternative suggestions as to how these problems should be solved.

By contrast, in Chapter 3 Keith Blois starts out with a discussion of market forms, which he defines in a specific and concrete way using two cases. The two cases from P&O and Intel give reasons to identify and discuss a variety of market forms. Blois then reviews how these forms are changing; he claims that most market forms will move toward the classical market form over time. In this way the classical market concept becomes a strong attractor. By contrasting economic and social dimensions he reaches a different conclusion from Ivan Snehota's. Snehota uses a deductive approach and Blois a case study approach to discuss the market concept.

In Chapter 4 Geoff Easton uses a bottom-up method based on a critical realist approach to identify important internal and external contingent relations. Easton begins with a single focal exchange and tries to identify some specific entities that will always affect it and others that are more contingent in nature. The author identifies a large number of necessary as well as contingent internal and external relations. The conclusion is "there is a variety of possible influences". Easton demonstrates how difficult and critical all our assumptions are regarding this very basic unit. In the second section of the chapter the emergent character of an aggregated structure is discussed and different ways to conceptualize market forms are suggested.

Taken together there are two major conclusions that can be suggested. The first is the need to find and develop better descriptive models to portray the richness and variety in what is taking place in any market; this is explained in terms of both the exchanges taking place in interactions between buyers and sellers and in the roles of third parties who might influence these exchanges. The second general conclusion is the need for new normative models of markets. There seems to be a need to find at least one alternative to the classically dormant view. The classical market model was developed for a certain specific purpose: resource allocation. However, it appears to be not especially relevant for other issues, such as resource development. The latter is probably one of the most important issues, both in developed and less developed economies.

Reference

McCloskey, D.N. (1990). *If You're So Smart: The Narrative of Economic Expertise.* Chicago: University of Chicago Press.

Perspectives and theories of market

2   *Ivan Snehota*

Introduction

There is a link between pictures, images and behaviour. Behaviour, in general, and purposive action, in particular, are guided by how the objects and phenomena, on which they are directed, are framed and interpreted. Pictures and images depend on the perspective, the angle from which objects and phenomena are observed. The purpose of this chapter is to explore how the perspective taken on the "market" affects the picture and interpretations of it that is the concept and theories of market.

Any object or phenomenon can be observed and approached from different angles, and the different perspectives result in different pictures of the landscape. Dependent on the perspective some features are brought to the foreground and others relegated to the background or hidden. The same feature assumes major or minor proportions depending on the perspective. Every perspective thus entails "distortions" of the object or phenomenon, but then again no picture can embrace all perspectives and any picture always implies a certain point of observation. The question is not whether images are distorted, but to what extent they are suited for the purpose at hand and what guidance they offer for action. The perspective affects explanations in that it points to features and phenomena that need to be explained. It matters especially when we face complex phenomena (Hayek, 1978).

Images of "market", the concept of the market and what the notion of market evokes, do not seem to bother most of those who refer to it in everyday language. They appear to know the meaning of it, and it seems to work perfectly well as a notion that conveys connotations that many apparently can share and occasionally act on. The situation appears to be different for those who are, for various reasons, more extensively and deeply concerned with markets and dependent on how markets work. This is the case for economists, economic historians, sociologists and, not the least, marketers and business managers. Each of these fields approaches "market" from somewhat different angles, depending on their research agendas. The different angles bring into the forefront different features of "the market". Since they approach the market from different angles, agreement on what connotes and defines markets is only partial.

We owe to economists, in particular those of the neoclassical tradition, the most coherent and elaborate concept of the market. It reflects the primary concern of economists with the efficient allocation of scarce resources in society. The neo-classical conception of market as the price determination mechanism is attractive. It has the support of much of the theorizing in economics, is parsimonious and coherent and has gained a special status as the dominant perspective. It has been challenged and questioned for different reasons from many directions, not least among economists themselves. Despite the diffused criticism the neoclassical economist's concept of market has been accepted and is used in several other disciplines, including management, in general, and marketing, in particular.

This chapter is written from the perspective of business management, in particular marketing, for which "market" is an important if not the central phenomenon in the context of managerial action. The need for a concept of market and theories of it that offer guidance to management is paramount. The perspective of neoclassical economics has inspired much of the research in management and marketing, even if other perspectives have been explicitly proposed in the past (e.g., Alderson, 1965). The problem is, as will be argued in this chapter, that the neoclassical perspective on the market often provides only limited guidance for how to act within a market. This is because it leaves unexplained several features of the market that loom large in the management perspective. The proper perspective on the market in the management and marketing disciplines would certainly be one "from within".

The chapter proceeds as follows: in the next section we will review the archetypal conception of markets and briefly review the grounds on which it has been repeatedly questioned; the chapter continues by summarizing some of the empirical research highlighting market phenomena that the traditional market conception does not account for. We will in particular explore the findings of the market-as-network research tradition that focuses primarily on business markets. We will then turn to the elements of an emergent market conception that could provide an account of the empirically observed market phenomena. The last section is devoted to consequences of the emergent conception of markets for management and for further research.

Economists, markets and the critique

Even though economics is generally credited for the most consistent and complete conception and theory of markets, it is not easy to find a summary statement of the market conception in economics. Not even textbooks, introductory or advanced, offer much assistance on this (e.g., Samuelson, 1967; Mankiw, 2001). The Nobel Prize Winner in economics, Douglas North, once observed: "it is a peculiar fact that the literature of economics and economic history contains so little discussion of the central institution that underlies neo-classical economics – the market" (North,

1977, p. 710). This comment remains pertinent even today. A plausible explanation is that, contrary to general belief, most economists are not really concerned with the conceptualization or explanation of the "institution" market. They are mostly concerned with the role of the market in choice behaviour in the situation of resource scarcity, which is the explicit central issue in economics (Robbins, 1932). The market is but a tool in solving the problem of economizing on the use of scarce resources, and such a perspective, therefore, has led to the focus on market as a price mechanism. Indeed, it has been observed that the neoclassical economist does not have a proper market theory but rather a theory of price.

The conception (picture) of the market institution resulting from the neoclassical perspective appears to be widely accepted not only by economists but by other disciplines as well, however. Such a conception of market has become the norm to which most relate, either explicitly or implicitly.

Since mainstream economists are not primarily concerned with the market as an institution it becomes somewhat problematic and arbitrary to outline the conception of the "market" from the neoclassical perspective. It requires grasping the features of the market institution as they can be derived from the assumptions underlying the price theory. So, what are the main features of the market institution that can be derived from the price theory? There are at least three aspects of the market in the neoclassical conception that are relevant for our purpose here; these relate to the boundaries of the market, the nature of relationships among market actors and the dynamics of the market.

With regards to the issue of boundaries, the market is defined as the demand and supply of a product and its substitutes (e.g., Tirole, 1989). It is thus assumed that the boundaries of a market are given by the product. The product is the parameter of the market, while price is the variable over which market actors exercise influence and on which they mostly compete. The actors who form the market are the buyers and sellers of the given product. Basically, every product has a different market in the sense that it has a different set of producers/sellers and consumers/buyers. Market is two-layered in terms of roles: buyers/consumers of the product on one side and sellers/producers of the product on the other side.

Second, the neoclassical conception of markets assumes that interaction among buyers and sellers in the market is restricted to carrying out exchange transactions and price signalling. The importance of other information and interaction among the actors is limited because prices convey all (or nearly all) the necessary information to clear the market and make the exchange happen; this is because both sellers and buyers know the needs and capacities of each other and share the meaning of the product. The exchange takes the form of single discrete transactions, with counterparts offering and agreeing to the "best" price available. The needs and preferences of the buyers and the production possibilities of the sellers are exogenously given and relatively stable. The relationship between a buyer and a seller is only virtual; it consists of instantaneous transactions. No other links exist, nor should they exist for the effective functioning of the market.

Finally, it is assumed that markets are stable and move toward equilibrium on both the seller and buyer side. Markets and their structures can change, but it is a consequence of changes elsewhere that can but not necessarily will be brought into the market. The exogenous factors that can induce change in the market can be the technology that affects the production function of the seller and/or the social sphere that affects the preferences of the buyers/customers. Once such exogenous changes in technology and preferences are imposed on the market, the conduct of market actors tends to lead to equilibrium. The tendency toward equilibrium, thus stabilizing the market, is the consequence of the competition for each transaction among buyers and sellers.

The three features above that can be ascribed to the institution market from the perspective of neoclassical economists are not the fruit of empirical observations. They are derived from the broad assumptions of price theory. The central assumption of price theory in this respect is that buyers and sellers behave rationally, having perfect knowledge and correct expectations. It is not the assumption of rationality (or capacity of purposive behaviour) as such that leads to the conception of a product-defined market with an atomistic structure moving toward equilibrium. It is the assumption of perfect knowledge (or accurate correct expectations), and thus of the possibility of "calculative rationality of market actors" applied to discrete exchange transactions, that is the basis for the conceptualization of market as a price mechanism.

The conception of market stemming from the economist's perspective, characterized by the above features, is widely accepted and used in economics and other disciplines, not the least in management. Yet, it has also been frequently challenged and criticized from different perspectives. The main critique comes from those who were interested in a particular aspect of the market institution and originates generally from dissatisfaction with what such a conception allows in terms of explanations and predictions of certain specific market behaviours and phenomena. What the "critics" appear to have in common is not so much the claim that the neoclassical conception of markets "is wrong", rather it seems to be that the perspective of the market as a price mechanism is insufficient to explain several empirically observable phenomena that characterize the evolution of markets and the behaviours of market participants.

Even among economists the three aspects of the market, as derived from price theory, have been questioned with the argument that such a conception of market does not account for important observable market phenomena. It has been argued that product is a variable rather than a defining feature of the market. The first seed of this argument is present in Chamberlin (1933) and has been taken further, among others, in the tradition of Austrian economics (e.g., Kirzner, 1973). The autonomy of market actors, which is the absence of idiosyncratic mutual orientation and relations, has been questioned by economists belonging to the institutional school and the Austrians. It has been observed that, apart from transactions, continuous interaction is common in many markets and that such interaction appears to be instrumental for the co-ordination of market participants and is needed in order to complement price signals (e.g., Richardson, 1972; Coase, 1988; Lindenberg and Frey, 1993). The notion that the dynamics of markets is simply a matter of exogenous factors (technology and socially determined preferences) has been questioned repeatedly (e.g., Schumpeter, 1934; Penrose, 1959; North, 1990; Langlois and Robertson, 1995). Instead, it has been argued that technological development and preferences to a large extent originate within markets.

Several of those who expressed disappointment with the prevailing conception of markets argued, to put it broadly, that there is a need to explain the dynamics of change in markets and their evolution. It has been repeatedly discussed that the perspective of the market as the pricing mechanism has not much to offer in order to explain economic development; this is because it relegates the factors of change to forces that are external to the market (Schumpeter, 1934; Hayek, 1945; Kirzner, 1973; North, 1977; Coase, 1988). A related issue on which there is some agreement among the critics of the prevailing perspective is that it yields "a theory of value allocation, but it lacks a theory of value creation" (Lazonick, 1991, p. 65). Others have pointed to phenomena that are empirically observable but lacking sufficient explanations in prevailing market theory, such as the growth of the firm and existence of buyer–supplier relationships, similar to the findings of the market-as-network perspective (e.g., Penrose, 1959; Richardson, 1972). More recently, an institutional perspective has found many advocates in order to produce a better understanding of the observable dynamics of markets (e.g., North, 1990; Loasby, 2000).

Disappointment with the dominant market conception has been expressed also in other disciplines concerned with markets and market behaviours. Those concerned primarily with choice behaviour in a market context observed that calculative rationality is not the only form of purposive action and that under conditions of ambiguity (or even uncertainty) "rational choice" is not and should not be following the norms of calculative rationality (e.g., Tversky and Kahneman, 1974; Loasby, 1976; March, 1978; Simon, 1978). Therefore, even without re-nouncing the rationality assumption the assumption of perfect knowledge and accurate expectations provides predictions of market behaviour that simply ignore some important empirical manifestations of the market phenomenon. Building on a long tradition, several sociologists and historians approaching and observing some market phenomena have discussed the difficulty of separating the working of the market from the social and institutional sphere (e.g., Polanyi, 1967; Granovetter, 1985; Smelser and Swedberg, 1994; Lindblom, 2001). Others have been concerned with the relationship between the social structure of markets and economic action (e.g., White, 1981; Willer, 1985; Burt, 1992; Podolny, 2001).

Whatever the ground for the disappointment with the prevailing conception of markets that results from the neoclassical perspective, the critics appear to share the view that alternative conceptions of the market are needed. The discontent with the limitations of the market concept and market theory borrowed from neoclassical economics has also been discussed in management.

The market and management

Interest in the functioning of markets has always been central to the disciplines that have as their main focus studies of business behaviour that we here refer to, somewhat broadly, as the discipline of management; this is only natural given that business conduct is invariably linked to the behaviour of various market actors. Marketing, in particular, has always been concerned with the functioning of the market institution. More recently, research on business strategy has focused on various aspects of market behaviour and generated a number of observations that are difficult to link to the economist's conception of market as a price mechanism.

Much of the early research in the marketing discipline was devoted to the functioning of the market/distribution system (e.g., Alderson and Cox, 1948; Cox and Goodman, 1956); this led to the formulation of elements of a distinct conception of market as an organized behaviour system considered appropriate for business management (Alderson, 1965). Other branches of research in marketing (e.g., consumer behaviour and distribution) remained only loosely related to the dominant market conception and theory.

A shift in attention took place in the marketing discipline in the late 1960s. What happened during that period was that the main thrust of interest and research moved toward management of marketing. In other words, it turned to the various activities and practices involved in managing the market from the perspective of producer/seller organizations (Verdoorn, 1956; Borden, 1964). As attention in research has shifted toward the practices of market management the interest in research on market institutions and processes has diminished. The research and theorizing has drawn heavily on the market conception prevailing in economics. The elaboration of a market concept suitable for management has been left to "applied economics", in particular to industrial organization (e.g., Bain, 1959; Scherer, 1970) and to parts of consumer behaviour research.

There has been, however, a stream of research in marketing that continued to explore the institution of market; namely, research regarding business markets (markets where both buyers and sellers are business organizations). The apparent reason for the origin of that stream of research is that the market conception borrowed from economics and the normative postulates of marketing are of limited use both to gauge and explain various aspects of business markets and to provide guidance for practitioners. The research tradition that would later become the one following the market-as-network perspective (the IMP, or industrial marketing and purchasing, research tradition) started at the end of the 1970s, apparently because of problems met when exploring business markets from the dominant perspective of market as a price mechanism (Håkansson and Snehota, 2000). Such a perspective simply did not permit the explanation of certain features of business markets observed in various empirical studies.

Further, it was building on previous research that observed evidence of several "peculiarities" in business markets (e.g., Levitt, 1965; Ames, 1968).

Empirical research on business markets has produced a substantial amount of empirical evidence of various phenomena in industrial markets that have not been foreseen by the available market theory nor could be easily explained by it. The first, documented in numerous studies over a period of more than two decades, has been the existence of recurrent exchanges and continuous interactions when buyers and sellers are business organizations (Håkansson, 1982). This coincides with the observations of Richardson (1972) on inter-organizational market relationships. There was little in the available market theory to explain why business between two organizations should be conducted on a continuous basis. In light of the prevailing market conception such relations could only be considered dysfunctional or as a sign that business marketing practices were lagging compared with those in consumer markets.

Further empirical research into what characterizes these buyer–seller relationships has brought in relief several features. One of these was the balance of initiative and, thus, the interactive nature of the relationships. Another observation was that social exchange (trust building, commitment) played an important role in developing the economic exchange. It also became apparent that continuous interaction was important for various reasons for both buyers and sellers, in particular for specifying and developing the objects of exchange among the parties. It produced evidence that the continuity of buyer–seller relationships often tends to be superior to the life of a product.

Another phenomenon or aspect of the business markets highlighted by the empirical research was the numerous interdependencies between the relationships of a company, in the sense that what happened in one relationship could produce effects in another. It has been observed that what could be achieved in one relationship was largely dependent on what was happening in other relationships of the two parties, either direct or indirect (e.g., Anderson et al., 1994; Håkansson and Snehota, 1995). The interdependences, when further explored, have turned out to be generalized in business markets. At a later stage, such findings have been formulated in terms of relationships between buyers and sellers in business markets forming an interdependent network-like structure. Further, it has been observed that, because of these interdependences, the continuous adaptations in their content is the rule (Hallen et al., 1991) and the mechanism that not only accommodate but also generate continuous change in market relationships and, thus, in the structure of the market.

Neither the existence of relationships nor the network structures of business markets, both main empirical observations of IMP research, finds an explanation in the conception of market as a price mechanism. Once observed they became the problem of theory and assumed centre stage. Subsequent research has focused more on relationships and their role for market actors and attempted to find explanations for their existence. The perspective, here labelled as "market-as-network", thus yielded different pictures and some hypotheses about how the unexpected phenomena – the development of buyer–seller relationships and interdependences – could be explained.

The mounting empirical evidence has led to formulating numerous hypotheses regarding critical relationship processes and the role of relationships for the market actors involved. The hypotheses that emerged appear to fall into three broad categories: the first is that social relationships play an important role and affect in various ways how the business relationship develops (e.g., Håkansson, 1982; Easton and Axelsson, 1992); the second is that interdependences and continuity in relationships favour, in particular, the development of new technical and other solutions in business (e.g., Håkansson, 1989; Lundgren, 1995; Håkansson and Waluszewski, 2002); and finally, that continuity is important for economy in the use of resources in business enterprises not only within given resource structures but also over time (e.g., Håkansson and Snehota, 1995; Gadde and Håkansson, 2001).

Those who study business markets have not been the only ones to find that the concept of market concept resulting from the market-as-mechanism perspective is of limited use for their particular purposes. Within the marketing discipline there was, until the dominance of marketing management, a long tradition of approaching the market from a distinct perspective. It pointed to the systemic dimension of the markets and postulated the notion of market as a complex behavioural system (e.g., Alderson and Cox, 1948; Cox and Goodman, 1956; Alderson, 1965) in which various actors interact with different roles. Similar arguments seem to be underlying much of the research in marketing on distribution systems and channels (Stern and Reve, 1980). Likewise, research on markets for services appears to yield empirical observations that emphasize the role of relational exchange (e.g., Gronroos, 1994). There are thus various research streams dealing with the functioning of markets that appear to point to the same phenomena (Webster, 1992) and tend to conclude that there is a need for an alternative concept of market and theories to explain the functioning of the market institution.

The empirical research in the market-as-network perspective has found support from many of those who found the application of the dominant market conception from neoclassical economics problematic, not only within the discipline of management but also in economics, sociology, economic history, etc.; this has oriented the empirical research and inspired the conceptualizations in the market-as-network tradition that have drawn heavily on concepts elaborated elsewhere. The market-as-network perspective yields a conception of market that is equivalent to the idea put forward in some of these disciplines that market is, primarily, an institution. The argument has been that it is an institution in so far as it consists of a set of actors connected by exchange relationships to a network-like pattern of behaviours. The conception of market as an institution means that its form is always specific, resulting from interaction of its elements: the single actors that form the institution and the institution are formed by evolutionary processes. It also implies that institutions are the structures in the context of action which impose limits on but also enable action.

However, the broad implications of the network perspective for conceptualizing markets and theory have not been addressed systematically. Rather, the implications have been discussed with respect to one or other partial aspect of the picture produced from the market-as-network perspective. Seldom has the discussion been at the level of the market concept as a whole (for an exception see Ford et al., 2003). In taking a broader perspective of the findings of this research tradition, we could paraphrase Coase's (1988, p. 1) argument: "the very arguments of the market-as-network perspective appears as so simple that they seem to be self-evident, their rejection or incomprehensibility would seem to imply that others have a different way of looking at the market and do not share such a conception of the marketing subject." Indeed, this appears to be the case.

Given the quest for an alternative market conception and theory both in management and other disciplines, it appears timely and desirable to link the various empirical observations and partial hypotheses and to sketch a coherent conception of markets and elements of an emergent theory of markets.

The essence of market as a network

When we confront the conception of market resulting from the neoclassical perspective with the conception of market as a network we face two pictures that differ significantly on several aspects of the phenomenon, aspects that appear not to be marginal for the behaviour of a market actor. The question remains whether these differences matter.

The issue that we will turn to next is not whether the picture of the market from the market-as-network perspective is realistic nor is it whether and to what extent it has been adopted, rather it is whether the differences matter for the market actor's conduct. The position that we will take here is that pictures matter because of their impact on how those involved act on or within the market. Conception is important in the context of social reality, where the map is not only guidance for action but also the foundation of the actual future context within which actors will perform. Such a stance is hardly debatable as it has been voiced and accepted in several disciplines (e.g., Thibaut and Kelly, 1959; Loasby, 1976; Coase, 1988; Moran and Ghoshal, 1999).

The picture of the market produced in these empirical studies of business markets and emerging elsewhere stands in marked contrast to the prevailing neoclassical conception. First, it emphasizes rich communication and interaction between market actors (mainly buyers and sellers), entailing not only information exchange but also important elements of social exchange. Building some degree of trust and commitment appears a necessary condition for conducting economic exchange transactions. The interaction and communication tends to have a time dimension; there is some need for mutual adjustments and, thus, for continuity. The past and expected future interaction tends to bind selectively specific actors and creates specific interdependences.

It indicates that markets tend to consist of a variable set of actors connected by continuous relationships within which different goods are transacted. What characterizes and defines the market is the set of actors and relationships rather than the product. Product is a variable in the single exchange relationships and across relationships between actors. All market actors are differentiated (hetero-geneous) with respect to the products they demand and offer. They are also differentiated with respect to their roles they are set. Sellers are not necessarily manufacturers, and buyers not necessarily consumers; their sets of relationships can overlap, but are never identical. As a principle the market appears as a net of relationships that is difficult to confine, if not endless. Setting boundaries becomes somewhat arbitrary. A market can be defined as a subset of relationships and actors that are "relevant" for a certain focal actor. There are significant interdepen-dences and cross-effects between these subsets (actor-relevant markets).

Finally, despite the evident continuity the market appears to be inherently unstable (evolutionary) as the participants continuously change and revise their plans and modify the content (also in terms of product) of their relationships. They mutually adjust to each other's behaviour and to exogenous changes. Such adjustments produce endogenous dynamics in technology and resource conception. On the whole the picture of the market based on the findings of research adopting the network perspective suggests that there is a need to reconsider the notion of "economic logic" and to focus on the dynamics of markets as a result of market actors' behaviour. Two broad considerations can be made.

The first is related to the time dimension. Focusing on relationships and postulating relationships as a central phenomenon in the market landscape amounts to introducing the time dimension in the market concept. Relationships arise over time and because the past is projected on the future. In fact, saying that the market-as-network perspective produces a picture, as we have done several times above and will continue for the sake of simplicity to do in the following, is somewhat misleading. The perspective produces snapshots of a movie, but emphasizes that the interpretation of a picture is as a part of a sequence and only has meaning with respect to the preceding and subsequent pictures; this, of course, has some implications for what can be observed and how it can be analysed.

The underlying theme is that buyers and sellers, being limited in their knowledge and understanding of the context in which they act or bounded in their rationality, do find in continuous market relationships (and interaction) a way to overcome their own limitations. In particular, relationships become a way to deal with the unpredictable and unforeseeable future. Continuous interactive market relationships permit not only access to the resources of others but also the ability to find and work out solutions to problems they meet by drawing on the experience and capabilities of others. Relationships that exist in the market appear thus to be instrumental to solve, broadly, the resource problem of the actors under conditions of uncertainty (Ford et al., 2003). The market, with its network of patterned relationships, thus appears as more than the mechanism to facilitate exchange, as implied in the market-as-price-mechanism perspective. It appears as a platform that facilitates the economic behaviours of the boundedly rational market actors.

The second consideration broadly regards the "economic logic". There is often a common and evidently dubious conclusion that some draw from the picture of a market as a network-like set of relationships that connects actors. It is that many markets certainly display the continuous relationships between buyers and sellers, but that these are due to other factors that interfere with the concern about economy. The relationships arise because other factors, such as politics and socially motivated behaviours, sometimes prevail and interfere with the pursuit of "economy" by the market actors. There is nothing in the research findings that actually supports such an opinion, rather the contrary is the case. We can point to the fact that the findings of network-like structures stem primarily from observations of markets where "economy" in the broadest sense is of primary concern for both buyers and sellers. These are markets where both buyers and sellers are businesses that systematically and explicitly declare that they pursue "economic returns" and apply as a rule the criterion of economic impact of their market conduct on their own organization.

The empirical observations suggesting the network structures of market do not necessarily imply "economic inefficiency". Economy remains the leitmotif in the conduct of market actors, even when it gives origin to a network-like structure. It may be more dependent on how the "economy" or economic efficiency is conceived. If "economy" is taken broadly and is not limited to the efficient allocation of existing resources, but referred to making the best use of past, actual and future resources, it is not incompatible with a network structure of markets. It also seems consistent with broader formulations of the nature of the economic problem, not uncommon even in economics (e.g., Hayek, 1945; Coase, 1988; Lazonick, 1991; Moran and Ghoshal, 1999).

An emergent conception and theory of markets: some conjectures

A fully-fledged alternative conception of markets and related theory has yet to be elaborated. However, the various empirical observations and hypotheses generated in the research reviewed here (in particular, but not exclusively, the one adopting the network perspective on business markets) suggest some central "issues" that have to be addressed. The issues originate in the phenomena observed and attempts and conjectures to explain them.

The conjectures below on the issues an alternative conception and theory of markets should address are stimulated by research on business markets that certainly display several peculiar features. Certain aspects, such as the role of continuous buyer–seller relationships, interdependences and change processes, become much more visible in business markets. The question becomes whether such features and aspects can be extrapolated to markets in general. As we pointed out earlier there is some evidence that such features are present in other markets (e.g., service markets and consumer markets). Another factor to consider is that the economic relevance of "business markets" is anything but marginal. Business markets appear thus not only relevant but also emblematic of markets in general.

The first issue is related to the dynamics of market change. Market actors strive to act purposefully and pursue in many respects the "economic logic" of effective use of available resources for their purpose. In doing so they are limited in their cognitive capacity. Their rationality of action is bounded. They act and have to act with only incomplete and partial knowledge and information. Purposive action requires under such conditions that they operate a closure by framing and stabilizing their interpretation of the context (e.g., Thompson, 1967; Goffman, 1974). Being based on incomplete and partial knowledge any such closure and framing on the part of the actors is only temporary. Market actors continuously revise and adapt their framing, interpretation and behaviours as a consequence of experience. Interaction with others is a major source and factor in the continuous adaptations in the cognitive structures guiding their behaviours. The important source of change is, thus, the interaction within the market rather than simply adaptation to changes exogenous to the market; this makes markets inherently unstable and subject to continuous evolution. Like all institutions, markets are made up of actors whose behaviours are locked in a network-like structure that enables and constrains those that take part in it. Markets are thus in continuous making – an enacted evolutionary structure. Accepting such a notion we also have to accept that no market can ever become optimally structured unless all of its actors fully share the same way to frame and interpret the context of action.

The second issue is related to the role of "relationships" that arise between market participants. The striking propensity to engage in continuous interaction and exchange with a selected and restricted set of others appears instrumental to purposive behaviour. The often-observed processes of trust building and commitment underlying the formation of relationships suggests that continuous relationships are a way of operating the necessary closure of the context of action; this process is mutual, not unilateral. Mutuality in the formation of relation-ships permits collective action, in that it allows one actor to draw on the actions of others and to transcend their own limitations, thus creating interdependence; this also appears to be clearly relevant for the economy (the resource aspect) of the behaviour of market actors. It permits one actor to draw on other's resources and to become a resource element for anothers. Continuous interactive relationships, as the backbone of exchange transactions, thus become the means if not a necessary condition of purposive action with economic logic. They do not appear to be an impediment of "economic rationality".

The third issue regards the notion of the "entity" of the market. In taking the institutional perspective, markets are made up of the exchange relationships between participants. There are interdependences between the relationships and between the actors. New relationships develop and existing ones become modified over time. Actors enter and exit the market. The market institution is thus made of an endless web of a variable amount of interdependent relationships and actors. Products are but a means in the formation of the relationships and a factor in their structuring rather than the defining element of market boundaries. The neatly confined product markets are an abstraction. The substantive feature of the market is, thus, that there is hardly any given way to confine a portion of the endless market that is not arbitrary. If a relevant unit of analysis is to be proposed, then it seems to be the portion of the market network that lies within the horizon of an actor – which, alas, is always subjective and shifting. We have thus to cope with the variable unit of analysis, the set and the net of the relationship within the horizon of a "focal" actor.

The fourth issue regards the critical structural dimension of the market. If we rule out the possibility of defining a market on the basis of product homogeneity, then the critical dimension of the market structure cannot be reduced to the size and relative bargaining power of buyers and sellers of the given product. Hetero-geneity, in the sense of differentiation (of roles, relationship contents, objects of exchange), appears to be the critical structural dimension of markets. It is so both in the perspective of the single individual actor and in a collective perspective. To the extent that market relationships are enabling the purposive action of its participants it is the entire set of relationships that the single actor is involved in and the complementarity between them that matters. Indeed, actors appear to precisely exploit the existing variety of roles and relationships and their comple-mentarity to their own roles and sets of relationships. From a more collective perspective the continuous process of making the market, entry and exit of actors and the emergence and disappearance of relationships between them appears to drive the market toward ever-increasing differentiation of roles, positions and resource elements.

The fifth issue is related to the heterogeneity of the market and regards the critical process in the positioning of the various market actors in the market context. Heterogeneity, in the sense of variety and diversity of market relationships and roles, makes the latitude of the actor in the market network critical. The co-ordinates of the actor appear critical because it is these that ultimately enable and constrain the repertoire of the purposive action. The latitude of the actor is, however, neither given nor stable, but rather enacted; this makes "connecting" to others the critical process in the market. The broad generic notion of connecting apparently entails three aspects: it involves associating the heterogeneous categories of the context to a "justified whole", required in order to operate the closure necessary for a purposive action with limited knowledge and information;

it consists of combining heterogeneous elements on the basis of their complementarity for this purpose; and, finally, it implies the enactment of necessary couplings to the other actor's resources and activities.

Developing a conception and theory of markets which would meet the need for "guidance" for action in markets requires taking a stance on the above conjectures and above all accommodating the empirical evidence of the phenomena these have been derived from. As far as we can see it requires replacing some of the cornerstones of the prevailing neoclassical market conception. But, above all it seems to require reformulating the conception of economic rationality in order to accommodate the conditions of the context in which it is taking place. Among these the "genuine ambiguity" the market actors face and have to cope with appears to be the most critical.

Such a consideration makes the development of the alternative conception and theory of markets a formidable task that can hardly be accomplished within the bounds of marketing or, for that matter, the management discipline alone. On the other hand, it appears to be the task that besets not only the disciplines of management; we have pointed out that similar efforts are being made in several related disciplines. Such efforts are promising for the possibility to develop a conception and theory of market that is better suited for the purpose of guiding managerial action.

Implications for further research

Among the academics concerned with the various fields of management it is common to be explicit about the consequences of an empirical finding for the practice of management and research. Many have been advocating the need to explicitly link the research findings to management practice; others, however, have been taking the stance that the implications can only be gleaned by those who face the problem of practice, whether the practice is one of management or research. It lies in the nature of the task that any attempt to explore the consequences of a perspective is likely to meet scepticism with respect to this and that conclusion. Broad generalizations regarding research in a discipline tend always to be faulty and unfair, for any discipline tends to harbour at any time several different strands of research. But then, contrasting views and interpretations are a prerequisite for any advancement of "usable knowledge". The above discussion may not provide an exhaustive account of the emergent market conception, but there are several signs that a lot of research points to the need for a different conception and indicates the direction in which it is likely to be developed.

The discipline of marketing could be a suitable forum. Until the emergence and dominance of marketing management in the 1960s much of the research concerned the ways markets or market systems function. There is nothing wrong in the move to management practices in marketing or the normative ambitions if it works: that is, if it offers effective guidance for marketing practice. Observations of some practices that produce results need not be based on consistent explanations or theories. "Scientific" marketing would require systematic explanations of why certain practices work and others do not. Indeed, such a concern may be pointless. However, those who advocate the "scientific grounding" have a point when they argue that systematic explanations (theories) make it possible to devise new practices, rather than relying on those traditionally in use. It raises the question whether we have workable conceptions and theories of markets for the purpose of marketing management. There appear to be signs that better theory is needed and that the interest in developing alternatives to the theory of markets is increasing (e.g., Venkatesh, 1999; Hunt, 2002; Levy, 2002).

There are several considerations for how research can be developed. One is that empirical research needs to be paralleled by more intense efforts in theory construction. It also implies that some of the empirical research needs to be devoted to more systematic testing of the hypothesis and the postulates resulting from the theory-building effort. In turn, this would require formulating hypotheses that are broader than what we currently see: that is, hypotheses deduced from empirical observations regarding some, more or less restricted, aspects of market and practices in market conduct. Another consideration regards the reach of the institutional perspective. The perspective appears fruitful, and resulting explanations are supported by the empirical findings that regard inter-organizational markets (business-to-business), but there are also signs it can be extended to other markets. Such an extension requires testing whether it yields workable explanations for other types of markets. There seem to be several signs that it might.

What issues should the research and conceptualization efforts focus on? This is a question that is even more difficult to answer. One issue is to explore and conceptualize the critical processes and variables in the formation and evolution of the institution "market". Another is the development of a conceptual framework to enrich the notion of economic logic, rationality and development. For our purposes here we can suggest two categories of such processes: those at work in single individual relationships and those that are at work at a collective network level. Processes that appear critical at the micro-level of interaction within a relationship are interesting. A common theme seems to be that they are related to mechanisms of cognition and communication: to framing of the problems and connections in interpretation of problems and conceptions of possible solutions. Exploiting the heterogeneity and the conflicts in framing the problems and devising solutions appears, thus, an area for future research and conceptualization. Another research area regards the issues that appear critical on a collective level, and this is one of connecting and disconnecting various network elements and balancing the forces of conforming and confrontation, consolidation and creation, and coercion and concession (e.g., Rosa et al., 1999; Loasby, 2000; Ford, 2003). On the whole it appears that what needs to be explored further is the socio-cognitive dimension of the market institution because it may provide the key to its dynamics which is what matters most as guidance to the behaviours of those that act on it.

References

Alderson, W. (1965). *Dynamic Market Behavior* (pp. 67–118). Homewood, IL: Richard D. Irwin.

Alderson, W. and Cox, R. (1948). Towards a theory of marketing. *Journal of Marketing*, **13**(2): 137–152.

Ames, B.C. (1968). Marketing planning for industrial products. *Harvard Business Review*, **46**(5): 100–111.

Anderson, J.C., Håkansson, H. and Johanson, J. (1994). Dyadic business relationships within a business context. *Journal of Marketing*, **58**(October): 1–15.

Axelsson, B. and Easton, G. (eds) (1992). *Industrial Networks: A New View of Reality*. London: Routledge.

Bain, J.S. (1959). *Industrial Organization*. New York: John Wiley & Sons.

Borden, N.H. (1964). The concept of the marketing mix. *Journal of Advertising Research*, **4**(June): 2–7.

Burt, R. (1992). *Structural Holes: The Social Structure of Competition*. Cambridge, MA: Harvard University Press.

Chamberlin, E.H. (1933). *The Theory of Monopolistic Competition*. Cambridge, MA: Harvard University Press.

Coase, R. (1988). *The Firm, the Market, and the Law*. Chicago: University of Chicago Press.

Cox, R. and Goodman, C.S. (1956). Marketing of house building materials. *Journal of Marketing*, **20**(July): 36–61.

Ford, D., Gadde, L-E., Håkansson, H. and Snehota, I. (2003). *Managing Business Relationships* (2nd edn). Chichester, UK: John Wiley & Sons.

Gadde, L-E. and Håkansson, H. (2001). *Supply Network Strategies*. Chichester, UK: John Wiley & Sons.

Goffman, E. (1974). *Frame Analysis: An Essay on the Organization of Experience*. New York: Harper & Row.

Granovetter, M. (1985). Economic action and social structure: The problem of embeddedness. *American Journal of Sociology*, **91**(3): 481–510.

Gronroos, C. (1994). From marketing mix to relationship marketing: Towards a paradigm shift in marketing. *Management Decision*, **32**(2): 4–20.

Håkansson, H. (ed.) (1982). *International Marketing and Purchasing of Industrial Goods: An Interaction Approach*. New York, John Wiley & Sons.

Håkansson, H. (1989). *Corporate Technological Behaviour: Cooperation and Networks*. London: Routledge.

Håkansson, H. and Snehota, I. (1995). *Developing Relationships in Business Networks*. London: Routledge.

Håkansson, H. and Snehota, I. (2000). The IMP perspective: Assets and liabilities of business relationships. In: J.B. Sheth and A. Parvaktiyar (eds), *Handbook of Relationship Marketing* (pp. 69–94). San Diego, CA: Sage.

Håkansson, H. and Waluszewski, A. (2002). *Managing Technological Development.* London: Routledge.

Hallen, L., Johanson, J. and Seyed-Mohamed, N. (1991). Interfirm adaptation in business relationships. *Journal of Marketing,* **55**(2): 29–37.

Hayek, F.A. (1945). The use of knowledge in society. *American Economic Review,* **35**(4): 519–530.

Hayek, F.A. (1978). The pretence of knowledge. In: F.A. Hayek (ed.), *New Studies in Philosophy, Politics, Economics and the History of Ideas* (pp. 23–34). London: Routledge & Kegan Paul.

Hunt, S.D. (2002). *Foundations of Marketing Theory* (pp. 3–30). New York: M.E. Sharpe.

Kirzner, I.M. (1973). *Competition and Entrepreneurship.* Chicago: University of Chicago Press.

Langlois, R.N. and Robertson, P.L. (1995). *Firms, Markets and Economic Change.* London, Routledge.

Lazonick, W. (1991). Business Organization and the Myth of the Market Economy. Cambridge, UK: Cambridge University Press.

Levitt, T. (1965). *Industrial Purchasing Behavior.* Boston: Harvard Business School, Research Division.

Levy, S.J. (2002). Revisiting the marketing domain. *European Journal of Marketing,* **36**(3): 299–304.

Lindblom, C.E. (2001). *The Market System* (pp. 1–107). New Haven, CT: Yale University Press.

Lindenberg, S. and Frey, B.S. (1993). Alternatives, frames and relative prices: A broader view of rational choice theory. *Acta Sociologica,* **36**: 191–205.

Loasby, B.J. (1976). *Choice, Complexity and Ignorance.* Cambridge, UK: Cambridge University Press.

Loasby, B.J. (2000). Market institutions and economic evolution. *Journal of Evolutionary Economics,* **10**: 297–309.

Lundgren, A. (1995). *Technological Innovation and Network Evolution.* London: Routledge.

Mankiw, N.G. (2001). *Essentials of Economics* (2nd edn). Fort Worth, TX: Harcourt College.

March, J.G. (1978). Bounded rationality, ambiguity, and the engineering of choice. *Bell Journal of Economics,* **9**(2): 587–608.

Moran, P. and Ghoshal, S. (1999). Markets, firms, and the process of economic development. *Academy of Management Review,* **24**(3): 390–412.

North, D.C. (1977). Markets and other allocation systems in history. *Journal of European Economic History,* **6**(3): 703–716.

North, D.C. (1990). *Institutions, Institutional Change and Economic Performance.* Cambridge, UK: Cambridge University Press.

Penrose, E.T. (1959). *The Theory of the Growth of the Firm.* Oxford, UK: Blackwell.

Podolny, J. (2001). Networks as pipes and prisms of the market. *American Journal of Sociology,* **107**: 33–60.

Polanyi, M. (1967). *The Tacit Dimension.* Garden City, KS: Double-Anchor.

Richardson, G.B. (1972). The organisation of industry. *Economic Journal,* **82**(September): 883–896.

Robbins, L. (1932). *An Essay on the Nature and Significance of Economic Science.* London: Macmillan.

Rosa, J.A., Porac, J.F., Runser-Spanjol, J. and Saxon, M.S. (1999). Socio-cognitive dynamics in a product market. *Journal of Marketing*, **63**(Special issue): 64–77.

Samuelson, P.A. (1967). *Economics*. New York: McGraw-Hill.

Scherer, F.M. (1970). *Industrial Market Structure and Economic Performance*. Chicago: Rand McNally and Co.

Schumpeter, J.A. (1934). *The Theory of Economic Development*. Cambridge, MA: Harvard University Press.

Simon, H.A. (1978). Rationality as process and as product of thought. *American Economic Review*, **68**: 1–16.

Smelser, N.J. and Swedberg, R. (1994). *The Handbook of Economic Sociology*. Princeton, NJ: Princeton University Press.

Stern, L.W. and Reve, T. (1980). Distribution channels as political economies: A framework for comparative analysis. *Journal of Marketing*, **44**(Summer): 52–64.

Thibaut, J.W. and Kelly, H. (1959). *The Social Psychology of Groups*. New York: John Wiley & Sons.

Thompson, J.D. (1967). *Organizations in Action*. New York: McGraw-Hill.

Tirole, J. (1989). *The Theory of Industrial Organization*. Cambridge, MA: MIT Press.

Tversky, A. and Kahneman, D. (1974). Judgment under uncertainty: Heuristics and biases. *Science*, **185**: 1124–1131.

Venkatesh, A. (1999). Postmodernism perspectives for macromarketing: An inquiry into the global information and sign economy. *Journal of Macromarketing*, **19**(2): 153–169.

Verdoorn, P.J. (1956). Marketing from the producer's point of view. *Journal of Marketing*, **20**(January): 221–235.

Webster, F.E. (1992). The changing role of marketing in the corporation. *Journal of Marketing*, **56**(October): 1–17.

White, H.C. (1981). Where do markets come from? *American Journal of Sociology*, **87**(3): 517–547.

Willer, D. (1985). Property and social exchange. *Advances in Group Processes*, **2**: 123–142.

The "market form" concept in B2B marketing

3

Keith Blois

Introduction

A firm will typically create a number of different product families[1] (goods, services or a mixture of both). While the firm's overall aim must be to make a profit it is clear that this may not be the objective with regard to any individual product or, indeed, any individual exchange. Thus, while the sale of a particular product to an individual customer may not of itself realize a profit it could be undertaken because the management perceives that this action benefits the firm in some manner that cannot be precisely measured: for example, a firm might believe that being known as a supplier to a particular well-regarded customer will enhance its reputation. It consequently may make sales to that customer at a price that it knows does not generate an accounting profit, but it believes is justified because of the anticipated reputational benefits. So, while each product and exchange must be seen as adding to the value of the firm's position they will not all be even expected to generate a profit. Therefore, the discussion in this chapter will take the generic term "value creation" as the objective of the marketing of a specific product (hereafter referred to as the focal product).

There are arguably at least two categories of exchange with which a firm will engage: the first is expected to be profitable in its own right, but the second is only expected to contribute to the company's overall profitability in an indirect manner. Both these types of exchange will involve direct contact with other organizations in the form of "restricted exchanges" (Bagozzi, 1979) and as such these organizations are identifiable.

There is, however, the possibility that a third group of organizations exist which will impact on a firm's ability to create value; this is the case even though these organizations are not competitors, potential market entrants or suppliers of potential substitute products nor is there currently any exchange between the

---

[1] A "product family" is a set of products that share a common platform (i.e., the design and components are shared by a set of products), but have specific features and functionality required by different sets of customers. For ease in the rest of this paper "product family" will be abbreviated to "product" (Meyer and Utterback, 1993, p. 30).

firm and them. Because of this it is argued in this chapter that an extended view of "the market" is called for so that this third group of organizations can be incorporated in the analysis. This extended view will be labelled the *market form*.

Given the disparate conditions under which products are marketed this chapter will take the view that, except for single-product firms, there cannot be just one relevant market form, but that a firm is likely to be involved with a series of market forms. Indeed, given that an industrial product may often have numerous alternative uses, possibly more than one for each product. There may well be very close links between these various market forms, but in this chapter the concept of market form will be considered with regard to a single product.

Two examples of complex market structures are first presented, and from this a definition of the term market form is proposed. A discussion of the nature of exchanges within a market form then follows and the manner in which they might be expected to evolve is considered, taking particular account of the role of social relations in exchanges. Finally, the reasons these social relationships may be expected to weaken over time are set out and it is argued that there is a tendency for the market form's structure to converge toward the economist's perfect market model.

The intricacy of the market form phenomenon

Given both the historic and current importance of markets in the development of society it is not surprising that they are a major topic of study for a number of academic disciplines (see Swedberg, 1994 for a brief but insightful discussion of the history of the concept from the point of view of economics and, separately, of sociology). It is though surprising that there is so little agreement as to what a definition of market might be or how markets are constituted. Indeed, differences of view occur within academic disciplines and not just between them. However, in spite of the variety of views about markets the common position is that they provide a mechanism by which prices are determined.[2] Discussions of markets have therefore been concerned with understanding the manner in which the activities of a number of institutions and forces together determine the extent to which a firm has freedom to set prices and, thus, the extent to which it is able to create value realizable in economic terms.

As such, these discussions have been concerned with those organizations with which a focal firm engages in exchanges directly, as in the case of a customer or a supplier, or indirectly, as in the case of members of an established network. In

[2] The statement that "Economists understand by the term *Market*, not any particular market place in which things are bought and sold, but the whole region in which buyers and sellers are in such free intercourse with one another that the prices of the same goods tend to equality easily and quickly" (Cournot, [1838], 1927) is still widely quoted in economics texts.

addition, the threat of new entrants to the market or the developments of substitutes is also recognized and incorporated in many analyses.

However, this chapter will suggest that the ability of a firm to create value is often determined by the two types of entrepreneurial action identified by the Austrian School of Economists: the first involves linking two apparently separate activities, and the second involves identifying organizations with which the firm does not and sometimes cannot conduct exchanges, but whose actions can have a significant impact on the focal firm's value-creating activities. The chapter will thus be adopting the position recommended by Mason which is that: "the market, and market structure, must be defined with reference to the position of the single seller or buyer; [and that] the structure of a seller's market ... includes all those considerations which he takes into account in determining his business policies and practices" (Mason, 1939, p. 69). Furthermore, the level of analysis adopted will be an organizational system perspective that views marketing as a technology used by organizations "to elicit desired responses from other organisations or individuals" (Sweeney, 1972, p. 4).[3]

Two examples

P&O Logistics

P&O Logistics[4] runs a large lorry fleet and contracts with companies wanting their products delivered to business customers. One of P&O's customers was a producer of cutting oils and had contracted for P&O to make deliveries of cutting oil to medium and small engineering firms. Jones, a manager concerned with delivery of these cutting oils, had a chance contact with Smith who was a manager in a separate division of P&O which delivered oil to power stations for use as a power source. Smith had expressed annoyance that he had recently lost some business because the power stations had started, as a result of government incentives, to meet a proportion of their total oil needs by burning waste oil (i.e., oil that has been used and cannot be recycled).

Following this chance encounter Jones enquired of the engineering firms to whom he delivered cutting oil what they did with their waste oil (Figure 3.1). He thus discovered that these firms were finding the disposal of their waste oil increasingly problematic due to the mounting awareness of environmental issues. However, he also discovered, through Smith, that the power stations would only purchase waste oil in far greater volume than any individual engineering firm could supply. He then recognized that he could accumulate sufficient volume to

---

[3] Space limits the discussion of the topics raised in this chapter to an organizational system perspective; this does not imply that either the distribution system perspective or the social system perspective is unimportant.

[4] P&O Logistics is a subsidiary of the Peninsular and Orient Steam Navigation Company. However, hereafter "P&O Logistics" will be referred to as "P&O".

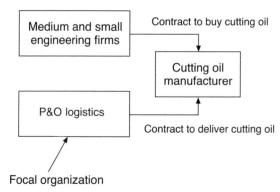

Figure 3.1—P&O's simple market form.

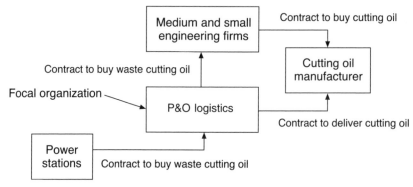

Figure 3.2—P&O's developed market form.

provide at least the minimum quantity that the power stations were willing to purchase if he collected the waste oil from all those firms to whom he delivered cutting oil. P&O then created a business that offered to take responsibility for removing waste cutting oil from those firms to which it delivered virgin cutting oil. A charge was made for this service, and P&O estimated this to be marginally lower than that which these firms were currently incurring by disposing of the waste oil themselves (Figure 3.2).

Intel

Intel has developed a new processor chip for use in laptop computers that will enable them to be connected wirelessly to local area networks (WLANs). The technical standards on which this chip is based are not proprietary and will be compatible with other wireless products. These standards are being set by the Institution of Electrical and Electronic Engineers (IEEE), and, in addition, the

British government (as do other countries' legislators) issues licences for the use of radio frequencies. It also allocates and monitors the use of spectral bands.

There are two main complementary technologies: one is *3G* (Third Generation) which is a mobile phone technology designed to allow Internet access over a wide area but at slower speeds than WLAN, and the other is *Bluetooth* which is a wire replacement technology designed to connect devices within the immediate vicinity of the user.

Intel supplies processor chips to computer manufacturers, such as Dell, but has a number of direct competitors. In addition, there is a group of companies that are not direct competitors because they concentrate on the manufacture of major communications equipment, but they are interested in producing chips for WLAN. This group of companies dominates the network interface card (NIC) and switcher/router segments. If consumers are to demand laptops with WLAN chips in them, it is essential that there are numerous "Wi-Fi hot spots" which use a small base-station plugged into a high-speed (broadband) connection to link laptops, within 50 metres of the base-station, to the Internet. Such hot spots are likely to be hotels, airports, cafes, etc. Owners of such locations will need to negotiate agreements with wireless Internet server providers (WISPs) who will provide the network services. Some central organization is needed to handle the billing for the use of these hot spots. Figure 3.3 sets out in simplified form the variety of organizations involved in this activity and some of their links.

The example shows that Intel's ability to create value for itself through the development of its new processor will be dependent on the behaviour of a large number of organizations, with some of which it does not, and given its current product range, will not have direct exchanges. Yet, these organizations' behaviour will impact on Intel's ability to create value with regard to this chip. Not only is the future of the product sufficiently important for Intel to invest considerable effort into influencing the behaviour of these organizations but also it is in a position to do so. Thus, it has appointed senior managers to lobby government and has a team working on those committees of the IEEE that are seeking to develop industry standards.

With regard to hot spots it has instigated studies of how best to finance the necessary investment and to develop a series of business models of income and expenditure appropriate to different types (e.g., hotels, airports, cafes, etc.) of site.[5] It is doing this not with the intent of itself being actively involved in the setting up of hot spots or supplying them with equipment, but to demonstrate to potential owners the benefits that they will gain by providing hot spots in their facilities.

---

[5] *The Economist* (31 May 2003, p. 64) commented, "Nobody is sure how commercial Wi-Fi hotspots will make money."

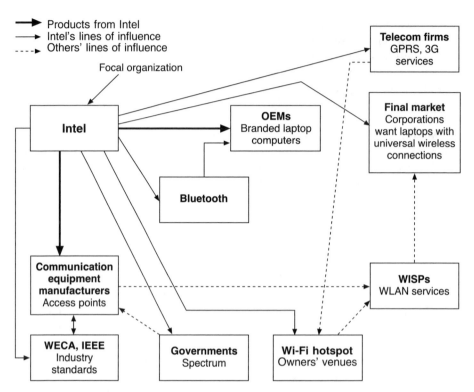

Figure 3.3—The market form for Intel's new chip.

The market form

A market form is considered to be a concept that encompasses all forms of exchange situation from the simplest dyadic or restricted exchange through to the most complex (Bagozzi, 1979). The market form will be defined as follows:

> *A firm's **market form** is comprised of those organisations whose activities it perceives: impact on its ability to create value; **and**, it can influence in a deliberate manner.*

A specific market form will be considered from the point of view of the firm supplying the focal product, and this firm will be referred to as the focal firm. The concept of market form is obviously very close to that of a "business network"[6] but there are some significant differences.

---

[6] Jarillo for example defines strategic networks as "long-term, purposeful arrangements among distinct but related for profit organizations that allow those firms in them to gain or sustain competitive advantage vis-à-vis their competitors outside the net" (1988, p. 32).

First, a business network is defined in relation to a specific organization, while a market form takes as its focus a firm's product family. Second, organizations within business networks are, by virtue of transacting business with each other, interdependent (Johanson and Mattson, 1992, p. 205). In contrast, not all the organizations within a market form are trading organizations and, even among those that are, not all necessarily have any buying or selling activity with the other organizations that make up the market form.

Third, interaction occurs within a network and a fundamental characteristic of interaction is that the parties are aware of each other's existence and try to understand and influence each other (Ford et al., 1986, p. 28). A market form differs in that it is possible for an organization within it not to be aware of the focal organization's existence or, even where it is aware of its existence, not to seek to influence the focal organization. Fourth, a common feature of the better known definitions of "networks" is that: "one party is dependent on the resources controlled by another, and that there are gains to be had by the pooling of resources" (Powell, 1990, p. 303). However, some of the organizations that comprise the market form have no need for or positive interest in pooling resources and, as such, present the focal firm with problems in formulating strategies by which they can influence such organizations' actions.

In P&O's case Smith had created a new market form that was comprised of his firm as the focus, the supplier of cutting oil, the engineering firms and the power stations (Figure 3.2); this is a relatively simple market form, and it might be argued that other actors should be included. For example, given that P&O's ability to create value in this way is dependent on the government's attitude to the disposal of waste oil, the government might be considered to be an actor in P&O's market form. Indeed, if an economical way for the users of cutting oil to recycle the cutting oil were discovered, then the government would probably stop encouraging power stations to burn the oil. However, the argument for not including the government in P&O's market form is that it is unlikely that P&O would be able to exercise much, if any, influence over the government's decision if such a circumstance did arise.

Thus, for P&O the government is not in the category of actors which meets the second criterion by which market form is defined; namely, it is made up of organizations that the focal firm "can influence in a deliberate manner". Moreover, given the small proportion of P&O's total profits that are derived from the sale of waste cutting oil, it would not make economic sense for P&O to expend much effort on attempting to exercise any such influence. Thus, the market form for the logistics company would not include the government agency concerned, even though its actions clearly do have an impact on P&O's ability to create value.

In comparison with P&O, Intel's market form is very complex, for it is comprised of all the organizations shown in Figure 3.3, with most of which it does not exchange the focal product. In comparison, P&O's market form (Figure 3.2) is comprised of only those firms with which it has contracted to purchase the waste cutting oil and those with whom it has a contract to deliver cutting oil.

The market form may include direct competitors, but does not necessarily do so any more than do networks. Nevertheless, as with networks, where a competitor's collaboration is required and actively managed (e.g., Kodak and Fuji working together on the APS film system) a competitor may be part of the market form. However, an important insight into the nature of the competition that will be faced is to seek to understand the competitor's perceptions of their market form. In many cases the market form so identified will be very similar. Thus, we would expect Intel's direct competitors to see the situation regarding the development of the WLAN market in a similar way as viewed by Intel. However, this will not always be the case, and understanding a competitor's market form may give useful insights into the appropriate types of competitive activities. Furthermore, the ability to perceive a market form with greater effectiveness than a competitor may provide the basis for competitive advantage.

Further, it is important to be aware that while Intel and its competitors are equally reliant on some of the organizations that comprise Intel's market form behaving in an "appropriate" manner, the effect of some of these organizations' actions might impact on Intel in different ways than they will on its competitors. The hot spot owners would fall into the former category, as the technology used will have a specification that all laptops equipped to work with WLANs will be able to use.[7] However, the timing, rather than the content, of the IEEE's decisions could have a different effect on Intel compared with its impact on its direct competitors because the stage of development of their technologies differs.

The nature of exchanges within a market form and the "strong attractor" model

The nature of the exchanges that occur between organizations constituting a market form will differ both in terms of the type of their governance and their "content". In this section, exchanges are considered from the point of view of the degree of economic rationality along a spectrum, ranging from strict market exchanges through to relational exchanges; that is, exchanges where, although direct monetary factors are not irrelevant, the personal relationships of those managing the exchange strongly influence the manner in which the exchange operates.

The former might be illustrated by the interaction between P&O and the oil company, as the market for contracts to deliver oil in the UK is close to being a commodity market. The latter could be illustrated by Intel's links with firms, such

---

[7] However, there is a complication in that at present it seems probable that owners of laptops with Wi-Fi capability will need to have multiple subscriptions if they are to be able to use their laptop in hotspots owned by different organisations! (*The Economist*, 28 June 2003, p. 86).

as Cisco and Dell, where those involved from both sides have often worked with each other over extended periods. As a consequence a considerable amount of mutual respect exists with regard to such matters as technical expertise, commercial probity, organizational competence, etc.

In spite of the increased interest, even on the part of economists, in other forms of market structures, the economist's perfect market model continues to act as "a strong attractor"[8] in two ways: first, its analytical clarity provides a clear benchmark against which any other forms of exchange governance can be compared and its characteristics are relatively well understood and agreed, and, second, it seems to be a form of exchange to which other forms begin to revert[9] under certain regularly occurring economic circumstances (namely, economic recessions).

In market exchanges the "instrumental rationality which includes consideration of costs and benefits" (Etzioni, 1988, p. 158) is dominant. In particular, under market exchanges any factor that might influence an exchange other than those things that either has an economic measure applied to them or to which an economic measure can be imputed are treated as "irrational". Indeed, Lane (1991) has suggested that there are four characteristics that differentiate pure markets from other systems of exchange. First, there is overspecification of the terms of exchange in that what might be intuitive behaviour is consciously evaluated and equivalences are sought. In a B2B (business-to-business) situation, both the supplier and the customer estimate the future "pay-off" of doing so before undertaking any actions that are not contractually required.

Second, the criteria for assessing this pay-off are narrowed to a single dimension, even though evidence of the success of an exchange could be based on multiple criteria. Such a one-dimensional assessment of an exchange will, for example, ignore the value that arises from any aspects of the exchange that give pleasure to the giver as well as the receiver. Thus, the use of a single dimension would lead to the satisfaction that, say, technical staff get from working on a particularly challenging problem that is being ignored.

Third, price is accepted as an exaggerated default value that is used as a surrogate for other information: for example, more expensive goods are thought to be "better" than cheaper ones. Such an interpretation of price occurs not just in B2C (business-to-consumer) markets but also in B2B markets (perhaps noticeably in the market for business consultants).

---

[8] There is always great danger in non-scientists using a scientific analogy, especially if it is drawn from chaos theory (which itself has been described as almost theological in its lack of clarity because of the disputes that exist between its supporters and their adversaries). Nevertheless, the use of the term *attractor* in the phrase "strong attractor" does have some similarity to the "attractors" of chaos theory which have been defined as a "set of points such that all trajectories nearby converge to it" and as representing the general trend of a system around which the details oscillate.

[9] An attractor is a "set of points such that all trajectories nearby converge to it" (see Footnote 8).

Fourth, under a non-market exchange at least part of the value that is gained by the parties is strictly non-transferable to a third party. Thus, when firms sell the design of or franchise the manufacturing of a product that they have developed, they often feel that they do not get the price they deserve. Obviously, sometimes this is a result of a naive or optimistic evaluation of the value of the product, but it may be a view distorted by the personal involvement of the firm's employees in the product's development.

These four characteristics mean that market exchanges reject the view that: "economic actions are truly social actions in a capitalist society" (Swedberg, 2001, p. 165). Indeed, market exchanges stand in sharp contrast to exchanges at the other end of the spectrum where social relations may dominate to such an extent that the decisions reached diverge radically from those that would be predicted on the basis of economic rationality. It has been asserted (e.g., Rangan, 2000; Swedberg, 2001) that one of the fundamental sociological propositions in this context is Granovetter's concept of "embeddedness" that he describes as follows:

> What I mean by "embeddedness" is that the economic action of individuals as well as larger economic patterns, like the determination of prices and economic institutions, are very importantly affected by networks of social relations. (Granovetter, cited in Swedberg, 1990, p. 100)

Granovetter's view is that networks of social relationships strongly influence the development of exchanges, and he argues that where relationships are embedded then behaviours "are so constrained by on-going social relations that to construe them as independent is a grievous misunderstanding" (Granovetter, 1985, p. 481).

For Granovetter, embeddedness challenges the economist's assumption of *Homo economicus*: that is, an isolated actor making rational decisions; this is something that can only exist when Lane's four characteristics are present and then "atomization" exits. Granovetter states: "The opposite of atomization is something I want to call '*embeddedness*'[10], and I believe that the usefulness of social structural analysis in economic life has to do in crucial ways with recognizing the importance of embeddedness" (Granovetter, 1982, p. 11[11]).

It is also important to note that the market form may also include actors that are not profit-making institutions. In the Intel example the IEEE and those government agencies responsible for allocating frequencies would fall into this category. Here again, the nature of the exchanges that occur between a firm, such as Intel, and these organizations can range from strictly bureaucratic and formal through to quite close. The former might be illustrated by civil servants refusing to hold

---

[10] Italics in the original.

[11] This reference is to an unpublished early draft of Granovetter (1985) that is not available to the author of this chapter, but is one that Swedberg (2001) quotes extensively.

meetings without formal minute taking, to accept even minimal informal contact, etc.[12] The latter could be illustrated by Intel's links with institutions, such as the IEEE, where those involved from both sides have known each other as scientists for long periods and the "bonding" through their professional status as scientists is very strong.

The factors that will determine the nature of those exchanges that occur between such non-profit actors and the private sector are different from those described above and will include such matters as the political philosophy of the government, the transparency of any negotiation processes, etc. In general though, such organizations are "rule-based" and "While these rules change over time, their adjustment to changed realities is frequently slow" (Etzioni, 1988, p. 171).

How market forms evolve

Keynes pointed out that: "Economists set themselves too easy, too useless a task if in tempestuous seasons they can only tell us that when the storm is long past the sea is flat" (cited in Skidelsky, 1983, p. 156). Indeed, in contrast to economists' (except the Austrian School) obsession with the stability of equilibrium, management theorists regard the investigation of how and why markets change to be a critical aspect of their studies.

A market form is "a creation" of the focal organization that arises from its assessment of the opportunities for creating value, and arguably networks of social relations are significant to its development. As such, once it has "created" a market form the focal organization will implement decisions as a result of which the market form will change. The reasons are twofold: first, the focal organization's own actions will often be designed to change the behaviour of other organizations in the market form, and, second, many of these organizations will themselves initiate actions in response to the focal organization's behaviour. The market form is therefore not static, but must be expected to be constantly developing.

This section will consider three of the several possible categories of influence that are likely to play a part in determining the way in which a market form evolves: entrepreneurial alertness, path dependence and replaceability.

Entrepreneurial alertness

Kirzner spoke of von Mises' view that "the market is a delicate *process*"[13] whereby, against the background of continually changing conditions and with information

---

[12] On one occasion the author, when working in industry, offered to buy a civil servant a cup of tea only to have the offer firmly rejected – but this was just after a high-profile court case involving the bribery and corruption of public sector employees.

[13] Italics in the original.

available only in a limited and piecemeal fashion, the decisions of market partici-pants are through their interplay in the market brought into a steadily dovetailing adjustment. In this process the key roles are played by "restless, ever alert en-trepreneurship, and by its counterpart, the merciless, ceaseless, impartial court of active competition" (Kirzner, 2000, p. 276).[14] However, there are two main views of this "alert entrepreneur": there is Kirzner's view of the entrepreneur as someone who reacts to the discovery of new opportunities, which is a quite different approach from that of Schumpeter (1943) for whom the entrepreneur is a creator of new opportunities via the implementation of both product and process innovations. These two views are illustrated by the examples of P&O and Intel.

The managers of P&O demonstrated entrepreneurship, which is "the capacity independently to size up a situation and more correctly reach an imagined picture of the relevant (as yet indeterminate) future" (Kirzner, 1996, p. 26), in that they observed behaviour in two quite distinct markets and brought them together. By so doing they created a new market form (see Figure 3.2) from two previously independent markets and provided a value-creating opportunity for them-selves.[15] This entrepreneurial capability of being alert to value-creating opportu-nities is a significant factor in the creation of new market forms.

In the Intel case the entrepreneurial activity is more Schumpeterian in that it sees the entrepreneur as a creator of a new disequilibrium. Intel understands that a value-creating opportunity exists if an appropriately dense network of hot spots can be developed and has worked out an initial perception of the appropriate market form needed if its new processor chip is to be a commercial success. If Intel is successful in encouraging the development of hot spots, then the development of the market for 3G will be disturbed and will also certainly change, if not disrupt, the market for Bluetooth.

An important result of entrepreneurial activity is, to extend Keynes' analogy, that one storm follows another and that not only is the sea never flat, but its current state of disturbance is partially determined by past storms. Indeed, Kirzner states: "today's expectations of future preferences and scarcities must acknowledge that these future preferences and scarcities will themselves be shaped by series of prospective creative, unpredictable decisions on the part of many entrepreneurs" (1996, p. 31). Thus, whether Kirzner's or Schumpeter's view of entrepreneurship is

---

[14] This was stated in a more down-to-earth manner by Kemmons Wilson, who built up the Holiday Inn Chain (starting his first hotel after an unpleasant hotel-based family holiday). He said: "Opportunity comes often. It knocks as often as you have an ear trained to hear it, an eye trained to see it, a hand trained to grasp it, and a head trained to used it."

[15] They also produce value for the creator of the waste oil who disposes of it at less cost than previously; this is possibly also the case for the power stations which by increasing the supply of the oil, thus helps them to meet Government targets and, by increasing the supply, may lower the price they need to pay for it.

accepted the activities of entrepreneurs will be factors that cause any market form to change continuously.

Although entrepreneurs are risk takers, if the actions of other individuals are too unpredictable then there is a risk of decision-making paralysis. However, as Boland (1979) highlighted, the scope of other agents' possible actions is reduced by the existence of norms, standards and conventions or even cultural taboos; these, while they do not erase individual freedom of choice, contribute to the convergence of plans by increasing the probability of one type of action within the choice set available. Certainly, such "controls" over behaviour arise within what Granovetter described as "networks of social relations" (Swedberg, 1990, p. 100). In both the P&O and the Intel cases, existing networks of social relations limited the uncertainties faced by each of the focal companies.

Path dependence

The concept of path dependence, which at the simplest level means "that history matters" (North, 1990, p. 100), is based on the understanding that historical events cause solutions to problems to become "locked in" which explains why sometimes apparently[16] superior innovations do not manage to supplant existing but inferior ones. Arthur (1994) has argued that there are four self-reinforcing mechanisms that create the possibility of this lock-in and the consequent path dependence effect; these are:

1. Large set-up costs leading to falling unit costs as output increases.
2. Learning effects which lower costs as products become more widely available.
3. Co-ordination effects which arise as other people take similar actions.
4. And adaptive expectations where belief in the product's success increases with increased presence on the market.

Arthur's case is based on the assessment of the success of technical innovations, but North applies Arthur's arguments to institutional change. However, he does this only after carefully evaluating the legitimacy of using the concept in this way and, having done so, he concludes that path dependence "is the key to an analytical understanding of long-run economic change" (1990, p. 112) and it "comes from the increasing returns mechanisms that reinforce the direction once on a given path" (1990, p. 112). North suggests changes to institutional structure

[16] There are numerous cases in which this type of lock-in has been asserted, and the QWERTY keyboard and the VHS video-recording format are among the best known examples of allegedly inferior product formats that dominate their markets. However, Liebowitz and Margolis (1990, 1999) present a compelling argument that there are no convincing instances of lock-in, but that these products succeeded because they were superior to their rivals.

will therefore be incremental and will result from managers' accumulation of knowledge, experience and information.

This would suggest that where a new market form comes into being, whether or not it is the most effective and/or efficient,[17] it would seem to have a momentum to it in those cases where increasing returns apply and there are also high transaction costs. In the case of P&O the costs incurred in establishing this new market form are low, as are the transaction costs. So, while the power stations seem unlikely to disrupt this market form by trying themselves to purchase the waste cutting oil from the engineering firms, many other organizations outside the market form could do so. In addition, as was suggested above, should an economical way to recycle waste cutting oil be discovered, then P&O's market form for cutting oil would presumably revert to that in Figure 3.1. Thus, P&O's market form for the handling of waste oil is not stable and may be short-lived.[18]

In the case of Intel's market form for the processor chip, increasing returns apply because of the substantial past investments by Intel in both the product and the relationships that underpin the market form. There are also high transaction costs in that the relationships between several of the organizations within the structure are based on intrinsic factors, such as mutual trust and respect of each other's knowledge, both of which usually take time to establish. The ability of any commercial organization to disrupt this structure by entry would seem low because of the problem it would face in matching Intel's investment and established contacts, plus the fact that a new entrant would need to establish its reputation.

It would therefore seem that, relative to the P&O case, Intel's market form is relatively stable. To a considerable extent this stability arises from the embeddedness that is represented by the networks of social relations existing between some elements of Intel's market form. Thus, path dependence operates in Intel's favour in many ways but not totally, because in the USA one national chain of coffee bars did install the necessary hot spot equipment, but lost money by doing so; this has left owners of other chains suspicious about the business case for becoming involved. The coffee bar chains, while not completely irreplaceable, are seen to be a very important element in the market form of the development of Wi-Fi

---

[17] Indeed, North does not seem to expect most market structures to be efficient by stating: "Throughout most of history the experience of the agents and the ideologies of the actors do not combine to lead to efficient outcomes" (1990, p. 96). He does not make it clear from which perspective he makes this judgment, but it would seem that it is an organizational system perspective rather than a distribution system perspective or a social system perspective (Sweeney, 1972).

[18] However, given the slim margins earned by firms delivering bulk materials, such as oil, it would not be worth the power stations cutting out P&O and collecting the waste oil themselves. The business model, on which the collection of the waste oil, its storage and subsequent delivery to the power station is based, only "works" for P&O because the cost of the journey to the cutting oil customer is covered by its contract with the supplier of the virgin cutting oil.

because they have large numbers of outlets with long opening hours and are based in central locations.

Replaceability

The issue that firms have to consider with regard to their own assets is not their value to somebody else, but how important their contribution is to the firm and how difficult it would be to replace them should the need arise. As Kay argues, the specificity of assets is a less important matter than their replaceability. In particular, he points out that from the transaction cost perspective: "asset specificity refers to the opportunity cost of assets *outside* the firm. However, this does not necessarily tell us anything at all about how the assets relate to other assets *within* the firm, and the ease with which they could be replaced if this proves necessary" (Kay, 1997, p. 44[19]). This argument holds true for those organizations that make up a firm's market form as much as it does with regard to individual assets.

There are degrees of "replaceability", as some assets cannot be replaced at all while others are almost commodities in terms of their availability. Similarly, with organizations within a market form, some are unique while others can easily be replaced by effectively identical organizations. Between these two extremes are replacements which while acceptable will require some adjustment in the behaviour of the focal organization. In the Intel case, although other types of hot spot location are attractive (e.g., hotels, transportation hubs, etc.) the larger coffee bar chains' characteristics are unique, and there is concern that if none "sign up" then in many senses they are irreplaceable.

One consequence of a focal organization recognizing that an organization in its market form is irreplaceable will be that it will accord it greater attention and may thus skew the "economics" of the case. In the Wi-Fi case, chains have shown some reluctance to make a commitment at present because they are aware of the failure of one chain to profitably establish hot spots. Thus, if the other coffee bar chains are to commit themselves, it may now be necessary to develop a financial model that initially allows them to earn higher profits than would otherwise be justified.

Issues arising from the existence of path dependence and replaceability can constrain the development of a market form. For, in its weakest form, path dependence can be no more than exaggerating the extent to which "history matters". As far as replaceability is concerned, sometimes thinking "out of the box" is required if a substitute is to be found.[20] In other words, entrepreneurial alertness, especially of the type envisioned by Kirzner (1996, 2000), may overcome this constraint.

[19] Italics in the original.

[20] For example, a food processor was facing inordinate difficulties in maintaining precise volume measures when packaging a relatively expensive product. Although no existing food packaging machinery could meet its requirements it was discovered that packaging machinery used in the pharmaceutical industry could do so.

Thus, a market form will evolve from its initial formulation due to the impact of these and other factors. It has been suggested that the existence of social networks will be a strong influence on its initial structure. However, Granovetter implies that, as forms of industrial organization mature, then the social networks approach may not be so useful in explaining what is happening because over time existing networks of social relations will weaken and, indeed, dissolve (Granovetter, cited in Swedberg, 1990, p. 104). The question, therefore, must be whether, just as Keynes' storm reverts to calmer weather before the arrival of the next storm, exchanges within a market form will move toward market-type exchanges before new market forms, within which social networks may have significance, evolve?

Embeddedness and the strong attractor

Why is it that networks of social relations might be weakened or even dissolved for, when they are, this allows the manner in which value-creating exchanges occur to migrate toward that of the pure market? Several reasons can be hypothesized, some of which are:

1. Market pressures.
2. Commoditization.
3. Increased managerial mobility.
4. New forms of business organization.

These reasons are often interdependent, but will initially be considered below individually.

Market pressures

There are a number of high-profile examples of customers, as a result of market pressures, acting in a manner that has resulted in the breakdown of social relations with their suppliers. For example, Marks & Spencer was once famous for its close and long-standing supplier relationships, based on shared values and understandings; this is illustrated by an M&S manager's comment that "they (viz. suppliers) are as much locked into our way of thinking as we are. These firms are more willing to take risks for M&S because there is more trust in the relationships. Should there be cutbacks, M&S would remain loyal to this group" (Lewis, 1995, p. 138). In spite of this, in 1999 M&S gave minimal notice of its intent to cease placing orders with a firm that had been a major supplier for 30 years. Without doubt the trigger for this action was that in 1998 M&S had registered its first loss for 30 years.

Similarly, in 2000, after several years of assiduously rebuilding relationships with its US suppliers, Chrysler without warning or discussion required all its suppliers to reduce their prices by 5% and demanded a further 10% decrease over the next two years. Chrysler too had suffered massive losses immediately prior to taking this action.

Granovetter makes it clear that his approach explains why forms of industrial organization are strongly influenced at an early stage in their development by social interactions and that they can become locked to a certain structure that may not be the most efficient. However, what is most efficient in a specific buyer–seller relationship is highly contingent on factors outside the firms' control. Indeed, in the cases of M&S and Chrysler, self-preservation became the dominant motivation, and the imperative of avoiding a loss-making situation in the short term overwhelmed any arguments about the future benefits of close relationships (Blois, 2003). As Swedberg (1994) points out, while Granovetter argues that social structure is important he does not claim that in their decision making the actors can ignore direct monetary factors.

Commoditization

The concept of commoditization is commonly associated with the situation where customers do not perceive any factor that differentiates the physical goods offered by competitors. However, true commoditization only exists where customers perceive there to be a uniformity of product offering between suppliers *and also* a uniformity of the manner in which suppliers will discharge their obligations.

Where such a situation arises prices will be driven down, and so a prime concern of all suppliers is to avoid the commoditization of their products.[21] Indeed, part of the rationale, at least from the supplier's point of view, behind the arguments for developing relationships with customers is to seek to differentiate the customer's perceptions of the manner in which the supplier will discharge its obligations in the future. The aim is to try to make "the relationship", where a major constituent is often the personal relationships between those managing the exchange, become "the product" (Blois, 1997, pp. 378–379). Then, even if the physical good is manufactured to internationally recognized standards and/or customers perceive competing suppliers' goods to be undifferentiated, the suppliers are still differentiated from the customers' point of view. Nevertheless, where the physical goods are perceived as being uniform the requirement for customers to be able to justify not purchasing from the lowest priced source can become intense and can threaten even those business relationships embedded in personal relationships.

---

[21] Much managerial and academic writing has been concerned with this issue (see Levitt, 1980 for one well-known example).

Increased managerial mobility

Granovetter pointed out that people have particular relationships that are overlooked if these relationships are defined by general role descriptions. Indeed, before 1999 M&S's view reflected this. Lewis commented that M&S believed that the long-term mutual learning and adjustment that arose between it and its suppliers benefited from low turnover among people at the interface. In addition, M&S understood that low turnover facilitated both the growth of trust and teamwork within relationships and the creation of shared habits that made each customer interface culturally distinct (Lewis, 1995). The implication is that a relationship may be disrupted by changes in any of the staff that interface with the supplier or vice versa. Thus, whether it results from staff being rotated between jobs or from them leaving the firm, a period of time is needed to rebuild those relationships disrupted by such changes.

A less direct but significant reduction in social cohesion occurs where a customer believes it may have to drop a supplier. As Humphrey and Ashforth (2000) have shown, a firm's managers become less friendly in their personal behaviour toward their suppliers' managers if they believe they *might* have to stop dealing with that customer.

It is arguable that staff changes that impact on supplier–customer relations are more likely to occur in large organizations, and, as Uzzi points out, "As firms grow, ties among individuals may become insufficient sources of embeddedness" (1997, p. 64). If this is the case, then this might give some grounds for confirming Granovetter's suggestion that his concepts are more useful for analysing small units than institutions (cited in Swedberg, 1990, p. 104).

New forms of business organization

Outsourcing has grown in popularity in recent years, as economic pressures have caused many firms to seek ways to strip out costs. IT, training, logistics, catering and facilities management are among the most common categories of outsourced activities. Where a firm outsources an activity it is common for the supplier initially to use some but not all of the firm's existing employees. However, it is evident that even where this happens the differing norms of the supplier will cause such employees to adapt their behaviour, and this can place strains on established social relations. In some cases there is a complete replacement of existing staff by the supplier's staff. In either case the management styles of many outsourcers seem to be to move staff around very much in the way in which consultancies manage their personnel. In addition, as it seeks to absorb the outsourcer's staff and to understand the norms with which they operate (Kern and Blois, 2002), there is often considerable social tension within the company that has made the outsourcing decision. Such a situation does not make it easy for established social contacts with others in the business network to be maintained.

A second new type of business organization has been the development of various types of e-business. Although e-business in B2B markets has not yet been as successful as was predicted, there is no doubt that it has had an impact on many firms. Together with other "electronic" developments (e.g., reverse auctions, EDI, etc.) there "are those who believe that e-procurement strategies will reverse the trend towards buyer–supplier relationship building" (Presutti, 2003, pp. 225–226).

It has been suggested that the issues (above) are among the factors that can lead to a breakdown in those social relationships within a market form that constrain exchange behaviour from being determined on the terms described by Lane (1991). Any one impact is likely to result from a combination of these factors: for example, market pressures on a firm's prices may lead to attempts to reduce costs through such activities as outsourcing and reorganizing managerial responsibilities. The progress of commoditization, which arises through a combination of more sophisticated buying practices, the breakdown in the limited brand loyalty that exists in B2B markets and new entrants to existing industries, again forces firms to re-examine their cost structures.

In some discussions of relationship marketing in B2B markets the fact that a buyer and supplier have traded with each other for a prolonged period is sometimes taken as indicating that "a relationship" exists; this is not necessarily the case, and to establish whether or not "a relationship" has existed requires detailed case analysis. Similarly, to understand whether or not networks of social relations have significantly influenced specific business exchanges throughout a specified period again requires detailed case analyses.[22] Without such analyses it can only be *assumed* that networks of social relations impact the way that economic decisions are taken and the manner in which economic institutions develop. What has been suggested above is that there are some recognizable features of economic behaviour that will from time to time undermine the influence of networks of social relations on the decision-making process.

Summary

Two examples have been used to propose a type of market organization labelled market form. The P&O example is of a very simple market form, but for Intel the market form is complex. The Intel example may appear to be an extreme case, but within the high-technology sectors of the economy such complex exchanges are not unusual. Indeed, they seem to be met more and more frequently in B2B markets, and the need to understand them is therefore of increasing importance.

It has been suggested that the focal firm needs to understand each of its products' market forms if it is to be successful. The essence of the concept is that creating value can involve complex interactions with many organizations, only some of which are parties that are "dependent on the resources controlled

---

[22] Even Granovetter quotes very few such detailed analyses.

by another" (Powell, 1990, p. 303) or that will perceive "there are gains to be had by the pooling of resources" (Powell, 1990, p. 303).

It seems that market forms will vary with regard to the amount by which they are influenced by non-economic factors. Indeed, within any particular market form there will be variance, with some dyads operating in a strictly economic manner while others are almost over-socialized. It has been suggested that there will be constant changes to the extent to which non-economic factors, such as social networks, influence actors who are primarily oriented toward economic objectives. In particular, the suggestion has been made that the economist's perfect market model is constantly a strong attractor not because price, as Rangan has said, is "the 'default mechanism'" (2000, p. 3), but because from time to time all resources are in short supply and, thus, economic pressures become dominant.

It is important for organizations to identify the market form that applies to their products. Failure to do so can result in them not dealing in an appropriate manner with organizations whose activities are critical to their ability to create value, such as the potential hot spot owners for Intel. Alternatively, they will fail to identify value-creating opportunities achievable through bringing together apparently separate markets – something P&O avoided doing. The capacity to identify these opportunities is what Kirzner called "entrepreneurial alertness" (1996, p. 26), which is the ability to appraise a situation and more precisely than others to reach an assessment of the (as-yet uncertain) future; this sounds remarkably like Levitt's statement that the marketing imagination "usually requires combining disparate facts or ideas into new amalgamations of meanings" (1983, p. 130).

References

Arthur, W.B. (1994). *Competing Technologies and Path Dependence in the Economy*. Ann Arbor, MI: University of Michigan Press.

Bagozzi, R.P. (1979). Toward a formal theory of marketing exchange. In: O.C. Ferrell et al. (eds), *Conceptual and Theoretical Developments in Marketing* (pp. 431–447). Chicago: American Marketing Association.

Blois, K.J. (1997). Are business to business relationships inherently unstable? *Journal of Marketing Management,* **13**: 367–382.

Blois, K.J. (2003). B2B "relationships": A social construction of reality? *Journal of Marketing Theory,* **3**(1): 79–95.

Boland, L. (1979). Knowledge and the role of institutions in economic theory. *Journal of Economic Issues,* **13**(4): 957–973.

Cournot, A. [1838] (1927). *Researches into the Mathematical Principles of the Theory of Wealth* (translated by N.T. Bacon). New York: Macmillan.

Etzioni, A. (1988). *The Moral Dimension: Toward a New Economics*. New York: Free Press.

Ford, D., Håkansson, H. and Snehota, I. (1986). How do companies interact? *Industrial Marketing and Purchasing,* **1**(1): 26–41.

Granovetter, M. (1982). Economic decisions and social structure: The problem of embeddedness. Unpublished early draft of Granovetter (1985).

Granovetter, M. (1985). Economic action and social structure: The problem of embeddedness. *American Journal of Sociology*, **91**: 481–510.

Humphrey, R.H. and Ashforth, B.E. (2000). Buyer–supplier alliances in the automobile industry: How exit-voice strategies influence interpersonal relationships. *Journal of Organizational Behavior*, **21**: 713–730.

Jarillo, J.C. (1988). On strategic networks. *Strategic Management Journal*, **9**: 33–41.

Johanson, J. and Mattson, L-G. (1992). Network positions and strategic action: An analytical framework. In: B. Axelsson and G. Easton (eds), *Industrial Networks: A New View of Reality* (pp. 205–217). London: Routledge.

Kay, N.M. (1997). *Pattern in Corporate Evolution*. Oxford, UK: Oxford University Press.

Kern, T. and Blois, K.J. (2002). Norm developments in outsourcing relationships. *Journal of Information Technology*, **17**(1): 33–42.

Kirzner, I.M. (1996). *The Meaning of the Market Process*. London: Routledge.

Kirzner, I.M. (2000). Ludwig von Mises. In: I.M. Kirzner (ed.), *The Driving Force of the Market* (pp. 275–277). London: Routledge.

Lane, R.E. (1991). *The Market Experience*. Cambridge, UK: Cambridge University Press.

Liebowitz, S.J. and Margolis, S.E. (1990). The fable of the keys. *Journal of Law and Economics*, **33**: 1–26.

Liebowitz, S.J. and Margolis, S.E. (1999). *Winners, Losers & Microsoft*. Oakland, CA: Independent Institute.

Levitt, T. (1980). Marketing success through differentiation – of anything. *Harvard Business Review*, **58**: 83–91.

Levitt, T. (1983). *The Marketing Imagination*. New York: Free Press.

Lewis, J.D. (1995). *The Connected Corporation: How Leading Companies Win through Customer–supplier Relationships*. New York: Free Press.

Mason, E. (1939). Price and production policies of large-scale enterprises. *American Economic Review*, **29**: 61–74.

Meyer, M.H. and Utterback, J.M. (1993). The product family and the dynamics of core capability. *Sloan Management Review*, **34**(3): 29–48.

North, D.C. (1990). *Institutions, Institutional Change and Economic Performance*. Cambridge, UK: Cambridge University Press.

Powell, W.W. (1990). Neither market nor hierarchy. *Research in Organisational Behavior*, **12**: 295–336.

Presutti, W.D. (2003). Supply management and e-procurement: Creating value added in the supply chain. *Industrial Marketing Management*, **32**(3): 219–226.

Rangan, S. (2000). The problem of search and deliberation in economic action: When social networks really matter. *Academy of Management Review*, **25**(4): 813–829.

Schumpeter, J.A. (1943). *Capitalism, Socialism and Democracy*. London: Unwin University Books.

Skidelsky, R. (1983). *John Maynard Keynes: A biography. Vol. 2: The Economist as Saviour, 1920–1937*. London: Macmillan Press.

Swedberg, R. (1990). *Economics and Sociology: Redefining Their Boundaries*. Princeton, NJ: Princeton University Press.

Swedberg, R. (1994). Markets as social structures. In: N.J. Smelser and R. Swedberg (eds), *The Handbook of Economic Sociology* (pp. 255–282). Princeton, NJ: Princeton University Press.

Swedberg, R. (2001). New economic sociology: What has been accomplished, what is ahead? *Acta Sociologica,* **40**(2): 61–182.

Sweeney, D.J. (1972). Marketing: Management technology or social process? *Journal of Marketing,* **36**(4): 3–10.

Uzzi, B. (1997). Social structure and competition in interfirm networks: The paradox of embeddedness. *Administrative Science Quarterly,* **42**(1): 35–67.

Market forms and market models

4   *Geoff Easton*

Introduction

Markets are complex economic, social and technological systems. They are also crucial to everyday life. Yet, while we constantly experience markets our understanding of them remains partial and fragmented. Markets are seen through different lenses by many different disciplines. Economists were the earliest to theorize about them, and their notions of what constitutes markets and how they operate have tended to dominate the prevailing discourse. Marketing academics by and large have taken a rather limited view of markets, and for them *market form* is inextricably linked to the notion of segments.

Despite these uncertainties it is not difficult to accept the idea that markets can take different forms. But what does the term "market form" imply? First of all, it entails the idea of some grouping of markets that are similar within but different between. The alternative would be to believe that all markets are the same, which some economists assume, or that they are all different, which is what some marketing practitioners might suggest.

Form is a particularly general term, and according to the *Oxford English Dictionary* means variously "shape, arrangements of parts, visible aspect, mode of existence or manifestation, state or disposition, make-up or constitution". It is a way of characterizing the nature of an entity; in this case a market. It answers the question: if markets are different in what ways are they different?

It should be obvious that the definition of market and its form are mutually constitutive. At its simplest this means that we need to know what a market means before we can go about describing what its nature and characteristics are. More subtly, definitions often spring from empirical descriptions of the subject's nature and constitution. In the former case we have something close to a deductive approach and in the latter case an inductive one.

Similarly, in the academic world we create theory from defined concepts, such as market, and relate them by means of formal logic to other concepts, such as exchange, creating, hopefully, a consistent system of meaningful ideas that seeks to represent the world. The existence of such a system is a necessary but not sufficient condition for claiming understanding of the world. There must also exist referents that link the theoretical system to the empirical world.

To reiterate, define a market in one way and the forms it can take are at least partly determined. Similarly, describing market forms helps to delineate how markets might be constituted. The conclusion must be that if we seek to understand markets more clearly one fruitful line of attack is to approach the phenomenon by theorizing about the forms markets take.

In this chapter my objective is limited to outlining an approach to the description and analysis of market forms rather than a taxonomic listing of what they might be. The specific route chosen was to build a theory/model/framework (after model) of markets using the ontology of critical realism (e.g., Bhaskar, 1978; Sayer, 1992, 2000; Lawson, 1997; Ackroyd and Fleetwood, 2000), a description of which is given in the next section.

Critical realist approach

Critical realism and causality

In a recent paper (Easton, 2002) I argued that critical realism is an ontology that is particularly suited to the study of complex socio-technical systems, such as markets. Critical realists use causal language explicitly. They define entities that they seek to understand, specify necessary relationships among them and attribute to them causal powers, which may or not operate in particular circumstances, to cause events to occur by particular mechanisms. Entities can be material, social, intangible or, indeed, anything that is believed to have causal powers and which can be included in the theoretical formulation that is being developed.

The initial stage in this process is to define the event to be understood and the entities that are believed to cause it to occur in that particular form.

Markets and exchanges

The problem with building a model of markets is that they are essentially complex aggregate phenomena. It was decided, therefore, in the first instance to work "bottom-up" with an exchange as the simplest event to be explained. This line of attack provides a complementary approach to the basically "top-down" approach adopted by Håkan Håkansson and Frans Prenkert (Chapter 5 in this book). These authors apply, parameterize and articulate the generic activity system due to Engeström in order to typify four different types of typical exchange systems. They do so by a process they describe as closing the open systems that are implied by the complex nature of markets; this involves making some key constraining assumptions about the nature of the relationships among the entities and concepts that they include in their analysis.

By contrast I have chosen to work with the "deeper" ontology of critical realism which involves fewer, simpler and more universal assumptions, but at the same time offers only a general approach to the issue of understanding market forms rather than their more detailed typological forms provided by Håkansson and Prenkert.

Exchange, while regarded as the central concept in the discipline of marketing, has been relatively little used in its theoretical development (for a major exception see Bagozzi, 1975, 1978, 1979); this may very well be because it is too even-handed in its nature to be much employed in marketing management-oriented research and theorizing. Nevertheless, it offers a unit of analysis and a building block simple enough to allow a critical realist-based model to be developed.

Exchange in this context refers to voluntary economic exchange. As usual, there are boundary issues. At what point does an exchange lose its economic character? When does an exchange become involuntary? Is it possible to have interactions between actors in any social system that are not in some sense exchanges as opposed to unilateral acts? While these are real problems they can only be tackled, if at all, when we understand more about what happens away from the phenomena boundaries (i.e., that we perceive of as typical).

Business-to-business or, more generally, organization-to-organization exchanges are more likely, for reasons that have been exhaustively rehearsed in publications by the IMP Group, to occur within the context of strong, long-term relationships that also provide the conditions for "action at a distance" that are the hallmark of industrial networks.

Exchanges in this setting are viewed as events, activities or processes that are the outcomes of a causal mechanism. Again, there are boundary issues involved. Can we only consider an exchange event to have occurred when the buyer is in possession of what they have bought and the seller has received payment for it? Exchanges may be regarded as instantaneous, as in e-commerce, but what about the long-drawn-out processes involved in projects where stage payments are made? Nevertheless, in all cases there will be process forms that can be empirically described. Perhaps the most profound process type is the presence or absence of an exchange event. Critical realists accept the idea that the non-occurrence of an event when one is expected not only requires explanation but may also provide very useful insights into the nature of the event.

Necessary relations

A critical realist approach to the nature of exchanges starts with the question; why did a particular exchange event of this type take place between this seller and this buyer involving these exchange entities at this time and in this way? A simple model of a single exchange event suggests that there is what critical realists describe as a *necessary relationship* between buyer and seller and what was

Figure 4.1—A simple model of exchange.

exchanged; these are the core theoretical entities in this situation, and they serve to define each other and the framework of causality. A buyer has the power to buy, a seller has the power to sell and the exchange entities have the power to influence, and all these powers are mobilized in this particular situation, causing an exchange event or outcome to occur. Buyers, sellers and exchange entities have other powers that may or not be invoked in particular exchanges. Any change in any of the three elements of the model – a different buyer, seller or exchange entity – would have created a different event or even non-event. Such is the basis of necessity. Buyer, seller and exchange entities are the key elements of the model and the basic unit of empirical analysis as shown in Figure 4.1.

The powers and liabilities of each of these components may help to cause particular market forms to occur: for example, a buyer may have chosen to enact their powers of purchase on a particular occasion as a result of the perceived power of the seller.

Asymmetry in power relations may be a key phenomenon that creates particular exchange forms. Similarly, a seller may have been liable by virtue of their cash flow situation to have undertaken an exchange that they wouldn't otherwise have enacted.

The nature of exchange entities differs from that of buyers or sellers since they are non-human and may even be intangible actors. Nevertheless, in line with actor network theory, they are accepted as having causal powers; for example, if the exchange entities are both tangible products as in barter situations or are very complex or rather simple these factors will have a profound effect on the nature of the exchange.

Contingent relations

Not all relations as prescribed in critical realism are necessary. A contingent re-lationship exists between entities when one *may* have the power to affect another, but will not always do so. If, in the case described above, an exchange event occurs, then there must be a buyer and a seller, but there need not be a competitive seller. If there is one, then that entity may affect the nature of the exchange, but does not do so necessarily. It is important to emphasize that the theoretical framework chosen governs the difference between necessary and contingent. If industrial net behaviour was chosen as the outcome to be understood, then a competitive seller would most likely have the necessary rela-tionships with buyers and other sellers in that net.

Put another way, adopting the exchange event as the outcome to be explained is a deliberate, albeit contestable choice since it implies that there may be important network effects that influence dyadic exchanges, but that is not necessarily always the case. In theory, it could of course be argued that there will always be some effects, but given the crudity of our research methods they may simply be un-detectable and, therefore, we are forced to ignore them in pursuit of the simplest explanation.

As with necessary relationships it is crucial to ask what it is about the contingent entity that causes or helps particular events to happen or, in the language of critical realism, what is the mechanism by which the causality operates? For example, competitors can affect exchanges both directly and indirectly or sometimes not at all. A direct mechanism could work by way of a direct offer from the competitor to the buyer. An indirect mechanism may operate by way of the perceptions of the competitor in the minds of the seller, which cause it to behave in a particular way.

It is a major advantage of critical realism that mechanisms can take many forms: for example, at the rather formal level, non-linear theories, such as chaos (Hibbert and Wilkinson, 1994), catastrophe (Oliva et al., 1995) or complexity theory (Easton et al., 1998), could be used as possible market mechanisms. However, less formally, ideas or concepts or any kind of metaphor (Easton and Araujo, 1993) could be used, such as network (Axelsson and Easton, 1992), marriage (Guillet de Monthoux, 1975) and dancing (Wilkinson and Young, 1994), providing they are consistent at some acceptable level with the data.

Competitive sellers, governments or even the weather are entities that are labelled *external* because they exist outside of and separate from the entities in necessary relations. It is important to make a distinction between external contingent relations and the simpler notion of contextual variables. In positivist quantitative modelling, contingency is defined in terms of the linear correlation between certain contextual variables in the "environment" of the key relationship and the dependent variable (e.g., Zeithaml et al., 1988). In the case of critical realism the entity should not only be defined but the form of the causal relationship should also be clearly set out.

However, there are also *internal* contingent entities and their relationships. In the case of the exchange event it is clear that buyers, sellers and the exchange entities will be quite different in different situations. One way to handle this situation would be to use a superficial contextual approach and simply categorize buyers, sellers and exchange entities and look for empirical regularities. Large firms buy in this way, German sellers sell in this way and products are different from services in the ways in which they are bought and sold.

However, the critical realist approach is to argue that the internal nature of these entities should be modelled in the same way as the higher level exchange between those entities; this is done by identifying the crucial entities and proposing the necessary relationships among them. For example, there is a great deal of research on organizational buying behaviour that could provide useful guidance in this process; for example, the occurrence of a purchase may only be explicable in terms of the necessary social, technical and economic relationships among the members of the entity called the buying task group.

However, critical realists acknowledge that the relationship between the internal contingent and focus-level model entities is by no means straightforward. In general, entities can be analysed at a number of different levels of aggregation. The social/biological/chemical/physical hierarchy is one of the most fundamental and hotly disputed. A crucial critical realist assumption is that for entities at a higher level of aggregation emergence is not necessarily a simple summative process. The properties of the higher level emerge from those of the lower level, but are not easily derived from them. For example, organizations have emergent properties that are more than the sum of the actions of their employees. They have corporate images, legal rights and obligations and cultures. Similarly, entities at a higher level cannot simply be reduced to the sum of their parts. The current lack of a biochemical basis for consciousness provides a case in point.

Emergence will be dealt with at some length later in the chapter in reference to markets and their forms. However, in this instance it is emergence as adopted by critical realists with which we are concerned and the internal contingent structure of buyers, sellers and exchanges that is important. Each of these entities emerges from structures of relationships within them, which affect the ways in which their powers are enacted. Organizations have different internal structures, processes and histories; exchanges may involve simple or complex products and be consummated through different media.

Contingent relations provide a basis for beginning to suggest what forms markets may take. All exchanges are influenced and affected by particular contingencies. An analysis of the internal and external contingencies and, more importantly, the mechanisms by which they work might provide a means of categorizing market forms. In the next two sections a first attempt is made to suggest some of the possibilities.

Internal contingent entities

One internal contingency of particular importance in this chapter is the *nature of the buyers and sellers*. Since buyers and sellers are market components by virtue of the definition of the exchange model, then their internal contingencies are likely to be crucial in determining market form.

B2B (business-to-business) markets are identified by the fact that both the buyers and sellers are organizations. However, while B2B is the current currency, it should be remembered that governments, NGOs, not-for-profit organizations and retailers should be included since they are also organizations that are market-involved.

What is it about organizations as sellers and buyers that is likely to affect their exchange behaviour? At a very high level of generalization it could be argued that all organizations do much the same things. They take in resources from the environment and use other resources to transform and create resources that they then exchange in some way with the environment. Differences arise, however, in terms of the kinds of resources and activities that are involved and the necessary relationships among them. A retailer not only utilizes quite different resources and activities from a car assembler, a local government organization or an international aid charity but also organizes them in different ways. Put another way the mechanisms will differ; for example, a crucial difference that can occur in business-to-retailer markets is that for a manufacturer the process is creating bulk while in the latter case it is breaking bulk, leading to particular kinds of timing problems and different ways of solving them.

The internal structures and activities of organizations differ considerably, particularly in terms of the array of variables normally associated with traditional models of organizational buying behaviour (Sheth, 1973); these might include size and composition of the group influencing the buying process (Lau et al., 1999), the social and political processes involved (Pettigrew, 1975) and, at a lower level of aggregation, the particular perceptions, attitudes and preferences of the individuals concerned (Crow et al., 1980). In addition, it seems obvious that the same set of internal contingent entities would be likely to distinguish selling organizations, although it is impossible to know whether this is the case since research on this topic is limited in both scale and scope.

Organizations differ from individual consumers in another major way: the scale of operations. They buy more and sell more, and this has implications in terms of returns to scale and concentration and the possibility of specialization in resources and processes (e.g., key account management, specialist buyers, customization, etc). Size also affects the complexity of organizational structure, control and culture. In each case it is possible to see how any one of these internal entities may affect the parties it chooses to exchange with and the forms of the exchanges. *Exchange entities* have a major impact on the nature of market forms. Organizational services such as consultancies, any form of outsourcing and any pre or post-sale services involve the organization and exchange of human-based resources (Halinen, 1996). These are necessarily much less tangible and more prone to quality problems, increased uncertainty and strongly affect the choice of exchange partner. They also involve quite different operations systems.

The function that the exchange entity has to perform is also a crucial contingent factor. For the buyer it may be important, visible, product-incorporated and complex or the opposite of all of these things. For the seller it can be important, profitable, problematic or a loss-leader. The media of exchanges has been changing in recent years with the growth of B2B e-commerce (Easton and Araujo, 2003), while barter represents another somewhat more antique type of exchange medium.

Where what is exchanged takes time to create we enter the world of project marketing. Here market forms are complex, time-varying and limited instantiations of particular meta-networks that exist without exchange, where links are based on past experience and assessment of present capabilities (Cova et al., 2002).

Exchange relationships

Exchanges exist within and influence a framework of more extensive dyadic phenomena known as relationships. The empirical work of the IMP group leads us to consider whether relationships *per se* are the most enduring feature of B2B markets (Ford, 2002). Within this paradigm exchanges are regarded as one kind of episode or event that occurs between firms that are in a relationship. Given that the single exchange event was defined as the primary outcome to be explained, the existence of a relationship between the buyer and seller can be handled in two different ways in the model.

The first of these is to treat a buyer–seller relationship as existing as a contingent entity located within the buyer and seller entities. The most obvious evidence of such a relationship would be the adaptations and specialized resources that each has invested in to service that relationship. Other resources include the social capital created within each actor that relates to the other, including the records of the history and experience of the relationship. The exchange event in this model has been defined as an economic exchange. However, relationships are sustained and enacted by means of many forms of non-economic exchange, so that the exchange entity can also be considered to have a contingent structure. Again, the important question to ask in this articulation of the model is what are the mechanisms that reproduce the relationship over time?

The second way to handle a relationship is to argue that it is externally contingent to exchanges. Sayer (2000) argues that non-tangible entities can also be used in explanation, and, indeed, at the level of individual behaviour the use of entities, such as attitudes, is almost mandatory. Moreover, social capital might be a candidate for one structural entity that can be said to incorporate the social capital built up by past exchanges. Put another way, relationships may be more or less socially embedded.

Both these alternatives are clearly dealt with in a summary fashion here. The intention is simply to offer an example of the alternative ways in which explanatory models might be built, noting that critical realism imposes a useful discipline in terms of definition of entities and the logic of relationships.

External contingent relations

A key external contingent relation for any dyad is with other exchanges that the actors in the dyad are involved in. In this way we move from exchange and relationships to networks. In what might be called *horizontal* relationships the most obvious proximate relations can be described, quite simply, as *competition* (Easton et al., 1993). Competition, in the sense of sellers competing for the exchanges of buyers, is an indirect network process. Thus, in most markets it is assumed that buyers mediate the relationships between competitors. In a similar way but under different market conditions (e.g., monopoly), sellers could mediate relationships between buyers.

Other proximate actors include buyers' customers, sellers' suppliers, complementary suppliers, subsidiaries and holding companies, joint venture and other partners and any other actors that are involved directly with the buyers or sellers to influence an exchange event. It is clear at this point that a network of external actors can be involved. This network view will be explored in more depth later in the chapter.

The economic system within which exchanges take place is replete with external entities that will affect those exchanges. While few centrally planned economies still exist, there remain very many different forms of economy with different institutions, both national and local. An agrarian economy (e.g., the USA's) is likely to have quite different economic structures and processes than one that is manufacturing or service-based; for example, seasonality would be important with the resulting issues of famine-and-feast situations and spare processing capacity. Countries where corruption is endemic would offer an interesting contrast with those where this is not the case. In the former case, economic exchanges at the firm level are influenced by other external economic exchanges at the individual level.

Space and time can be regarded as external contingencies. Distance between the buyer and seller is a relational contingency derived from the location of each entity; for example, various kinds of industrial districts and localized clusters depend on proximity for their existence, but again the relationship may be necessary but not sufficient. In addition, the social embeddedness that is also a product of local closeness may play a powerful role in supporting these clusters. Physical distance is also mediated by psychological and cultural distance, which affects international market forms in particular ways (Swift, 1999).

Time in various ways strongly impacts on market forms. The history of previous exchanges between buyer and seller are hugely important, whether a relationship can be said to exist or not. While this can be in part considered an internal contingency it also exists outwith the actors as a contingency external to them in terms of the social capital existing in the extended networks to which they both belong; for example, a buyer may be wary of buying from a particular seller that has a reputation for either reneging on its contracts or that seeks to lock in customers to its offerings.

Time is also reflected in the frequency of exchange that distinguishes between capital goods and consumable/component exchanges, for example. In the former case there may be intense relationships over short periods of time (computer installations). In the latter case (steel for car bodies) the market may exhibit rather stable structures over time. In both cases there is a mutual causality between product form and exchange behaviour over time.

The *social and cultural milieu* affects market forms in profound ways. There are huge differences between, for example, the Japanese and American ways of doing business and the resulting market behaviours. Again, it is important to try to understand the exact mechanisms by which the social institutions of a particular nation affect outcomes at the level of a single exchange event. For example, the importance of face-to-face involvement in at least initial exchanges involving personnel from buyer and seller firms varies from culture to culture. Arabic nations tend to require it, while northern Europeans are less concerned and are more ready to use impersonal media, such as e-commerce systems.

The *political* institutions surrounding an exchange may also exert profound influences; for example, market behaviours are regulated in various ways by governments. Two of the most powerful influences are anti-collusion/monopoly regulation and the control of marketized government services.

What this epigrammatic analysis demonstrates is that even at the level of a single exchange event there are a multitude of different entities both internal and external to the exchange that could influence its nature through a variety of different mechanisms. In this way they are likely to be the factors affecting and may even be constitutive of market forms.

In this very brief summary of possible external contingencies what is only too obvious is the variety of possible influences that can cause a particular exchange to occur between two focal actors at a point in time. It emphasizes the point that seeking universal explanations cannot exist. What critical realism does offer, however, is the possibility that entities, their relationships and generic types of causal mechanism may be unearthed or developed that do serve as a set of options or building blocks that help us move beyond the hopelessness of the idea that every event is essentially unique.

Aggregation and emergence

The unit of analysis thus far has been the buyer/seller/exchange triad of entities. However, in the vast majority of contexts we would expect to treat a market as a plurality involving multiple buyers, sellers and exchanges. Some method of aggregation is required.

Critical realists can offer a route since they assume the emergent properties of social systems. What should be emphasized is that this assumption is both theoretical and analytical and ranks alongside the critical realist concept of the real world as something that can only be adduced and never fully known. What emergence means in this case is that a market is not simply an aggregation of all the properties of buyers, sellers and exchanges involved; it has other properties that are attributable to the collectivity. A simple example would be the fact that actors in a "market" perceive it as such and their behaviour is affected by that perception.

The emergent relationship between exchanges and markets is difficult to conceptualize. How do markets come to have properties that are more than simply the sums of the individual characteristics of the exchanges involved? Are there any mechanisms that can be used to relate one to the other?

One answer to these questions might emerge from the observation that exchanges are not independent entities. Their very interconnectedness comes to the rescue. What happens in one exchange can affect what happens in another, whether there exists a strong long-term relationship or not. The latter point needs clarifying. A focal actor may be exchanging with other actors in a transactional, atomistic way and playing the market. But, it is still likely that what happens in one exchange (increase in price of a raw material) will affect what happens in another exchange (purchase of a component), for example, a focal firm putting pressure on a component supplier in order to offset the price increase in raw materials. This connectedness explains how and why whole economies work to satisfy demands of buyers by transforming the resources available.

At a more general level it could be argued that emergence must always involve some element of connectedness; for example, biology could be regarded as an emergent from chemistry in the sense that it is the combinations and connections among chemical entities that create and underpin biological process. The social world is only understood through the connections between the people that comprise that society. Closer to home the properties of organizations stem in part from the connections among the individuals and groups they contain.

This is not to argue that all emergent phenomena can be understood by recourse to the notion of connectedness; for example, in the case of organizations there are clearly other emergent properties that are not necessarily due to connectedness. Organizations offer scale economies that are not available to individuals and have hierarchical structures and cultural norms that control at least to some extent individual behaviours.

An important implication of this conceptualization of emergence is that the forms and processes of interconnection of entities at a lower level of analysis will often be crucial in determining emergent properties at a higher level; for example, where exchange connections are, in theory, relational we might expect certain market properties to emerge. Where they are transactional we might expect quite different market behaviour.

Market definition

Whether relational or transactional it follows that rather than define markets in terms of "homogeneous" groups of independent exchange dyads they could be defined in terms of sets of connected exchange dyads. There then arises the problem of when to stop aggregating. Using the theoretical model presented at the start of this chapter the conclusion would probably be that there is only one market, since all dyads are connected to some extent and no bounds can be set. All buyers, sellers and exchanges are to be included.

While the above statement is ontologically correct in terms of practical research and sensible theorizing, bounds have to be placed around any system, physical or social, which is studied. Therefore, it is suggested that markets could be defined in terms of the relative density of connections. Put another way, markets can be bounded where their *influence*, through exchange dyads, becomes small. The economist's notion of a gap in the chain of substitution measured by the cross elasticity of demand represents a similar approach, although it is limited to "horizontal" markets where buyers' reactions to changes in sellers' offerings set the limits for the market.

The definition used here is closer to the technique of clique detection in social network analysis where the density of any and all connections determines the existence of a clique or cluster of entities; for example, how much does the purchase of an office PC influence and affect the purchase of a grinding wheel by the same firm or the sale of industrial diamonds to the grinding wheel manufacturer? Of course, influence is rather difficult to define and smallness is an arbitrary criterion, but we cannot expect anything else given the complexities of real life markets.

Market models and forms

Defining markets through their connectedness provides a novel way of thinking about market models and forms. It can best be described in terms of a research proposal of daunting difficulty, the purpose of which is a thought experiment rather than the presentation of a set of ready-made doctoral research projects. Beginning with a single exchange it would be possible to map out the other exchanges that each of the (organizational) actors is involved in and to estimate the extent to which other past, current or possible future exchanges influence or are influenced by the focal exchange. The data collected might include past case episodes, participant perceptions or purchase/sales data analysis. It is to be hoped that some form of the 20/80 rule would operate in that most other exchanges would not affect the focal exchange, but a few would in a significant way. Cut-off points would either suggest themselves by the nature of the data or would need to be made arbitrarily and sensitivity analyses performed.

However, markets defined in this way would be unlikely to be uniform in terms of the strengths of the connections. We might have to abandon the term "market" as the sole descriptor of such clusters and borrow from consumer marketing and think about such concepts as segments, micro-segments and fuzzy sets.

The result of this research and analysis would be sets of patterns of actors and exchanges, or nets in IMP terminology. However, since the object is to find a way of defining and characterizing markets the term "net" could be used for the raw data and "market model" used for net patterns that are empirically observed.

The notion of market model is somewhat analogous to the business models so beloved of marketing strategists in that they attempt to capture typical ideal forms.[1] In the case of business models the actor provides the focus and the objective is to understand how value is added in their relationships with other actors. However,

---

[1] I am grateful to Thomas Ritter for pointing out this relationship.

in the market models case it is the market that is categorized, and the aim is clearer definition and greater understanding of markets and their forms.

The next stage in the process would be to examine the nets and attempt to categorize and label them in terms of canonical market model forms. The labelling could be of two types. First, the actual data would be nets (i.e., structures relating actors, their connections and the processes implied by the exchanges). As a result market model-form labels might be almost geometrical in nature, using terms such as vertical, horizontal, narrow, broad, striated, concentrated, diffuse, etc., or they might be described in more imaginative and metaphorical ways, such as small tightly connected nets portrayed as cysts or large and widespread nets stemming from a single customer depicted as deltas.

Second, market model forms could also be labelled in ways that correspond to the common characteristics of the actors or the exchanges or, indeed, any other putative causal factor that might be shown to lead to the particular market model (e.g., manufacturing, project, distribution, transactional, relational, electronic, etc.). In the latter case there is the beginning of a process that attempts to give market model forms theoretical meaning and usefulness, albeit in a rather crude way.

Modelling market forms

The term "form" as a conceptual device implies that it has meaning and can be helpful in explaining the phenomena researched. In simple terms we need to ask why the market models we have uncovered are what they are. Two ways, among the many possible, immediately suggest themselves.

One possible way to do this would be to draw on the critical realist models of dyads and their emergent properties as described in previous sections. For each of these market models it would be necessary to try to explain their patterns and structures in terms of both the necessary and contingent factors in individual dyads and the necessary emergent market processes. For example, at the dyadic level, it may be that a "horizontal"-form market model is explained by the fact that it includes both capital products and the services purchased to maintain them. The purchases are intimately connected.

Another example involves contrasting what we might expect from transactional and relational exchange connections. In the former case it might be predicted that, in general, influences would be small away from the focal exchange. Therefore, transactional markets might be conceived of as relatively tightly clustered patterns of exchanges. By contrast, exchange relationships would "carry" influence further and with more effect, leading to larger and more diffuse markets.

Common to both of these examples is the fact that the links between exchanges are mediated through actors. The horizontal market is created in the first example by the requirement that buyers need complementary products/services by virtue of their internal production technology, an internal contingency. In the second case the constant switching of transactional buyers means that they cannot hope to influence the sellers they switch between, leading to smaller nets than relational buyers would be involved in.

In both cases the mechanisms by which actors link exchanges to each other clearly have to be modelled and understood before any attempt can be made to understand the ways in which market forms emerge. Easton and Lundgren (1992) provide some suggestions, treating such links as flows through nodes. However, this bottom-up approach will always be problematic given the complicated structures of the market models and the possibility of multiple mechanisms working at once.

The second approach is to concentrate on the processes of emergence rather than micro-level mechanisms. An example of such an approach is provided by some recent work on network process modelling using complexity theory (Easton et al., 1998). Starting with simple market models the sequencing of exchanges was simulated using Boolean logic to describe the flow through nodes operation of the simulated actors. The simulated systems, suitably constrained, flowed into system attractors that modelled stable but dynamic states. These states emerged given any possible starting point for the simulated system, and this emergent process is one that is a central component of complexity theory. One set of results demonstrated, for example, that the requirement for tight sequencing of exchange events, as required by many service systems, tends to lead to narrow vertical market forms.

Conclusions

There are several conclusions that emerge from the arguments presented above. The first is that it should be fruitful to problematize the whole notion of what a market is and what forms it can take. It is only too easy to continue to take for granted the definition of a concept that in part demarcates the discipline that some of us claim to inhabit. Second, the relationship between the concepts of market and market forms has also been identified as problematic since market is a social phenomenon, and consequently the forms it can take are part of both its constitution and definition and they are therefore mutually determining.

Third, a new market definition has been offered that defines markets in terms of influence among and between exchanges. It is argued that this approach offers quite a different view of market properties and forms. For example, in vertical terms, where middlemen are involved, exchanges involving manufacturer to distributor and distributor to final organizational customer would probably need to be included in the definition of a market. In terms of horizontal relationships, complementary suppliers and competitors might need to be involved. It also distinguishes between market forms that are structural/processual and those that are taxonomic.

Fourth, critical realism offers a way to theorize about and research markets defined in this way. It can provide modes for modelling exchanges and linking them to market models, although it has to be admitted that the task is never going to be easy. It also presents an opportunity to think about the concept of emergence, which has always been an incipient problem in industrial networks research. What are the links that exist between the small nets that we tend to research and the greater networks of which they are a part? How do nets and networks affect individual exchange relationships and vice versa? What are the properties of nets and networks that cannot be adduced from their constituent parts? These are huge questions and ones that deserve greater attention than we have given them in the past.

References

Ackroyd, S. and Fleetwood, S. (eds) (2000). *Realist Perspectives on Management and Organisations*. London: Routledge.

Axelsson, B. and Easton, G. (eds) (1992). *Industrial Networks: A New View of Reality*. London: Routledge.

Bagozzi, R.P. (1975). Marketing as exchange. *Journal of Marketing*, **39**: 32–39.

Bagozzi, R.P. (1978). Marketing as exchange: A theory of transactions in the marketplace. *American Behavioral Scientist*, **21**: 535–556.

Bagozzi, R.P. (1979). Towards a formal theory of marketing exchanges. In: O.C. Ferrell, S.W. Brown and C.W. Lamb Jr (eds), *Conceptual and Theoretical Developments in Marketing* (pp. 431–447). Chicago: American Marketing Association.

Bhaskar, R. (1978). *A Realist Theory of Science*. Hemel Hempstead, UK: Harvester Press.

Cova, B., Ghauri, P. and Salle, R. (2002). *Project Marketing*. Chichester, UK: John Wiley & Sons.

Crow, L.E., Olshavsky, R.W. and Summers, J.O. (1980). Industrial buyer's choice strategies: A protocol analysis. *Journal of Marketing Research*, **17**: 34–44.

Easton, G. (2002). Marketing: A critical realist approach. *Journal of Business Research*, **55**(2): 103–109.

Easton, G. and Araujo, L. (1993). Language, metaphors and networks. In: D. Sharma (ed.), *Advances in International Marketing* (Vol. 5, pp. 67–85). Greenwich, CT: JAI Press.

Easton, G. and Araujo, L. (2003). Evaluating the impact of B2B e-commerce: A contingent approach. *Industrial Marketing Management*, **32**(5): 431–439.

Easton, G., Burrell, G., Shearman, C. and Rothschild, R. (1993). *Managers and Competition*. Oxford, UK: Blackwell.

Easton, G. and Lundgren, A. (1992). Changes in industrial networks as flow through nodes. In: G. Easton and B. Axelsson (eds), *Industrial Networks: A New View of Reality*. London: Routledge.

Easton, G., Wilkinson, I. and Georgieva, C. (1998). Towards evolutionary models of industrial networks: A research programme. In: H.G. Gemünden, T. Ritter and A. Walter (eds), *Relationships and Networks in International Markets* (pp. 273–293). Oxford, UK: Elsevier Science.

Ford, D. (ed.) (2002). *Understanding Business Marketing and Purchasing*. London: Thomson Learning.

Guillet de Monthoux, P.B.L. (1975). Organizational mating and industrial marketing management. *Industrial Marketing Management*, **4**(1): 25–32.

Halinen, A. (1996). Service quality in professional business services: A relationship approach. *Advances in Services Marketing*, **5**: 315–341.

Hibbert, B. and Wilkinson, I.F. (1994). Chaos theory and the dynamics of marketing systems. *Journal of the Academy of Marketing Science*, **22**(3): 218–233.

Lau, G.T., Goh, M. and Phua, S.L. (1999). Purchase-related factors and buying center structure: An empirical assessment. *Industrial Marketing Management*, **28**(6): 573–587.

Lawson, T. (1997). *Economics and Reality*. London: Routledge.

Oliva, R.A., Oliver, R.L. and Bearden, W.O. (1995). The relationship among consumer satisfaction, involvement and product performance: A catastrophe theory application. *Behavioural Science*, **40**(2): 104–132.

Pettigrew, A. (1975). The industrial purchasing decision as political process. *European Journal of Marketing*, **9**(1): 4–14.

Sayer, A. (1992). *Method in Social Science; A Realist Approach* (2nd edn). London: Routledge.

Sayer, A. (2000). *Realism and Social Science*. London: Sage.

Sheth, J. (1973). A model of industrial buying behaviour. *Journal of Marketing*, October, 50–56.

Swift, J.S. (1999). Cultural closeness as a facet of cultural affinity: A contribution to the theory of psychic distance. *International Marketing Review*, **16**(2–3): 182–201.

Wilkinson, I. and Young, L. (1994). Business dancing: An alternative paradigm for relationship marketing. *Asian–Australian Marketing Journal*, **2**(1): 67–80.

Zeithaml, V.A., Varadarajan, P.R. and Zeithaml, C.P. (1988). The contingency approach: Its foundations and relevance to theory building in marketing. *European Journal of Marketing*, **22**(7): 37–64.

Part Two
Interaction between market actors

Investigation of the role of marketing when market exchange is characterized by the interaction of heterogeneous resources involves a first prerequisite of delving deeper into what is going on between individual market actors. The following five chapters (Chapters 5 to 9) all start out from the individual exchange between two business actors. Chapters 5 and 6 investigate the basic foundation of markets: Chapter 5 explores the content and function of exchange, and Chapter 6 examines the content and function of interaction. If these two contributions outline the constitution of markets when resources are heterogeneous and business actors interdependent, the following two chapters (Chapters 7 and 8) consider the opportunities and restrictions of exchange in such a context. Chapters 7 and 8 discuss marketing from the perspective of the selling company and highlight its possibility of influencing and utilizing exchange. Chapter 9 focuses on the role of the buying side, which presents itself rather differently in a market situation characterized by resource heterogeneity and interdependence between business actors. A common theme of all the chapters is the examination of the opportunities (and restrictions) the individual business actors face in relation to their counterparts and, particularly, how these possibilities can be identified and analysed.

In Chapter 5, Håkansson and Prenkert use an activity system model to examine different ways to identify exchange activities and to discuss the understanding of the market exchanges they produce. The authors suggest that there are four main ways that exchange activities have been defined in both the academic and business worlds: the first focuses on products, the second on facilities, the third on co-operation and the fourth on networks in terms of connection between relationships. The main difference between these approaches to market exchange is that the content differs in terms of central "exchange object", something that also has an effect on the view of the business actor and the context.

Each approach to market exchange is preceded by a discussion of the viewpoints of different theoretical schools, but they can also be identified in empirical order of exchange. Certainly, each way has its merits and, depending on the situation and ambition, they can all be beneficial to companies. However, each has special consequences, and business actors must adapt to each type in order to treat exchange in an efficient or effective way. In the future each type will probably be developed further, but we might also expect a number of new combinations. One theoretical contribution is the possibility of examining the exchange process in terms of the large variety involved: something that is difficult to handle both for the academic scholar and the business actor, but which gives the two focal counterparts in an exchange situation more freedom to decide where to put the boundaries/limitations.

In Chapter 6, Ritter and Ford focus on interaction and discuss both why there is such a restricted amount of economic research focused on this important phenomenon as well as identifying some areas where it has been explored in one way or another. One major reason behind the neglected interaction is claimed to be the underlying assumption of classical marketing approaches. With a focus on the individual, independent company marketing and purchasing simply becomes an issue to handle in isolation. However, an exception to the traditional approaches is constituted by distribution scholars; it is here the authors find the earliest attempts to capture interaction effects on market exchange.

This research is later followed by the IMP (industrial marketing and purchasing) approach, including the network approach. (The latter research stream is used in the final section of the chapter to formulate an approach where interaction is one of the central concepts.) The discussions lead to the identification of six concepts that can all be related to interaction and its effect on change and stability. These six are broken down into three pairs: confront and conform, consolidate and create, and coerce and concede. The central theme of Chapter 6 is a need to include two active partners that both contribute to all of the key processes that occur in the marketplace.

The customer portfolio perspective in Chapter 7 is used by Selnes and Johnson to develop a theory of marketing strategy. The starting point is a typology of exchange relationships. Three types of products (parity, differentiated and customized) are combined with two types of transactions (continuous and repetitive). The typology is first used to discuss the six different cells in a static way, describing the differences between them. In a second step the typology is used in a more dynamic way, as the same product can appear in several of the cells and that this is not by chance but follows certain patterns due to hetero-geneity, innovations and competitive moves. The article stresses the importance of finding ways to capture dynamic situations where even those dimensions that in most earlier analyses were seen as constants, such as the product, are changing!

Chapter 8 by Anderson is about the creation of value for customers. Compared with Chapters 6 and 7, this chapter can be seen as an attempt to help sellers manage the interaction. Anderson starts out from different definitions of customer value and concludes with one value equation, where the value minus price for the offer from the focal supplier is compared with the value minus price for the best alternative. The author then discusses and compares value expressions based on ratios, using an approach based on differences. One important issue is related to value ambiguity and the importance this gives to reference dependence. The final section of Chapter 8 is a step-by-step suggestion for how to develop a value calculation for a selling company's product. One important feature of this chapter rests in its demonstration of how actors are involved in and wrestle with economic consequences. The difficulties lie both in their own limitations and in analysing highly complex economic influences.

Chapter 9 by Gadde and Persson looks at developments within purchasing. During the last decades a dramatic shift has appeared within this company function; this also is an indication of how industrial marketing has changed. The change is described in three interrelated aspects: purchasing efficiency has been reformulated, from focusing on price for single products to the total costs associated with inputs; the role of purchasing has changed from being mainly operative to having severe strategic implications; and, finally, relationships with suppliers are looked on more from a revenue side. All these changes can be seen as the mirror image of a number of the challenges on the selling side that we identified earlier.

In summary, Chapters 5–9 bring two major conclusions concerning market exchange to the fore: first, the exchange processes are clearly interactive, varied and dynamic, underlying the need for better models for capturing what's happening in the marketplace; and second, this variation also affects economic logic due to differences in how exchanges or interactions are formed and utilized. This is a strong argument for the need to develop new economic normative models that have a dynamic base.

Exploring the exchange concept in marketing

5   *Håkan Håkansson and Frans Prenkert*

Introduction

That exchange activity is at the core of marketing has been claimed by, among others, Alderson (1957, 1965), Kotler (1967), Bagozzi (1975a, b), Snehota (1990) and Kinner et al. (1995). However, conceptualizations of *what* the exchange is vary between these researchers (Khodabandehloo, 1995). This variation is at the heart of this chapter, and we will try to explore and analyse the consequences of it.

One very basic characteristic buried in the word "exchange" itself is that it requires two actors (i.e., there is a need of both an actor, such as a company, and a counterpart, such as a customer or a supplier), as recognized by Kotler (1972, p. 47). It is a simple and still quite dramatic requirement because it introduces not one but several dynamic elements as soon as we recognize the existence of some differences between the two sides; for example, in the way the actors utilize the specific exchange in relation to other internal or external activities and processes they are involved in. In this case the dynamic aspect of the exchange process itself is not just emphasized, but gives rise or extra energy to other dynamic processes.

In this chapter we will see how these dynamic aspects have been identified and conceptualized in earlier approaches. Our ambition is to systematically describe and compare these approaches in order to identify their consequences. The starting point will be taken in business-to-business exchange relationships, but the discussion is also relevant in business-to-consumer situations.

Content of exchanges

One suggestion made in a number of studies is that the exchange activity contains both social and economic elements. For example, Bagozzi (1975b) argued that exchanges could be of three types: utilitarian, symbolic and mixed. Of these three, most empirical studies seem to suggest that in business-to-business marketing situations the typical case is that the utilitarian aspect dominates, but that symbolic social elements also play a fundamental role; this is partly due to the fact that the two parties have significant social features, but is also due to the fact that there are important uncertainties and ambiguities in the utilitarian aspects. An important part of these uncertainties is related to technological factors. Thus, in order to be utilitarian in the long run the immediate purpose of an individual exchange on a "business-to-business market" could be multiple. "Economic, technical and social elements" have to be involved in these exchange activities.

Paralleling the idea put forward by Granovetter (1985), the type of exchange activity we are interested in is embedded; it is not purely social and symbolic – that would be to over-socialize it – and neither is it purely economic utilitarian – that would be to under-socialize it (Granovetter, 1985; Uzzi, 1997). In our case this social embeddedness also includes technical items. Thus, embeddedness in social and technical dimensions is often of significant importance.

There are two main consequences: one is that despite the basic economic utilitarian purpose we have to consider the inclusion of social aspects; and the second and more important one is that we have to consider the possibility that exchange, embedded in technical and social items and structures, changes the economic logic. One consequence, if that is the case, might be that the utilitarian dimension will influence the behaviour in a different way to that postulated in economic theory (i.e., that perhaps the pure market will not auto-matically give the most efficient use of resources).

Direction of exchange

McInnes (1964) discusses a broad conceptualization of marketing where exchange can be identified, although he never uses the word "exchange":

> *A concept of marketing in its widest sense, therefore, **is any activity which actualizes the potential market relationship between the makers and users of economic goods and services**.* (McInnes 1964, p. 57, emphasis in original)

If we translate or combine this conceptualization of marketing with exchange we can suggest that actualization of market potential is achieved through the exchange. The exchange processes actualize the latent potential since they establish a boundary-crossing contact. One consequence is that there is a certain direction in exchange since this way of conceptualizing marketing indicates that it is a "motion" or a force, as Shaw suggested in 1915. McInnes (1964) expresses it as:

> *Marketing is the creative force which reacts on these potentialities as material. Hence it is necessary to analyze marketing activity, an activity which in its essential and generic meaning is actualization.* (McInnes, 1964, p. 61).

These activities are of a genuinely boundary-crossing character and suggest that business exchange has a certain direction – a dynamic dimension. The exchange results in something new or, in the terminology of McInnes, something is being actualized through the process.

It has been suggested in earlier business-to-business studies that business exchange activity equals the view on and conceptualizations of interaction (e.g., Håkansson, 1982; Håkansson and Waluszewski, 2002a). Although the word "interaction" is used to denote approximately the same thing as exchange, it can be of interest to note that the word "interaction" has a direction in its meaning as well.

Interaction can be seen as a dialectic process characterized by two-way activities across borders between two parties, hence constituting an element of social behaviour (Buber, [1927] 1970; Homans, 1951). The two parties interact with each other, and from this interaction something new arises. Hence, there is a sense of direction in the dialectic process toward something novel. It is a progressive development. Hegel's dialectic is defined as the process of necessary change involving three elements: an existing thing or thought, its opposite or contradiction and the unity resulting from their interaction. This heritage from Hegel is an important distinction compared with a reciprocal process, which is of a mutual character as similar to the dialectic process, but lacks this sense of direction. Interaction in terms of business exchange activity can accordingly be seen as a two-way dialectic process across boundaries, creating new solutions as well as linking two parties to each other. The parties could be any type of actor, ranging from individuals to social collectives, such as departments, organizations or nations (Kotler, 1972), including more or less of technical and human parts.

Context of exchanges

As we have seen above, business exchange activity implies exchange behaviour and, according to most business-to-business research during the last 20 years, business exchanges are to be understood as unfolding over time in an exchange relationship. This exchange relationship supplies one critical element of the contextual situation of the exchange.

However, it also actualizes another issue: as the exchange unfolds over time it can become embedded in the context in different ways. In other words, it can be related to other processes within the two parties and between other actors in what Bagozzi, with inspiration from Alderson, termed an "organised behavioural system of exchange" (Bagozzi, 1974, p. 78). Due to the way the two parties integrate the exchange into other activities the effects will be different. The way will even influence the principal nature of the exchange activity.

The process unfolding over time can be seen as a way to close something that in principle is an open "system". The reason to close it is to achieve efficiency in the exchange (i.e., to achieve utilitarian goals). However, this will at the same time define the character of the central activity in question. Different ways to close the system will be a way to define and specify what kind of process it is through relating it to specific surrounding processes. The parties can in this way be seen as choosing (consciously or not) how they want to embed the exchange activity. Business exchange activity can in this way be seen as a truly complex human activity that, potentially, includes a large number of facets. It is like an untreated diamond, which can be made into a number of different jewels with different surfaces reflecting the light in many ways. However, when the two parties have embedded the exchange in a certain way it will affect what can be done later. Closing it to one specific activity "system" means implicitly that other possible closures into other possible systems are disregarded.

Within the area of research labelled "cultural psychology" (Cole, 1990; Cole et al., 1997), a model has been developed to analyse complex human-organized activity systems. This model is based on the works of Vygotsky ([1934], 1986, 1978, 1981) and puts forward the cultural and contextual interdependence between human activity in society and individual cognitive development.

This interdependence is manifest in the model in that it is based on the notions that humankind and society are integral systems rather than separate entities, requiring a system view, and that this system of humankind and society is characterized by continuous qualitative transformation, requiring a historical view. Departing from these two requirements the activity system model is based on the principle of *cultural mediation*; this means that the relation between subject and object of an activity is mediated through various kinds of tools and instruments deployed to manipulate the object. However, it also means that the relation between subject and context in which the subject is embedded is mediated through various institutionalized structures, such as rules, norms, power and roles. Thus, we have a notion of "double mediation" as we set out to analyse human activity in an activity systems model. Due to this notion of mediation the activity systems model is graphically depicted as a triangular shape in accordance with Figure 5.1, so as to depict these mediating relations between elements of human activity.

According to the analysis of Engeström (1987) in developing the model, the nodes of the model represent the constituent parts of any generic human activity and this activity always simultaneously encompasses instances of production, exchange, distribution and consumption. Although each part of the model in Figure 5.1 is related to the others, let us, for the sake of clarity, examine them more closely as we go through the nodes *A* to *F*:

- Node *A* denotes the *object* and the *outcome* of the activity performed within the activity system (Engeström, 1987, pp. 65–66). The object of activity represents the entity toward whose transformation the activity is geared. The outcome of the activity corresponds to the goal of the collective in question, although in any given concrete activity system, deviations between the actual outcome and the goal of the collective as well as of individuals occur.

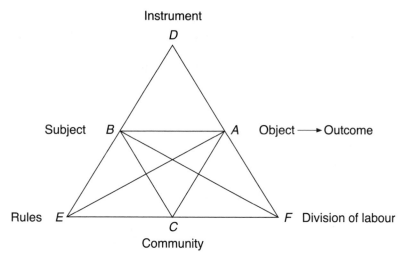

Figure 5.1—The constituent parts of the generic activity system.
Adapted from Engeström, 1987, p. 78.

- Node *B* denotes the subject performing the activities depicted in the activity system (i.e., the agent). This agent is not isolated but linked to the community as well as to other nodes, as is indicated in the activity systems model. This agent could be a collective subject consisting of a number of individuals (Engeström, 1987, p. 70).
- Node *C* denotes the *collective* of subjects to which the activity system pertains and represents the social context of the subject of the activity; this is essentially a result of the adoption of the theoretical idea of the hierarchical levels of human activity. Engeström asserts that "[h]uman labor, the mother form of all human activity, is co-operative from the very beginning" (Engeström, 1987, p. 66).
- Node *D* denotes the instruments used by the subject to perform the activities so that a certain outcome is achieved and so that the object of activity is transformed. As we have already seen, these instruments are of both material and psychological character (Engeström, 1987, p. 60). Examples of such instruments are; language, knowledge, algebraic symbol systems, abstract models, maps, drawings, physical tools (such as hammers, nails and machinery), computers, production systems, manufacturing facilities, etc. These instruments could be viewed as technology and techniques used to transform the object of activity and to achieve the desired outcome of the subject.
- Node *E* denotes the institutionalized structures in the form of explicit rules as well as the more implicit norms and conventions used to mediate the relation between a subject and a community; these are socially infused and structured as the interaction between subject and community is of a social character. As with the collective node, this is also essentially a result of the adoption of an activity

theoretical idea. In this case it is about the sociality that distinguishes humankind from the animal kingdom in which every subject exists (Engeström, 1987, pp. 74–78).

- Node *F* denotes the organization of tasks of the subjects into certain areas according to the institutionalized structures of a *division of labour*. The division of labour of the activity system links subjects performing actions to the wider activity, which, according to Engeström (1987, p. 82), is the fundamental source of contradiction. The contradiction arises as a result of the confrontation of subactivities determined by the division of labour and the total activity system.

Nodes *A* to *C* represent the core elements of human activity, while nodes *D* to *F* represent the mediatory elements. The distinction is central as it means that any one of the core elements may relate to any other core element not only directly but also by way of any one of the mediatory elements. The mediatory elements are never directly related, but serve only as mediators between the core elements; this is illustrated in Figure 5.1, which shows that each of the core elements has five ways to relate to the other elements, as indicated by the lines originating at the core element nodes. Two of these lines refer to the other two remaining core elements, while the remaining three refer to the three mediatory elements. The mediatory elements each have only three ways to relate to the other elements, their lines *always* referring to the core elements, *never* to another mediatory element.

To summarize, an activity system model is a model for analysing purposive goal-directed actions performed by subjects with certain tasks and who are socially related to each other in a collective entity. These actions are enhanced by the use of material and psychological tools and performed within socially negotiated and institutionalized contexts composed of tacit norms and values, as well as of explicit rules and regulations. When taken together these various activities of subjects in a social context, with assigned tasks and using instruments to transform the object and to bring about an outcome, embody an activity system.

The model above is described at the most general level. One important dimension of the model is that it points out that there is a close and unavoidable connection between the single activity and the activity system it is part of. A certain way of looking at the activity also influences the way the activity system has to be delimited. Here we want to use the model to identify how different ways to define or delimit exchange activities will affect the related activity systems. In this way we can both characterize different theoretical ways to approach the concept of exchange and discover how companies can choose to use exchange.

Closing exchange systems

The starting point for our discussion is that the exchange process, by definition, is an open process, but for it to create any type of efficiency it has to be closed by the two involved parties. This process is what we referred to as business exchange activity earlier and, borrowing the terminology from Bagozzi (1974, p. 78), we have also called it an "exchange system". The exchange system is in principle open in character and could be potentially closed in many different ways by the two involved actors (i.e., they can choose to "develop or extend" the content of it to a larger or lesser extent).

We suggest that the activity systems model can be used to model in detail these closures, and we will use it in this section to illustrate four different ways of closing exchange systems. These four different types of exchange are chosen to represent what seem to be the most used by companies and to represent the most typical cases from a theoretical point of view.

They are identified in terms of which resources are involved in the exchange and the four can be labelled: (1) *buying/selling* when the closure starts out from the product or service, (2) *producing/using* when it takes the production facilities as the focus, (3) *co-operation* when it takes the total relationship between the two, or the alliance, as the basic unit and (4) *networking* when it also includes other relationships in the basic unit. These four types have been suggested by Håkansson and Waluszewski (2002a). Here they will be used to identify typical ways to define and relate the business exchange activity in terms of exchange systems, thereby relating them to other internal and external processes. The four activity systems produced in this way can be identified as four alternative ways of interpreting the central activity in the business exchange.

All four types have been subject to investigations in prior research, but seldom combined or analysed in the same setting. The first one, being the most restricted, is close to the classical way of defining market exchange as transactions: isolated or in a series. It is used in transaction costs analysis (Williamson, 1971, 1975, 1985; Williamson and Masten, 1999; Rindfleisch and Heide, 1997), as well as in the marketing mix approach (e.g., Kotler, 1967; McCarthy, 1960). The second has been identified by Richardson (1972) and has been further analysed within the markets-as-networks approach by Dubois (1994, 1998) and Håkansson and Snehota (1995) and within the resource-based view (e.g., Foss, 1997; Loasby, 1991). The third has been studied in research on strategic co-operation by such researchers as Axelrod (1984), Lorange and Roos (1992), Ring and Van de Ven (1992), Clarke-Hill et al. (2003). The fourth has been studied in some network-oriented studies (e.g., Blankenburg and Johanson, 1992; Håkansson and Snehota, 1995; Håkansson and Waluszewski, 2002).

Four ways of closing exchange systems

We will start the analysis with the buying/selling exchange activity followed by producing/using, co-operation, and networking, respectively. In so doing we will adhere strictly to the structure given in the activity systems model as devised by Engeström (1987, p. 78), hence discussing the logical object, subject, community, instruments, rules, division of labour and outcome elements, respectively, for each of the four exchange activities. By so doing we achieve four typical closures and see how this will affect the constituent elements of the four activity systems.

The buying/selling activity system

Object. Market theory can be used as the starting point for this case, because it suggests that buying/selling activity revolves around products. We define products as the total offer of an actor to its customers, including tangible as well as intangible elements. The substantiated resource called "products" displays physical as well as social properties, although the physical properties may in certain situations be emphasized; this parallels the discussion in cultural psychology, where Leontyev (1978, 1981) asserted that, while focusing on the physical object in a material sense, these objects also include socially determined properties. Hence, the object could be seen as a system of physical things and social entities making sense in a social setting. Products as objects of buying/selling activity fit nicely into this description.

Subject. The firm is the classical subject in market theory (e.g., Coase, 1937). The firm is supposed to try to maximize its profit, which also is supposed to be the only goal in *each transaction.*

Community. The community is in this case termed the "market" and it is generally characterized in terms of product differentiation and number of sellers and buyers.

Instruments. Given that a focal firm is identified as the subject, its products as the object and the market to which it caters as the community, the instruments used are very limited – none if the market is perfect. If the market is more or less given, the company can only use different internal rules to adapt to it.

Rules. The basic rules are given by the economic interest of the firm in combination with the given market. The basic rule is to optimize the economic result, which is translated into choosing the counterpart with the best value/price ratio. Some other common rules governing buying/selling activity are associated with industry-wide norms and standards; these are manifest through certifying organs, quality-issuing organs and other types of quality control, such as ISO standards.

Division of labour. In the buying/selling activity the division of labour is based on the specialization of a market player in supplying standardized products with the potential to solve certain specific problems of the customer. The customer, too, is specialized but in terms of *their* products solving specific problems of *their* customers in a completely different market. A division of labour emerges as a consequence of this state of play, where the market players are specialized in its respective offers in the market. The division of labour arises from the fact that two market players that interact *actually are different.* This difference has its roots in that the two are specialized in different knowledge areas.

This difference in specialization (Piore, 1992) is what we here call the division of labour of the buying/selling activity. Indeed, the difference in specialization is the very reason the buying/selling activity can exist at all. Hence, the buying/selling activity is the means used to bridge between two otherwise different firms and, by so doing, creating a minimum common denominator; this may be compared with the notion of different product markets and the entrepreneurial function through which they are linked (Kirzner, 1973, p. 96).

Outcome. Given the fact that the object of the buying/selling activity are the products of a focal market player, the subject is that market player and the community is a market, the outcome is identified as pertaining to the exchange of resource elements that generate the lowest costs and, hence, are the most efficient exchanges. One major part concerns the prices paid, which are de-termined by negotiation between the interacting parties in the market, and a second part concerns the costs of performing the transaction (i.e., for using the price mechanism).

The first part has been analysed in great depth in classical economics, while the second part was first identified by Coase (1937) and more extensively analysed in the transaction cost paradigm, starting with Williamson (1971) and Alchian and Demsetz (1972). Within the transaction cost paradigm there are an abundance of studies identifying when the firm should choose different ways to adapt to the market situation due to variation in transaction costs (i.e., the use of vertical integration and the use of relationships with single counterparts). For overviews see Rindfleisch and Heide (1997) and Williamson and Masten (1999, part III).

The producing/using activity system

Object. When we go from the buying/selling to the producing/using activity the *production facilities* on both sides are emphasized (Håkansson and Waluszewski, 2002b). These facilities are the basic resources that the exchange activity activates. The production facilities of two or more actors become connected through exchange activity; this creates some specific problems or opportunities, as Richardson (1972) first observed and analysed. The exchange creates an inter-dependence that can be handled in different ways given its characteristics. Complementarity and similarity are the two dimensions used by Richardson (1972, p. 890ff) in order to differentiate between three solutions. These co-operation forms are direction through planning (hierarchy), standardization in order to use the market and the matching of plans (co-operation). It is the third solution that becomes important in situations in which there are close complementarities and low similarities when performing two related activities.

Subject. There is no change in the subject in relation to the first case. It is still the firm, but it has now come to include some technological dimensions. It has in this way got some substance, which will influence the behaviour compared with the first situation.

Community. In accordance with the above the community is identified as the market, but there are certain specific interdependencies. Thus, there are some systemic aspects that are enhanced, which is why we can describe the community as a "market system". However, this is not an aspect discussed by Richardson (1972). In a work highly related to Richardson (1972), Dubois (1994) discusses this systemic aspect more thoroughly and then uses networks to characterize the community.

Instruments. What a technological firm involved in the producing/using activity supplies is in fact not primarily material products, but rather *solutions* to handle co-ordination problems based on technological interdependencies. The instruments that are being used are represented with *adaptation*. Through co-operation, both business units can adapt to the given problem and situation in order to find a solution by matching their plans (Richardson, 1972).

Rules. The rules governing the producing/using activity are of a somewhat different character than those of the buying/selling activity. In the producing/using activity, trust in each other of being able to solve technological problems in adherence to given standards and within certain limits govern the activity. Soft rules in terms of confidence in each other's area of expertise and technical knowledge becomes important. The overall governing mechanism is confidence in solving the specific problems arising in a situation.

Division of labour. Compared with the first case this situation also starts out from specialization, but adds the integration dimension more explicitly. Specialization drives the process of integration, as recognized by Piore (1992), in which specialized business units tend to integrate their activities when they are similar and complementary (Richardson, 1972). If they are dissimilar and complementary they can be handled by market exchange, but it is when they are closely complementary and dissimilar that we need the special type of quasi-integration labelled "co-operation" by Richardson (1972). In the producing/using activity this third type of integration has a larger impact in creating an efficient division of labour (i.e., the specialization can be driven one step further). When it comes to the producing/using activity, specialization and integration have to be combined in order to reach a higher level of division of labour. This technological specialization and integration, which is developed through the activation and creation of resources with other technological actors, creates a technological identity of a given actor that reflects the inherent division of labour.

Outcome. Given the fact that the object of the producing/using activity are production facilities, the subject is a firm with a technological substance and the community is the market system, the outcome is identified as pertaining to how well the technological firm solves co-ordination problems that relate to important counterparts. In other words, this has to do with a given firm's efficiency in solving another firm's problem; this means that one technological firm's producing activity is linked to another's using activity through the outcome of the joint producing/ using activity.

The co-operation activity system

Object. Co-operation always comprises a collective notion with at least two entities co-operating for one reason or another. Co-operation emerges due to resource dependencies between two actors (see Axelrod, 1984 and Pfeffer and Salancik, 1978) and is seen as an ingredient in the interaction between them (Håkansson and Waluszewski, 2002b). Co-operation and co-operative relationships have been recognized in strategic management literature as an "alternative form" of governance (e.g., Ring and Van de Ven, 1992) between markets and hierarchies and have been at the core of the discussion in research on strategic alliances (Ghoshal, 1987; Lorange and Roos, 1992; Nohria and Eccles, 1992; Niren et al., 1995; Clark-Hill et al., 2003).

The impact of strategic alliances has been investigated in such different areas as new product development (e.g., Kotabe and Swann, 1995) and third-party logistics (Hertz and Alfredsson, 2003), to name but two. Sometimes, the focus has been directed toward partnering (e.g., Anderson and Narus, 1991; Dubois and Gadde, 2000; Gadde and Snehota, 2000) and vertical co-operative relationships between the firms in business markets (e.g., Eccles, 1981; Dwyer et al., 1987; Johnston and Lawrence, 1988; Anderson and Narus, 1990) rather than on strategic alliances. Regardless of what kind of manifestations the co-operation activity takes – alliance, partnering or anything else – it is suggested that co-operation activity in general is performed within a *dyadic business relationship* (Anderson et al., 1994; Blankenburg et al., 1996, 1999). Hence, we contend that it is around business relationships that the exchange activity revolves and that these relationships constitute the objects of the activity.

Subject. The typical subject in all the studies above is the focal business unit. We prefer to use business unit instead of firm because the strategic, social and technical features are more emphasized than strict, economic ones. Thus, the point of view adopted is that of one of the business units that partake in co-operation in a dyadic relationship (Anderson et al., 1994).

Community. Despite the fact that the object of the activity is a specific business relationship and that the subject of co-operation is a business unit within that relationship, the most used type of community in the studies above is still the market in which the two business units in question are situated. Thus, the dyadic relationship is seen as an exception and as floating around in a more or less atomistic market.

Instruments. What we chose to label *proximity* can be identified as an important instrument used in co-operation; this has to do with knowledge about others and means knowledge about the other actor in terms of activities and resources. This knowledge is used as an instrument in co-operation as it smooths the relationship in question. Proximity could essentially be of two types: first, one has to do with the actual physical distance between the two co-operating parties, and, second, the other has to do with the "perceived distance" between the two business units; this has to do with the ability to work together in a business relationship. When it comes to proximity as the ability to work together, it has to do with two things: speed and readiness. First, speed is essential in the co-operative activity since some problems require immediate attention so as to, for example, avoid costly interruptions in logistical flows. Second, readiness ties into the former in that it means the readiness to solve a problem regardless of its character and context (i.e., whenever and wherever it occurs).

Rules. The rules governing the co-operative activity between the two actors could be both formal and informal in nature. Informal rules are mainly implicit and take the shape of *expectations* toward the other party's behaviour rather than explicit rules. These expectations are socially negotiated in the activity, are highly implicit and function as norms governing the behaviour based on trust in the counterpart. The formal rules include contractual agreements (e.g., MacNeil, 1980), standardized routines and protocols for behaviour, etc.

Division of labour. The assumed division of labour in the co-operative activity is based on the combination of the existence of specific co-operations within a market community. The basic division resembles the one identified in the buying/selling and producing/using activities earlier. But, one more element needs to be added. The reason that two business units collaborate is that there are some specific dependencies between their two sets of resources. These dependencies are unique and can only be utilized through close co-operation. Thus, specialization has created these interdependencies, and by combining the resources extra revenues can be created. The division of labour will consequently include an element of "focusation" where the resources, in terms of the type of products offered, the production facilities used to produce the offer, the competence and knowledge of the people involved and/or the financial resources available, are directed toward a specific counterpart.

Outcome. We started out our analysis of co-operation by referring to Pfeffer and Salancik (1978), who established that co-operation arises as a consequence of resource dependences between business units. This dependence requires co-operation to get access to the resources in question. It is contended here that the outcome of co-operation is an increase in a business unit's effectiveness through what Alchian and Demsetz (1972) labelled *team effects*. The idea of team effects means that the utilization of resources can be improved over time and, thus, is never a priori given. Hence, such resources are given their economic value on the basis of how they are combined with other resources, and the overall effectiveness of the business unit is consequently enhanced by the realized outcome of co-operation; this means that through co-operation the use of resources of a focal business unit becomes closely related to some resources of a co-operating partner, which will improve their value.

The networking activity system

Object. The object of the networking activity concerns the business relationships that are connected directly to the focal relationship. Influence and change are achieved by the networking activity in terms of actions channelled through a given relationship that will have repercussions in the connected relationships.

This connectedness is the object of networking. What happens in one business relationship has repercussions in the other, due to their connectedness. Thus, a change in the relationship between two actors may have effects on another relationship and vice versa (e.g., Blankenburg and Johanson, 1992; Håkansson and Snehota, 1995).

The connection illustrated in Figure 5.2 means that changes in the business relationship between actor *A* and *B* will have consequences for the business relationship between actor *B* and *C*; this is the triadic unit that is defined as the object of the networking activity. In principle, connectedness may exist between any relationships, not only those in proximity within a triad, thus invoking a picture of relationships "channelling" influence. However, not all changes in a relationship result in changes in the connected relationships (Halinen et al., 1999), although changes concerning such issues as technology usually have a spreading effect in the network (Håkansson and Waluszewski, 2002a, p. 196).

Departing from the role of the single dyad as a mechanism for change in business networks (Anderson et al., 1994; Håkansson and Snehota, 1995), Halinen et al. (1999) developed a framework for analysing change as confined or connected. Confined change means such changes that are limited to the dyadic exchange relationship, whereas connected change means changes that spread to the wider network through the relationship connections. The networking activity

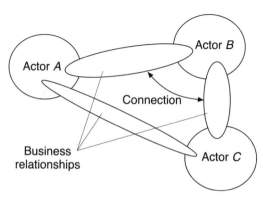

Figure 5.2—The triadic structure of connected business relationships.

could also be directed toward distanced business relationships farther away from the focal relationship. In these circumstances the networking activity changes the network structure as it loosens or tightens it, thus increasing or decreasing the space available for manoeuvring in the network.

Subject. The subject that is in focus is the focal business unit. This business unit is trying to utilize the connections between its relationships in order to exert influence on others to try and achieve a better position or a better economic outcome.

Community. The word "networking" indicates that the larger community is seen as a network. The connections serve as the institutional context. Here, the direct relationships between single business units in the industrial network are only the starting point, and the existence of important effects of indirect relationships is emphasized. This web of business units, made up of direct and indirect relationships, creates the community where different units try to mobilize support for creating or hindering specific changes in the network.

Instruments. The prime instruments in networking are business relationships. They are used to exert influence on other business relationships in the focal net. The use of a business relationship as an instrument in networking could be separated into three distinct primordial types: linking activities, tying resources and bonding actors, based on the substance layers of business relationships (Håkansson and Johanson, 1992; Håkansson and Snehota, 1995). Pressure to change is produced in the network, because these three substance layers of a business relationship are linked to the three substance layers of another proximal business relationship (Håkansson and Johanson, 1992; Håkansson and Snehota, 1995).

These vectors of change could be generally described as attempts to connect activities to the total activity pattern in a network, as attempts to influence the web of actors through politics and social pressure and as attempts to embed resources in an underlying resource constellation. These activities are all examples of networking, although they focus on different aspects of the business relationship being used to exert influence on the network.

Two types of instrumental uses of business relationships can be identified in networking: first, a given business unit could use the relationship to leverage its position in order to exert influence in the network; this has to do with knowledge *about* the network, its parts and connections, its history, dominating actors and the division of labour structure (business units use this knowledge and its position to leverage influence in the network), and, second, a given business unit could use the relationship to leverage its role in order to exert influence on the network; this has to do with knowledge about *how to* network, what the different types of business relationships may be used for, in what way, to what end and how this use will affect the relationship in question. A certain use of a certain relationship may not only lead to a desirable end but also cause harm to the relationship in question. There could be a trade-off of this kind. Business units use this knowledge too and its role to leverage influence in the industrial network.

Rules. When discussing the influence of institutionalized structures in the buying/selling activity, we recognized that they might have both restricting and enabling effects on a focal business unit's locus of activity, with special reference to the market tools to be used. However, this has wider principal implications, as was observed by Håkansson (1989, pp. 15 and 26), as this creates a dualistic character of the network, meaning that it may function as both a constraining factor and an enabler for change.

From the perspective of the focal business unit, networking activity is thus a matter of mobilizing support from the network in order to carry through desired changes and is highly influenced by institutionalized structures. In networking, previous interaction in the form of co-operation seems to be of extra importance, since such activity may have created memories and attitudes for the people involved; this is beneficial for the networking actor in that it may have created a capital of trust. This capital of trust is based on a notion of a person being trustworthy, something that could be created by memories of prior interaction in the co-operation activity. Such trustworthiness, stemming from relationship connections, adjoins other ingredients to form the power necessary to be able to exert influence.

Other ingredients of this power may be the direct possession of resources or the indirect control of resources through various business relationships that are being exploited in the networking activity. Hence, power to exert influence in networking mainly stems from two sources: first, power that stems from authority based on trust and trustworthiness, what we could call "social arguments", determines the extent of influence and behavioural restrictions in the activity; and, second, power that stems from resource access, what we could call "technical arguments", determines likewise the extent of influence and behavioural restrictions.

Division of labour. In networking the division of labour between business units is based on the number and types of connections to other business units. This connectedness profile is based on the pattern of connections between business units and business relationships within the network of the focal business unit; this creates a unique connectedness profile for each business unit in terms of its connections with various resources in the network. This profile functions as the basis for parcelling out rewards and distributing influence.

With many connections of great substance the prospect of both influencing and being influenced increases (Håkansson and Ford, 2002). Existing forces may be able to influence by networking, which means that a business unit may mobilize support for an idea that may eventually result in a change in an institutionalized structure, as is the case of the interplay between new ideas and already activated structures in technological development (e.g., Håkansson and Waluszewski, 2002a, pp. 82–83). This mobilization of support is done through combining resources. Identity is another way to express this. As a consequence, identity is something that can neither be created nor maintained by an isolated business unit, but is dependent on interaction with others (Håkansson and Waluszewski, 2002a, p. 154f).

Outcome. In order to gain access to certain resources the network must continuously be changed. When attempting to gain access, a business unit could attempt to exert influence through its business relationships, using them as a tool. Influence of this type is exerted by means of the networking activity. As a consequence of this networking activity, pressure to change emerges. This pressure could be seen as attempts to change the network or as vectors of change (Håkansson and Snehota, 1995). Whether successful or not, it is usually a matter of what type of change is being initiated and whether it counteracts institutionalized structures or not. While one motive for networking is resource access and the intention is to exert influence, the outcome of networking is an attempt to change the current structure of the overall network so as to increase the effectiveness of the subject business unit. Another and often more important motive for networking is to increase the utilization of resources.

One outcome of networking is to increase a business unit's effectiveness through *resource embeddedness.* The concept of embeddedness is borrowed from Granovetter (1985) and has been elaborated by Wedin (2001) and Håkansson and Waluszewski (2002a) for single resources. It means that resources, through being used together, give each other features (i.e., become embedded in each other). One important consequence is that a resource (technical or organizational) is never given a priori, but that its features are created in interaction with the context in which it is embedded (Håkansson and Waluszewski, 2002a, p. 32). Hence, resources are given their economic value from their relations with other resources with which they interact, and the overall effectiveness of the business unit is the realized outcome of networking.

Comparing the four activity systems

A summary of the four identified activity systems is presented in Table 5.1. These four activity systems representing four alternative closures of an exchange system show an interesting pattern. First, there is a systematic change from left to right with an increased complexity in terms of the number of dimensions or aspects involved. However, there is at the same time a more fundamental change from the first to the second compared with the first to the third; this regards how the community is defined.

In the producing/using activity system there is a systemic aspect included in the community that is often neglected in approaches based on the co-operation activity system. In this way the networking activity system is a combination of two and three.

However, there is also an interesting difference in relation to outcomes, and this is the issue that we now turn to.

Table 5.1—Four possible closings of exchange systems

Generic activity system element	Buying/Selling activity system	Producing/Using activity system	Co-operation activity system	Networking activity system
Object	Products	Facilities	Business relationship	Triad
Subject	Firm (economic unit)	Firm (production and economic unit)	Business unit (technical, social and economic unit)	Business unit
Community	Market	Market system	Market	Network
Instruments	Market tools	Adaptation in products and facilities (co-operation)	Proximity	Business relationship
Rules	Market rules	Trust in problem-solving capacity	Trust in the counterpart	Technical and social arguments
Division of labour	Specialization	Integration	Focusation	Resource combining
Outcome	Efficiency	Efficiency	Effectiveness	Effectiveness

Outcomes: services creating value

One important effect of the variety in the contexts is that it changes the outcome of the exchange activity. Business exchange activity clearly indicates that there exists something that is exchanged, but what this is depends on how the context is delimited. If we start out from the buying/selling activity it is either a product/ system and/or a service that is exchanged for money. However, if we start from the producing/using activity it is utilization of capacity or capabilities. If we start from the co-operation activity the core is moreover general services or knowledge, and if we start with the networking activity it is a piece of the structure that is exchanged.

However, irrespective of whether physical objects or services are exchanged, Penrose (1959) concluded that physical resources, such as products, are not valued for anything more than the services they create. Thus, all exchange activities are conducted in order to realize services. Business exchange activity is characterized in that it is through exchange that the potential services of resources are released and value arises. In other words, the outcome of the business exchange activity is the services rendered, and the goal of business activity is to actualize the potential services buried in the innermost recesses of the included resources.

Actors do business by performing boundary-crossing activities that generate business exchange. This business exchange is seen as stemming from the realization of the potential services in resources, usually conceptualized as *value* (e.g., Snehota, 1990). Hence, business exchange activity comprises engagement in a mutual boundary-crossing value-creating process. The benefits are the activities of the potential services inherent in resources and are coloured by the contextual situation in which the exchange occurs.

The objective is to create value through the release of the services habituated within resources. The value comes into existence in the exchange of resources, while services are a function of how the exchange is embedded in the two parties' institutionalized context. Hence, the value of a given exchange to the two parties is dependent on the value of the services that the exchange resources render to the parties individually.

Based on the earlier discussion there are reasons to propose that there are two different types of processes involved that could be a factor fuelling business exchange activity. The major reason for this is a recognition of the heterogeneity of resources recognized by, among others, Penrose (1959), Alchian and Demsetz (1972) and Rosenberg (1982). This heterogeneity could then be a critical source for the importance of business exchange activity. The existence of the two types of value creation processes is illustrated in Figure 5.3.

The two types of value creation processes are closely related, but there is a problem in that they have different logics and contexts. The exchange value is determined in a process in which the two parties relate to each other and to others.

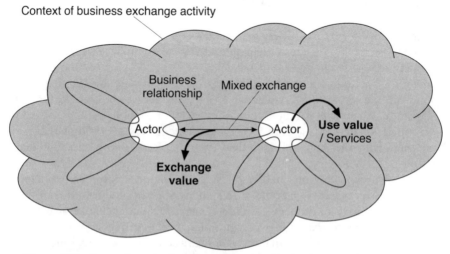

Figure 5.3—Two value creation processes related to business exchange activity.

Both sides have alternatives, even if they sometimes are of a quite different character; this is important and has been stressed in all market analysis. But, the two parties also have to relate to each other. In this process there is an important cost element, often depicted as transaction costs. Each party has, through the exchange, to discover the best way of utilizing the resources of the counterpart. Consequently, there is an important knowledge component.

In summary, the exchange value can be seen as a conceptualization of the *efficiency* of an activity system focusing on the *exchange* of resources. Even though every actor always has alternatives, once the choice about how to close an activity system together with another party has been made, this dyad becomes the benchmark for the efficient exchange of resources; this is the case with the buying/selling and the producing/using activity. As we saw in our earlier analysis, efficiency is emphasized in these activities as they are directed toward the very relation between input resource elements and the output, in terms of how well the acquired resource element produces a solution to a problem or caters to a need.

The use value is determined by the capabilities of each party to contextualize the resources rendered from a given exchange. Whatever is received through the exchange has to be combined with what is received from other exchanges, as well as with what is controlled or produced within the actor/company. It is this combining that is highly influenced by how the parties choose to close the "activity system": the broader the exchange the more different the types of resources. However, even when the exchange is limited to the buying/selling process there are a number of resources that can be related. It can especially be other products or facilities that can be adapted to the use of the exchanged product or service. Thus, the use value can be seen as a conceptualization of the *effectiveness* of an activity system, emphasizing the *utilization* of resources.

This effectiveness of the activity system is dependent on its relations with other activity systems, because the utilization of resources is highly contextual and embedded in existing resource structures in the network. These resource structures are manifest in the adjoining activity systems and function as the benchmark for the effectiveness of a given activity system, since the resources that are being exchanged sooner or later must relate to these existing structures. Thus, making the exchanged resource of a given activity system fit with the existing resource structure is an overall goal, the attainment of which determines the effectiveness of the activity system in question.

Distinct from the conceptualization of efficiency as dyadic based on exchange value, effectiveness is conceptualized as inherently contextual and networked based on use value. This latter case is illustrated in our earlier analysis of the co-operation and the networking activity, as these activities are directed toward how well a given resource may fit with the wider structural resource pattern. However, in order to determine how well a resource fits with a pattern the resource must be exchanged – it cannot be done a priori. Hence, use value cannot be achieved without exchange value, and an effective activity system always also implies an efficient activity system (but not the other way round). Whether a given activity system emphasizes one or the other depends on how it is closed in negotiation with a counterpart and how it relates to other arbitrary closures of activity systems in its context.

The embedded exchange

The picture emerging is rather complex. Exchange between two parties is basically an open process where whatever issue the two parties want to bring in can be brought into the process, but due to the discretion of the counterpart only some of these issues will be acted on. The exchange process is related to value creation and efficiency in two ways: first, the process in itself can be handled more or less efficiently, and, second, what is produced within the exchange can be more or less conceptualized. In order to be efficient the two parties have to agree and "close" the activity system. Thus, the creation of limitations or boundaries is a key ingredient in the interaction. The two sides need to find some common boundaries in the exchange (i.e., close the exchange process into a common activity system). At the same time, each of the actors has to close the internal activity system (i.e., how the outcome of the exchange process is embedded in the other processes each is part of). Here each of the two sides can make its own limitations, in so far as each is free to do whatever they want with the outcome of the exchange.

The exchange process will in this way become more or less embedded in a number of other processes and thereby into a number of different resources on each side. However, this will also affect how the two sides want to continue the exchange and will create a certain tension in the process. These tensions create the basis for the change and development of business exchange activity and serve as a hotbed for new and innovative ways of closing the exchange processes into common activity systems.

References

Alchian, A.A. and Demsetz, H. (1972). Production, information costs, and economic organization. *American Economic Review*, **LXII**(December): 777–795.

Alderson, W. (1957). *Marketing Behavior and Executive Action: A Functionalist Approach to Marketing Theory*. Homewood, IL: Richard D. Irwin.

Alderson, W. (1965). *Dynamic Marketing Behavior: A Functionalist Theory of Marketing*. Homewood, IL: Richard D. Irwin.

Anderson, J.C. and Narus, J.A. (1990). A model of distributor firm and manufacturer firm working partnerships. *Journal of Marketing*, **54**(January): 42–58.

Anderson, J.C. and Narus, J.A. (1991). Partnering as a focused market strategy. *California Management Review*, **33**(Spring): 95–113.

Anderson, J. C., Håkansson, H. and Johanson, J. (1994). Dyadic business relationships within a business network context. *Journal of Marketing*, **58**(October): 1–15.

Axelrod, R. (1984). *The Evolution of Co-operation*. New York: Basic Books.

Bagozzi, R.P. (1974). Marketing as an organized behavioral system of exchange. *Journal of Marketing*, **38**(October): 77–81.

Bagozzi, R.P. (1975a). Marketing as exchange. *Journal of Marketing*, **39**(October): 32–39.

Bagozzi, R.P. (1975b). Social exchange in marketing. *Journal of the Academy of Marketing Science*, 3(4): 314–327.

Blankenburg, D. and Johanson, J. (1992). Managing network connections in international business. *Scandinavian International Business Review*, **1**(1): 5–19.

Blankenburg, D., Holm, D., Eriksson, K. and Johanson, J. (1996). Business networks and co-operation in international business relationships. *Journal of International Business Studies*, **27**(5): 1033–1053.

Blankenburg, D., Holm, D., Eriksson, K. and Johanson, J. (1999). Creating value through mutual commitment to business network relationships. *Strategic Management Journal*, **20**(5): 467–486.

Buber, M. ([1927] 1970). *I and Thou* (translated by W. Kaufmann). New York: Charles Scribner's Sons.

Clarke-Hill, C., Li, H. and Davies, B. (2003). The paradox of co-operation and competition in strategic alliances: Towards a multi-paradigm approach. *Management Research News*, **26**(1): 1–20.

Coase, R.H. (1937). The nature of the firm. *Economica*, **IV**(November): 386–405.

Cole, M. (1990). Cultural psychology: A once and future discipline? In: J. J. Berman (ed.), Nebraska Symposium of Motivation, 1989: Cross-cultural Perspectives (pp. 279–336). Lincoln, NE: University of Nebraska Press.

Cole, M., Engeström, Y. and Vasquez, O. (1997). Introduction. In: M. Cole, Y. Engeström and O. Vasquez (eds), *Mind, Culture, and Activity: Seminal Papers from the Laboratory of Comparative Human Cognition*. Cambridge, UK: Cambridge University Press.

Dubois, A. (1994). Organising industrial activities: An analytical framework. Unpublished doctoral thesis, Chalmers University of Technology, Gothenburg.

Dubois, A. (1998). *Organising Industrial Activities across Firm Boundaries*. London: Routledge.

Dubois, A. and Gadde, L.-E. (2000). Supply strategy and network effects: Purchasing behaviour in the construction industry. *European Journal of Purchasing and Supply Management*, **6**(3-4): 207–215.

Dwyer, F.R., Schurr, P.H. and Oh, S. (1987). Developing buyer–seller relationships. *Journal of Marketing*, **51**: 11–27.

Eccles, R.G. (1981). The quasi firm in the construction industry. *Journal of Economic Behavior and Organisation*, **2**: 335–357.

Engeström, Y. (1987). *Learning by Expanding: An Activity-Theoretical Approach to Developmental Research*. Helsinki: Orienta-Konsultit Oy.

Foss, N.J. (1997). The classical theory of production and the capabilities view of the firm. *Journal of Economic Studies*, **24**(5): 307–323.

Gadde, L.-E. and Snehota, I. (2000). Making the most of supplier relationships. *Industrial Marketing Management*, **29**(4): 305–316.

Ghoshal, S. (1987). Global strategy: An organizing framework. *Strategic Management Journal*, **8**: 425–440.

Granovetter, M. (1985). Economic action and social structure: The problem of embeddedness. *American Journal of Sociology*, **91**: 481–510.

Håkansson, H. (ed.) (1982). *International Marketing and Purchasing of Industrial Goods: An Interaction Approach*. Chichester, UK: John Wiley & Sons.

Håkansson, H. (1989). *Corporate Technological Behavior. Co-operation and Networks*. London: Routledge.

Håkansson, H. and Ford, D. (2002). How should companies interact in business networks. *Journal of Business Research*, **55**(2): 133–139.

Håkansson, H. and Johanson, J. (1992). A model of industrial networks. In: B. Axelsson and G. Easton (eds), *Industrial Networks: A New View of Reality* (pp. 28–36). London: Routledge.

Håkansson, H. and Snehota, I. (eds) (1995). *Developing Relationships in Business Networks*. London: Routledge.

Håkansson, H., and Waluszewski, A. (2002a). *Managing Technological Development: IKEA, the Environment and Technology*. London: Routledge.

Håkansson, H. and Waluszewski, A. (2002b). Path dependence: restricting or facilitating technical development? *Journal of Business Research*, **55**(7): 561–570.

Halinen, A., Salmi, A. and Havila, V. (1999). From dyadic change to changing business networks: An analytical framework. *Journal of Management Studies*, **36**(6): 779–794.

Hertz, S. and Alfredsson, M. (2003). Strategic development of third party logistics providers. *Industrial Marketing Management*, **32**(2): 139–149.

Homans, G. C. (1951). *The Human Group*. London: Routledge & Kegan Paul.

Johnston, R. and Lawrence, P.R. (1988). Beyond vertical integration: The rise of the value-adding partnership. *Harvard Business Review*, **66**(4): 94–101.

Khodabandehloo, A. (1995). Marknadsföring som utbyte: En idéhistoria, en pluralistisk ansats. Unpublished doctoral dissertation, University of Stockholm, Stockholm [in Swedish].

Kinner, T., Bernhardt, K. and Krentler, K. (1995). *Principles of Marketing*. New York: Harper Collins.

Kirzner, I.M. (1973). *Competition and Entrepreneurship*. Chicago: University of Chicago Press.

Kotabe, M. and Swann, K. (1995). The role of strategic alliance in high technology new product development. *Strategic Management Journal*, **15**: 135–152.

Kotler, P. (1967). *Marketing Management. Analysis, Planning and Control*. Englewood Cliffs, NJ: Prentice Hall.

Kotler, P. (1972). A generic concept in marketing. *Journal of Marketing*, **36**(April): 46–54.

Leontyev, A.N. (1978). *Activity, Consciousness, and Personality*. Englewood Cliffs, NJ: Prentice Hall.

Leontyev, A.N. (1981). *Problems of the Development of Mind*. Moscow: Progress.

Loasby, B.J. (1991). *Equilibrium and Evolution: An Exploration of Connecting Principles in Economics*. Manchester: Manchester University Press.

Lorange, P. and Roos, J. (1992). *Strategic Alliances: Formation, Implementation, and Evolution*. Cambridge, MA: Blackwell.

Macneil, I.R. (1980). *The New Social Contract. An Inquiry into Modern Contractual Relations*. New Haven, CT: Yale University Press.

McCarthy, E.J. (1960). *Basic Marketing*. Homewood, IL: Richard D. Irwin.

McInnes, W. (1964). A conceptual approach to marketing. In: R. Cox, W. Alderson and S.J. Shapiro (eds), *Theory in Marketing*. Homewood, IL: Richard D. Irwin.

Niren, M.V., Williams, L.S. and Dennis, C.R. (1995). An analysis of strategic alliances: Forms, functions, and framework. *Journal of Business and Industrial Marketing*, **10**(3): 47–60.

Nohria, N.N. and Eccles, R.G. (eds) (1992). *Networks and Organisations: Structure, Form and Action*. Boston: Harvard Business School Press.

Penrose, E.T. (1959). *The Theory of the Growth of the Firm*. Oxford, UK: Basil Blackwell.

Pfeffer, J. and Salancik, G.R. (1978). *The External Control of Organizations. A Resource Dependence Perspective*. New York: Harper & Row.

Piore, M.J. (1992). Fragments of a cognitive theory of technological change and organizational structure. In: N.N. Nohria and R.G. Eccles (eds), *Networks and Organizations: Structure, Form and Action* (pp. 430–444). Boston: Harvard Business School Press.

Richardson, G.B. (1972). The organisation of industry. *The Economic Journal*, (September): 883–896.

Rindfleisch, A. and Heide, J.B. (1997). Transaction cost analysis: Past, present, and future applications. *Journal of Marketing*, **61**(4): 30–54.

Ring, P.S. and Van de Ven, A.H. (1992). Structuring cooperative relationships between organisations. *Strategic Management Journal*, **13**: 483–498.

Rosenberg, N. (1982). Technological interdependencies in the American economy. In: N. Rosenberg (ed.), *Inside the Black Box: Technology and Economics*. Cambridge, UK: Cambridge University Press.

Shaw, A.W. (1915). *Some Problems in Market Distribution*. Cambridge, MA: Harvard University Press.

Snehota, I. (1990). Notes on a theory of business enterprise. Unpublished doctoral dissertation, Uppsala University, Uppsala.

Uzzi, B. (1997). Social structure and competition in interfirm networks: The paradox of embeddedness. *Administrative Science Quarterly*, **42**(1), 35–67.

Wedin, T. (2001). Networks and demand: The use of electricity in an industrial process. Unpublished doctoral thesis, Uppsala University, Uppsala.

Williamson, O.E. (1971). The vertical integration of production: Market failure considerations. *American Economic Review*, **LXI**(2/May): 112–123.

Williamson, O.E. (1975). *Markets and Hierarchies: Analysis and Antitrust Implications*. New York: Free Press.

Williamson, O.E. (ed.) (1985). *The Economic Institutions of Capitalism*. New York: Free Press.

Williamson, O.E. and Masten, S.E. (eds) (1999). *The Economics of Transaction Costs*. Cheltenham, UK: Edward Elgar.

Vygotsky, L.S. [1934] (1986). *Thought and Language*. Cambridge, MA: MIT Press.

Vygotsky, L.S. (1981). The genesis of higher mental functions. In: J.V. Wertsch (ed.), *The Concept of Activity Soviet Psychology*. Armonk, NY: Sharpe.

Interactions between suppliers and customers in business markets

6   *Thomas Ritter and David Ford*

Introduction

Suppliers, customers and others interact in business markets. Each individual or company brings its own problems, abilities, knowledge, ideas, prejudices and experiences to its dealings with a counterpart. They may discuss, request, offer, demand, advise, inform and threaten each other. They may co-operate, disagree, develop, adapt, order and deliver, often simultaneously. Interaction has been at the core of business ever since people started to trade with each other; this leads to the simple, but profound conclusion that what happens between business companies is not within the complete control of either of them, but is the outcome of the interactions between them.

However, it is striking how much research into business markets, business marketing and purchasing takes the perspective of a *single company* as a sole actor and pays little attention to the interaction between companies. Because of this, the first aim of this chapter is to examine why research into markets and marketing has tended to neglect or oversimplify interaction. Following this, we take a look at some of the different streams of research in marketing and examine how they have approached the idea of interaction and the contribution that they have made to understanding it. Finally, we propose an approach to help us understand interaction in business markets which draws on research from a number of areas.

Difficulties and defence mechanisms in research in business markets

Social science research in general faces the difficulty of having to deal with situations where there are a large number of different influences on an individual or an organization and where those influences are likely to be from a number of other parties or observable phenomena. It is also concerned with situations where those influences are themselves interconnected. Social science research must also deal with the effects on an actor of *changes* in those influences and the effects on the influencers themselves of the process of influencing. Since it deals with living individuals it is also concerned with situations where the subjects of influence are also influencers themselves and where these processes are constantly evolving over time.

Business research almost always faces this situation of multiple parties, multiple phenomena and multiple influences. No individual or organizational actor exists, or can operate, independently. Each is subject to a large number of complex and varying influences, from both internal actors (e.g., colleagues, departments) and external actors (e.g., suppliers, customers and competitors). At the same time, the views, actions and expectations of an individual or organization are likely to affect numerous others, often in diverse ways. Thus, each actor that consciously or unconsciously influences another is itself subject to influence from those that it attempts to influence. In this way the knowledge, attitudes and actions of each actor are constantly evolving in the light of the actions of others and their experience of the effects of their own actions on others.

Defence mechanisms

These difficulties have led business and other social science researchers to employ a number of what might be termed *defence mechanisms*. All of these mechanisms have the effect of simplifying reality. But, each leads to other problems. In particular, each serves to de-emphasize, hide or even ignore the processes of interaction between different actors and the dynamics of that interaction. Some of these defence mechanisms are as follows:

- *Description*: Researchers often devote considerable attention to simply describing the situation of their subjects or the influences on them. These descriptions provide a rich and colourful representation of a business situation, but offer few insights into the processes of influence between those involved.
- *Isolation*: Researchers often examine a single phenomenon or its effects, assuming that each can be isolated from the effects of different phenomena. The "problem-solving" or normative orientation of much business research has meant that it has been carried out from the perspective of a single actor or "client", whether a marketing company, a purchasing company or a company seeking to develop strategy within some generalized environment.
- *Generalization*: Some research examines the overall effects of generalized external stimuli on a single subject. Other studies may consider phenomena in a single situation or at a discrete point in time and generalize from this to wider circumstances.

- *Simplification*: Some research expresses influences in terms of independent and dependent variables and, thus, infers that the process of influence takes place in a single direction, rather than interactively.

Approaches to marketing and interaction

There are a number of identifiable approaches to the general study of market behaviour and marketing activity, ranging from the early functional, institutional and utility approaches (e.g., Nystrom, 1949 and Cherington, 1920) to the more recent managerial and network approaches. There are also a number of important approaches to the examination of specific aspects of markets and marketing, such as distribution, international marketing or business relationships.

In this section we will explore two of these general approaches – managerial marketing and the network approach – and three specific approaches – distribution, international marketing and the IMP (industrial marketing and purchasing) approach to business relationships. We will use these approaches to illustrate the wide variety that exists both in the extent and the ways in which each addresses the issue of interaction between actors. We will then attempt to achieve some integration of ideas from each approach. We start with the managerial approach to marketing.

The managerial approach to marketing

The "managerial approach" to the study of marketing has predominated for many years, since the early work of Howard (1957), Stanton and Buskirk (1959) and Phelps and Westing (1960). This approach is firmly anchored in a single-company view, seeing marketing solely as a managerial problem for that company. In this, a single marketing company assembles a *marketing mix* and launches it toward a market with the aim of achieving the reaction of purchase. The perspective is that of action and reaction, rather than interaction.

Research within this approach frequently demonstrates some of the defence mechanisms we have referred to. Many studies attempt to describe or analyse the process of a single purchase by either consumer or business buyers (e.g., Robinson et al., 1967). Others examine the effects on that process of a variety of factors, both intrinsic and extrinsic to the buyer, which may be manipulated by a supplier (e.g., Sheth, 1973 and Boutilier, 1993). Some studies attempt to determine which of these effects may be successful in different circumstances in achieving *a single response* from the customer, usually a purchase. Examples include Fishbein (1967) and Aaker (1997). Many other studies are concerned with the process of "managing" by a customer of its purchases from a supplier, or of "managing" by a supplier of its customers within so-called CRM (customer relationship management), relationship marketing or supply chain management. Examples include Davis (1993), Grönroos (1994) and Christopher et al. (2003). Finally, there are widespread attempts to examine marketing, purchasing or overall strategy *from the perspective of a single company*, operating in a generalized "environment", concentrating on its analysis, its strategy and the supposed effects of this on its customers and/or suppliers. Some of the discussion of market orientation can be seen in this light as there is an underlying assumption of a generalized market or homogeneous segments to which a firm can be oriented (Narver and Slater, 1990; Jaworski and Kohli, 1993).

Over time the complexity of factors that have been considered has increased and the causal links have been analysed more finely. But, the processes have still largely been examined from the perspective of one of the participants, and the direction of effects has been seen to be largely one-way, rather than interactive.

Distribution

There was a strong interest in the specific issue of distribution during the period from the 1950s to the 1970s, which coincided with the development of the general managerial approach to marketing. The characteristics of distribution led researchers to directly face many of the common problems of business research that we have highlighted. The difference was that the multi-company characteristics of distribution make it difficult for researchers to employ the defence mechanisms we have noted:

> *(Distribution) channels have been neglected as a separate area of inquiry because their complexity discourages investigators. Channels in a very real sense are among the most complicated phenomena encountered in an advanced economy. . . . For this reason, if for no other, the nature of marketing channels has not been explored satisfactorily, either from an empirical or theoretical point of view.* (Mcammon and Little, 1965, p. 322)

Despite the problems, researchers into distribution did address the interactive aspects of channel behaviour, such as the conflicts that frequently occur between companies, how power might be exercised by different companies, what would be the reactions of those subject to it and which type of company is likely to become the most powerful, under different circumstances (Grether, 1937; Balderston, 1958; Revzan, 1961). A particularly important aspect of power and conflict in channels that concerned researchers is the tendency of companies to form alliances with others to increase their power over other types of channel members (Palamountain, 1955). Many channel writers were also interested in the difficulties that a company faces when trying to achieve change in a channel, against the opposition of surrounding companies. Researchers also tried to explain the inertia of both individual channel members and their collective tendency to react negatively toward change (Hoffer, 1951; Kriesberg, 1955; Mcammon, 1963).

Writers within the channel tradition were strongly aware of the importance of differences in the views of individual companies, whether producers, wholesalers or retailers, about the actions of others and of the channel as a whole. Channels were not seen to be designed by any one company, but to be the outcome of the decisions, aims and *interactions* of many companies. For example:

> *The middleman is not a hired link in a chain forged by a manufacturer, but rather an independent market, the focus of a large group of customers for whom he buys. After some experimentation he settles upon a method of operation, performing ... functions he deems inescapable in the light of his own objectives, forming policies for himself wherever he has freedom to do so. His choices are in many instances tentative. He is subject to much influence from competitors, from aggressive suppliers, from inadequate finances and faulty information, as well as from habit.* (Mcvey, 1960)

> *... In cohesive channels the firms think of themselves as being highly interdependent. In other cases the relationships between firms are loosely structured and fluid. Even in these situations there is interaction and interdependency. The behaviour of channel members is regulated by a code that specifies types of acceptable competitive behaviour.* (Wroe Alderson, 1957)

However, there was little transfer of ideas from the more interactive channel literature to those writers taking a managerial view; this was perhaps due to a lack of interest on the part of the latter or due to a realization that, the complexity revealed by the channel literature limits the independent action of an individual company and restricts the ability of marketing academics to give straightforward prescriptions to a managerial audience. Indeed, it is quite rare to find reference to the channel literature in today's writing.

International marketing

The channel literature was built on the idea that the interaction between any single company and those around it, rather than its own independent strategy, determines outcomes for a single company. In contrast, the international marketing literature mostly takes the perspective of a *single* company operating in or seeking to enter and affect a *generalized* environment. It infers that outcomes are largely the result of the actions of a single company, and it is concerned with the skills, resources, experience and attitudes of that single company:

> *International usually refers to either an attitude of the firm towards foreign activities or the actual carrying out of activities abroad ...* (Johanson and Wiedersheim-Paul, 1975, p. 306)

The single-company orientation of much of the international marketing literature can be seen in the many attempts to refine the stages in the process of a single company's internationalization and the factors that lead to shifts between stages (e.g., Perlmutter, 1969; Tookey, 1969; Simpson and Kujawa, 1974; Bilkey and Tesar, 1977; Johanson and Wiedersheim-Paul, 1975; Johanson and Vahlne, 1977). These studies suggest that internationalization is an incremental process, through which a single company builds on its own experience and acquires knowledge about specific markets gained in one stage, before moving to the next stage of greater export market involvement (e.g., Sharma, 1992). It sees the international marketer as a company that chooses where, how and through whom to market.

The IMP approach

The first book from the IMP Group (Håkansson, 1982) placed interaction at the centre of its research. This research took the perspective that business marketing and purchasing takes place within the context of *relationships* that are frequently close, complex and long term. Rather than taking a separate view of supposedly separate transactions or sales or purchasing actions, the research emphasized the interconnections between sales and purchases, *over time*. Both buyer and seller were seen as active participants in *interactions* that extend beyond the purchase of a predetermined standardized product so that both are likely to be involved in the design, development and fulfilment of complex offerings. In this way the work challenged the view of marketing as the manipulation of a marketing mix that is developed solely by a supplier. The study also emphasized the stability of market structures where the incumbents know each other well and are individually significant to each other, rather than being part of an anonymous, atomistic supply or customer market.

The network approach

The IMP approach was in some ways a precursor of the network view of business markets. Rather than being concerned with single relationships between companies or the portfolios of relationships of a single company, the network approach suggests that a company and its relationships can only be understood as part of a complex and dynamic network of interconnected relationships (Håkansson and Johanson, 1992; Johanson and Mattson, 1992).

The contrast between the network approach and previous literature can be illustrated very clearly in its approach to international marketing. Rather than a view that centres on the company itself and its strategy, the network approach sees international marketing development as a process involving: a company's existing home and overseas relationships; those that it may wish to establish in a new market; the effects of its attempts to develop relationships with new counterparts on its existing relationships of itself and its counterparts; and the actions of both the company *and of others around it*. In other words, the process is driven by the interaction of all of the actors in a network (Johanson and Mattson, 1988).

This interactive view does not focus solely on a single active producer and the passive responders to its actions, but on the purposeful interaction between many companies, such as retailers, wholesalers, importers and finance houses (Johanson and Mattson, 1988; Forsgren and Johanson, 1992; Hallen, 1992; Blankenburg, 1995; Blankenburg et al., 1997).

This analysis may highlight the difficulties encountered by a company in establishing a "position" in a new market, because of the interlinking network of relationships that may already be developed. Similarly, market entry may involve a complex set of relationships, so that companies that are competitors in one market co-operate in another and are suppliers and customers to each other in a third (Forsgren and Johanson, 1992). Finally, the complexity of foreign market development means that a company must continually review its actions in the light of ever-changing conditions; this makes following a pre-designed company-oriented strategy extremely difficult, as conditions are not easily predicted nor easily adapted to.

An integration of ideas on interaction from different approaches

Our examination of these general and specific approaches to business markets – the managerial approach, distribution, international marketing, the IMP and the network approach – highlights a number of issues that must be faced in trying to make sense of interaction in business markets, as follows.

The unit of analysis: The managerial and the international marketing literature inevitably restrict the ability to explore what happens in the interaction between companies, because their unit of analysis is not only a single company but also a single type of company – a producer. In contrast, the IMP approach takes its unit of analysis as the relationship; this concentrates attention on the interaction between customer and supplier. The IMP, distribution and network literatures show that an understanding of what happens between companies, or even within a single company itself, can only be achieved by employing a unit of analysis beyond that of the individual firm.

Conflict and co-operation: The distribution literature emphasizes conflict between companies and pays less attention to co-operation between them as part of their conflict with others.[1] In contrast, the view of customer–supplier interaction in both the IMP and the network literature emphasizes co-operation,

---

[1] In this way it did not take note of Wroe Alderson's (1957) assertion that marketing researchers concentrated too much on conflict in business or Gettel's view that companies were engaged in "pluralistic competition", comprising *simultaneous* conflict and co-operation with each other.

complementarity and co-ordination (Ford, 1980; Mattson, 1981, 1984, 1988; Håkansson, 1982; Johanson and Mattson, 1988; Easton, 1992). The international marketing literature finds difficulty in examining co-operation and conflict clearly because of its orientation toward the perspective of a single company. Companies are engaged in *simultaneous* conflict and co-operation with each other, and as such both elements should be looked at as part of their interaction with each other.

Position: The channel literature used the concept of *channel* position extensively as probably the single most important factor in a company's operations. But, it lay dormant until expanded on by the network literature a quarter of a century later. The managerial approach to marketing seeks to explain a company's position at any one time as the effect of its own strategy. But, an equally valid explanation of its position is as the outcome of its *interaction* in the relationships in which it is engaged (Håkansson and Ford, 2002).

Position is not simply a useful descriptive device, it also helps us to examine the alternatives open to a company and the extent to which it is influenced by others, often showing how relatively insignificant it really is, at least compared with its own self-importance! Positioning or strategizing in networks is a matter of interactions.

Relationships as resources: The distribution literature sees a company's relationships as important resources for its development. It also recognizes that the inertia and conflicting interests in relationships are simultaneously strong constraints on company development. This paradox was "re-recognized" in the IMP and network literature much later (Håkansson, 1982; Håkansson and Ford, 2002). It is implicit in the international marketing literature that internationalizing companies are attempting to acquire relationship resources, even though the literature only examines this process from the perspective of one of the companies involved. The network literature takes the issue further by not only considering relationships as resources but also emphasizing how each company's resources are developed and exploited *interactively* through them.

Postponement and speculation: The distribution and international marketing literatures and managerial marketing, in general, were developed during an era of mass production, in which products were produced speculatively and then had to be sold and distributed. The distribution literature reflected the need for producers to establish efficient channels to dispose of their products and, to a lesser extent, that intermediaries need to develop links with the optimum range of speculative producers to satisfy their customers' requirements (Bucklin, 1965). Similarly, the international marketing literature has its roots in the need for speculative producers to dispose of their production overseas, to achieve economies of scale or to generate a better return on development expenditure.

The IMP literature emphasizes the importance of relationships as sources of problem solutions, rather than as being simply the vehicles for the supply of a defined product. Customers' problems are individual and complex. Hence, their solution is likely to require a complex offering that can only be defined or even developed interactively between a supplier and a buyer, rather than being the result of speculative production. The network literature developed during a period when many different types of companies co-existed in business markets and provided a wide range of offerings, thus making markets more dynamic and making speculation risky if not impossible. A physical product is likely to be only one element of their offerings, and its "production" is likely to be postponed until much closer to the time of its consumption. Both timing and characteristics are determined *interactively*.

Even more importantly, the offerings for a single final consumer are unlikely to be the unchanged output from a manufacturer that has passed unchanged through a distribution channel. Instead, they are likely to be based on the respective technologies of and the interaction between many interdependent companies, including the final consumer.

The single channel, the single relationship and the supply chain: The distribution literature developed a *linear* view of the movement of goods to consumers, although it did examine the competition between alternative linear channels. This linear view is also implicit in the international marketing literature as it is primarily concerned with alternative, but single routes to market via a "supply chain". The network literature shows how relationships within the "chain" or "channel" are affected by each company's relationships outside the channel, as well as by those relationships that may seemingly be unconnected to it.

Thus, the network perspective emphasizes that it is only possible to make sense of interaction between any two actors by examining the *wider interactions* in which they are both engaged and which also takes place around them.

Control and efficiency: Each of the areas of channels, international marketing, IMP and networks has been concerned with the issues of control and efficiency. The channel literature plotted the evolution of channels in terms of the rise and fall of control by wholesalers, manufacturers or retailers. But, it later concluded that power was limited in any one company and was widely distributed throughout the channel. The international marketing literature infers that a producer has the power to choose its means to market, to manage its own evolution and to add or drop agents or sales subsidiaries, etc.

The IMP literature examined various ways to assess and manage both individual and portfolios of relationships (Ford, 2002; Håkansson and Snehota, 1995). The network literature has a thread that suggests that a company can act as the "hub" of a network or design its "own" network (Lorenzoni and Baden-Fuller, 1995). However, perceptions of the extent and location of control are inherently subjective and are based on an infinitely variable "picture" of the extent and characteristics of the network. Also, more recent network literature has demonstrated that not only is control extremely rare but, where it does occur, it is also likely to reduce the efficiency of the network as a whole (Håkansson and Ford, 2002).

Rather than unidimensional control by a single company, interaction between companies is likely to be based on their respective resources and abilities, and each company is likely to be able to exercise influence to some extent in some areas in its relationships. Similarly, efficiency in interaction is not a single dimension and it is important to analyse it at the different levels of the individual company, relationship, portfolio and network.

Stability and change: Stability and inertia both within and between companies is an issue in all three areas of literature, and each area highlights the importance of different precipitating factors in overcoming it. The channel literature concentrates on the role of outsiders in achieving change: those who may not know or choose to ignore the unwritten "rules of the game" in the channel. The international marketing literature also points to the changes inside or outside the company that may shift it from one type of international operations to another. The IMP literature has examined the dynamics of business relationships through various stage models (Ford, 2002). The network literature emphasizes the juxtaposition of change within overall stability and suggests that new ways of working may have to be developed within *existing* relationships or that new relationships will often have to be built with similar companies to those in a company's current portfolio.

Each area of literature shows at least implicitly that internal and external evolution is as much a function of unplanned events, the actions of others and interaction between companies as it is of analysis and strategy by one company.

This review of different approaches in the marketing literature shows that an understanding of interaction between companies may require a reappraisal of the nature of business markets, of what happens between the companies within them and of how to research them, as follows.

Interaction and interconnection: Each transaction is comprised of multiple interactions between two active companies and takes place within a relationship. Each interaction is affected by the other interactions of the two companies and by other interactions elsewhere in the network. Because the interactions between companies take place within a relationship, each will be affected by the previous experiences of the two companies and their expectations for the future; this means that each interaction between two companies, and each transaction, is interconnected with all other interactions. Thus, it is difficult to examine a relationship at a single point in time, unless due regard is given to the dynamics of the relationship of which it is part and of the network within which it exists. The study of interaction requires longitudinal studies (Pettigrew, 1997).

Interaction and heterogeneity: Networks are heterogeneous and consist of a large number of companies, each having a unique position within it. Each company has different resources, abilities, problems and relationships. Each interacts with others and seeks solutions to their different problems (Dubois, 1998). These interacted solutions will depend on the abilities and resources of many companies and will affect many others (Hertz, 1998); this leads to the conclusion that the study of interactions requires a multi-actor focus and must be situation-specific.

Interaction and interdependence: Interaction within business relationships is the outcome of the views and actions of at least two parties. Thus, a view of interaction alters ideas of managerial discretion. If interaction is purposeful for *both* of the parties, it means that neither of them can solely determine either their immediate interaction, the development of their relationship or the characteristics of the surrounding network. If its relationships provide the context for all of a company's external dealings, then this means that the company is very restricted in its ability to develop independent strategy. Companies are *interdependent* for sales, supplies, information, technology, development and for access to other companies elsewhere in the surrounding network (Hughes, 1987). The outcomes of the actions of any company will be strongly influenced by the attitudes and actions of those with which it interacts, and that interaction involves simultaneous elements of co-operation, conflict, integration and separation in the companies' relationships. Hence, the study of interaction requires focus on interdependency and co-evolution.

Interaction and its context: If interaction is conditioned by the experiences and expectations of the participants, then the analysis of that interaction cannot be confined to the interaction itself. Instead, it must take into account the other *specific* direct interactions and relationships of the participants and those other relationships in the wider network in which they are not involved, but which affect either their perceptions or their interactions. The study of interaction requires both a holistic view of the network and its specific elements rather than a view of a generalized and homogeneous environment.

Interaction and time: Interaction between companies changes over time (Ford, 1980; Dwyer et al., 1987; Hallén et al., 1991; Morgan and Hunt, 1994). The early stages of a relationship are associated with reduction in the social, cultural and technological "distance" between the companies and increases in their commitment to each other, expressed through adaptations in the offerings and operations of both companies. Long-established relationships may be associated with institutionalized interactions that no longer meet the needs of the counterparts or demonstrate commitment between them. The process of relationship development is not deterministic and there is no "ideal" relationship state. The assessment of a company's relationship and the management of its interactions within them are key management tasks. Interactions in business markets develop over time and, thus, are of a dynamic nature for which no optimum can be defined.

Interaction and value: Firms engage in the complex process of interaction in relationships in order to provide more value for both sides than in a purely transactional exchange. Value is provided by the interactions between the companies and exists in the relationship itself as a potential for future productive interactions (Anderson et al., 1994; Walter et al., 2001). The relationship enables companies both to exchange offerings that are more suitable for both sides, through adaptation and customization, and to reduce transaction costs between them. Within a network, a single interaction may have consequences (i.e., creating of destroying value) on four levels (Ford and McDowell, 1999). There is an immediate impact on the exchange in the relationship. Single interactions also have an impact on the relationship itself and its potential for future development. Also, as a result of relationships being interconnected, there is likely to be an effect on the other relationships between the two companies. Finally, there are effects on the wider network of indirect relationships. Interactions between suppliers and customers have a value-creating potential that can be realized not only within the given relationship but also elsewhere in the network.

Actor bonds, resource ties and activity links: Interactions between companies in a relationship may also be interpreted in terms of the development of activity links, actor bonds and resource ties between the companies (Håkansson and Johanson, 1992). Thus, the activities and resources of producers and users in business markets only have economic meaning when connected to each other. Tying resources and activities together is an interactive process with participation from both sides. The ability to interact productively is likely to be based on the development of bonds between the individual actors concerned. It is only through interaction that companies can move beyond the simple transactional buying and selling of a predetermined offering.

Interacting and networking

We have emphasized that interaction is not solely a dyadic phenomenon and that each interaction is affected by all of a company's other interactions with those in the surrounding network and by their interactions with others. It is for this reason that the term "networking" has been recently introduced to refer to interaction in networks (e.g., Ford et al., 2003).

Networking is simultaneously carried out by all of the companies in a network, and any interaction outcome is the result of all those interactions. But, companies have limited freedom and much of their networking will involve reaction to the actions of others; this will not only have to take into account the reactions of others but will also be moderated by these reactions. Networking involves combined co-operation and competition and simultaneous combinations of working with, through, in spite of or against others. A company's position in the network together with its experience and expectations are central factors in its networking. The company's networking will be based on its own view of that position and on its view of the positions of others and their likely reactions. Thus, networking is based on incomplete knowledge, and this means that "learning by doing" is one of its important aspects.

Networking has been associated with a large set of activities or tasks. Key elements have been the tasks of: exchanging information, goods and money; adapting to other actors needs; co-ordinating of processes; initiating of contacts; and controlling, reviewing and monitoring others' activities and outcomes (Helfert and Vith, 1999; Ritter et al., 2002; Walter, 2003).

The idea of networking allows us to separate the interactions in a network into three types. Each involves managerial choices for a company and each relates to three paradoxes of networks (Håkansson and Ford, 2002). However, when discussing choice it is important to emphasize that a company's choice is not "free", but simultaneously constrains and is constrained by the choices of others.

The first aspect of networking: interaction within existing relationships

This aspect of networking relates to the first network paradox: a company's relationships are the basis of its current operations and development. But, those relationships also restrict that development.

This paradox involves a company in choices of when to *confront* the status quo of accepted ways of interacting in its relationships and when to *conform* to particular ways of operating into which it is tied by its relationships. To some degree we could argue that the decision at this stage is a decision that hovers between collaboration and conflict. While conformation means the continuation of a known system, confrontation introduces change and very likely conflict. As many studies have shown, a certain level of confrontation (and thus conflict) is needed in relationships to allow them to develop further, to reinvent themselves (e.g., Wilkinson and Young, 1994).

The second aspect of networking: choices about position

The second aspect of networking is concerned with the connections between existing and new relationships and relates to the second network paradox: it is equally valid to say that a company defines its relationships or that a company is defined by those relationships.

Companies face important choices between accepting their current network position, as defined by their existing relationships, and initiating new relationships to change that position. A company's existing relationships, its network position and the company itself are the outcome of its past interactions. A company can accept this existing position and actively work to stabilize it by using the first aspect of networking (above) to improve efficiency and effectiveness. Alternatively, the company can seek to systematically change its position by combining its existing relationships in new ways or by building new relationships.

The second aspect of networking involves the choice for a company between when to *consolidate* by stabilizing and strengthening its existing network position or when to *create* a new position by changing the combination of its existing relationships or developing new ones.

The third aspect of networking: choices about how to network

Companies face decisions on networking both within and between their relationships. They must also consider how to interact with their counterparts, and this

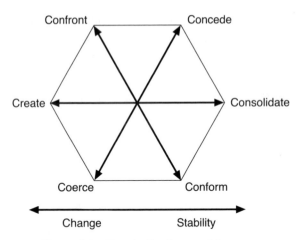

Figure 6.1—The six Cs of networking.

involves them in facing the third network paradox: companies try to control the network and want the benefits of control, but control has its problems and when it becomes total it is destructive.

Companies in networks are incomplete and depend on the resources and skills of others. They also depend on the initiative of others to generate change and improvement. Companies inevitably try to get their counterparts to do what they want, in such things as the offerings exchanged between them, the price charged, direction of development or the attention given to counterparts' other relationships. But if counterparts do what the company wants, they are acting on the basis of one company's ideas alone. They may have to disregard their own wishes and wisdom, and relationships will not have the benefit of the initiative of these counterparts. In a way the complexity reflected in the actions of the network is the complexity captured by a single actor. As that actor has only limited knowledge the network is less flexible, less realistic and less connected to the wider network. Thus, the development of the company's relationships will be limited by the company's own wisdom, and its counterparts may become unwilling participants.

Hence, companies face the choice of when to *coerce* others into carrying out their wishes and when to *concede* to the wishes and initiatives of others.

The six endeavours of networking are displayed in Figure 6.1. In the figure we have divided them into those intentions that more likely introduce change in networks as opposed to those that introduce stability.

Conclusions

In this chapter we have argued that researchers have tended to apply a set of defence mechanisms in order to reduce the complexity of business reality; this has meant that research into business markets has often neglected the interactive nature of what happens within them. Despite this, it is apparent that throughout the relative brief history of marketing research there has been some recognition of interaction as the driving force behind what happens in business markets and, at least, some attempts to analyse it.

An interaction approach to the study of business markets inevitably increases complexity when compared with a unilateral approach. But, if such an interaction approach is only applied at the dyadic level, then it will only provide a partial view at best and is likely to deceive as much as it informs; this is because no single interaction within a dyad takes place in isolation, but is affected by and affects numerous simultaneous interactions. This means that specific clear outcomes from a single interaction can never be identified, nor can observable events, situations or dynamics in a network ever be ascribed to a single or even to multiple interactions. It also means that success itself is a difficult concept to apply to interaction or networking, since not only is it multi-causal it is also time-dependent.

This limitation has profound implications for researchers seeking causal links and for managers predicting results from their actions or seeking to explain their apparent successes or failures.

References

Aaker, J. (1997). Dimensions of measuring brand personality. *Journal of Marketing Research*, **34**(August): 347–356.

Alderson, W. (1957). *Marketing Behaviour and Executive Action*. Homewood, IL: Richard D. Irwin.

Anderson, J.C., Håkansson, H. and Johanson, J. (1994). Dyadic business relationships within a business network context. *Journal of Marketing*, **58**(4): 1–15.

Balderston, F.E. (1958). Theories of marketing structure and channels. Paper given at *Conference of Marketing Teachers from Far Western States, University of California, September* (pp. 134–145).

Bilkey, W.J and Tesar, G. (1977). The export behaviour of smaller-sized Wisconsin manufacturing firms. *Journal of International Business Studies*, **8**: 93–98.

Blankenburg, D. (1995). A network approach to foreign market entry. In: D.T. Wilson and K. Moller (eds), *Business Marketing: An Interaction and Network Perspective* (pp. 375–410). Boston: Kluwer Academic.

Blankenburg, D., Holm, D. and Johanson, J. (1997). Business network connections and the atmosphere of international business relationships. In: I. Bjorkman and M. Forsgren (eds), *The Nature of the International Firm* (pp. 411–432). Copenhagen: Handelshøjskolens Forlag.

Boutilier, R. (1993). Pulling the family's strings. *American Demographics*, **15**(August): 44–48.

Bucklin, L.P. (1965). Postponement, speculation and the structure of distribution channels. *Journal of Marketing Research*, **2**(February): 26–31.

Cherington, P.T. (1920). *The Elements of Marketing*. New York: Macmillan.

Christopher, M., Payne, A. and Ballantyne, D. (2003). *Relationship Marketing, Creating Shareholder Value*. Oxford, UK: Butterworth-Heinemann.

Davis, T. (1993). Effective supply chain management. *Sloan Management Review*, **34**(Summer): 35–46.

Dubois, A. (1998). *Organising Industrial Activities across Firm Boundaries*. London: Routledge.

Dwyer, F.B, Schurr, P.H. and Oh, S. (1987). Developing buyer–seller relationships. *Journal of Marketing*, **51**(April): 11–27.

Easton, G. (1992). Industrial networks: A review. In: B. Axelsson and G. Easton (eds), *Industrial Networks: A New View of Reality* (pp. 3–27). London: Routledge.

Fishbein, M. (1967). Attitudes and predictions of behavior. In: M. Fishbein (ed.), *Readings in Attitude Theory and Measurements* (pp. 447–492). New York: John Wiley & Sons.

Ford, D. (ed.) (2002). *Understanding Business Marketing and Purchasing* (3rd edn.). London: Thomson Learning.

Ford, D., Gadde, L-E., Håkansson, H. and Snehota, I. (2003). *Managing Business Relationships*. Chichester, UK: John Wiley & Sons.

Ford, I.D. (1980). The development of buyer–seller relationships in industrial markets. *European Journal of Marketing*, **14**(5/6): 339–354.

Ford, D. and McDowell, R. (1999). Managing business relationships by analyzing the effects and value of different actors. *Industrial Marketing Management*, **28**(September): 429–442.

Forsgren, M. and Johanson, J. (1992). *Managing Networks in International Business*. London: Gordon & Breach.

Grether, E.T. (1937). Solidarity in the distribution trades. *Law and Contemporary Problems*, June: 376–391.

Grönroos, C. (1994). From marketing mix to relationship marketing: Towards a paradigm shift in marketing. *Management Decision*, **32**(2): 4–20.

Håkansson, H. (ed.) (1982). *International Marketing and Purchasing of Goods. An Interaction Approach*. Chichester, UK: John Wiley & Sons.

Håkansson, H. and Ford, D. (2002). How should companies interact in business networks? *Journal of Business Research*, **55**(2): 133–139.

Håkansson, H. and Johanson, J. (1992). A model of industrial networks. In: B. Aselsson and G. Easton (eds), *Industrial Networks: A New View of Reality* (pp. 28–34). London: Routledge.

Håkansson, H. and Snehota, I. (1995). *Developing Relationships in Business Networks*. London: Routledge.

Hallén, L. (1992). Infrastructural networks in international business. In: M. Forsgren and J. Johanson (eds), *Managing Networks in International Business* (pp. 77–92). London: Gordon & Breach.

Hallén, L., Johanson, J. and Seyed-Mohamed, N. (1991). Interfirm adaptation in business relationships. *Journal of Marketing*, **55**(2): 29–37.

Helfert, G. and Vith, K. (1999). Relationship marketing teams: Improving the utilization of customer relationship potentials through a high team design quality. *Industrial Marketing Management*, **28**(5): 553–564.

Hertz, S. (1998). Domino effects in international networks. *Journal of Business-to-Business Marketing*, **5**(3): 3–31.

Hoffer, E. (1951). *The True Believer*. New York: New American Library.

Howard, J.A. (1957). *Marketing Management: Analysis and Decision*. Homewood, IL: Richard D. Irwin.

Hughes, T.P. (1987). The evolution of large technological systems. In: W.E. Bijker, T.P. Hughes and T.J. Pinch (eds), *The Social Construction of Technological Systems: New Directions in the Sociology and History of Technology* (pp. 51–82). Cambridge, MA: MIT Press.

Jaworski, B.J. and Kohli, A.K. (1993). Market orientation: Antecedents and consequences. *Journal of Marketing*, **57**(July): 53–70.

Johanson, J. and Mattson, L-G. (1988). Internationalisation in industrial systems: A network approach. In: N. Hood and J.E. Vahlne (eds), *Strategies in Global Competition* (pp. 87–314). New York: Croom Helm.

Johanson, J. and Mattson, L-G. (1992). Network position and strategic action: An analytical framework. In: B. Axelsson and G. Easton (eds), *Industrial Networks: A New View of Reality* (pp. 205–217). London: Routledge.

Johanson, J. and Vahlne, J-E. (1977). The internationalisation process of the firm: A model of knowledge development and increasing foreign market commitments. *Journal of International Business Studies*, **8**(Spring/Summer): 23–32.

Johanson, J. and Wiedersheim-Paul, F. (1975). The internationalisation process of the firm: Four Swedish case studies. *Journal of Management Studies*, **12**(October): 305–322.

Kriesberg, L. (1955). Occupational controls among steel distributors. *American Journal of Sociology*, **61**(November): 203–212.

Lorenzoni, G. and Baden-Fuller, C. (1995). Creating a strategic centre to manage a web of partners. *California Management Review*, **37**(3): 146–163.

Mattson, L-G. (1981). *Interorganisational Structures in Industrial Markets: A Challenge to Marketing Theory and Practice* (Working Paper 1980/81). Uppsala: Sweden. Department of Business Administration, University of Uppsala.

Mattson, L-G. (1984). An application of network approach to marketing: Defending and changing market positions. In: N. Dholakia and J. Arndt (eds), *Changing the Course of Marketing: Alternative Paradigms for Widening Marketing Theory* (pp. 263–288). Greenwich, CT: JAI Press.

Mattson, L-G. (1988). Interaction strategies: A network approach. Paper given at *AMA Marketing Educators Conference, San Francisco, August*.

Mcammon, B.C. (1963). Alternative explanations of institutional change and channel evolution. In: S.A. Greyser (ed.), *Toward Scientific Marketing* (Proceedings of the Winter Conference, pp. 477–490). Chicago: American Marketing Association.

Mcammon, B.C and Little, R.W. (1965). Marketing channels: Analytical systems and approaches. In: G. Schwartz (ed.), *Science in Marketing* (pp. 321–385). New York: John Wiley & Sons.

McVey, P. (1960). Are channels of distribution what the textbooks say? *Journal of Marketing*, **24**(January): 61–65.

Morgan, R.M. and Hunt, S.D. (1994). The commitment–trust theory of relationship marketing. *Journal of Marketing*, **58**(3): 20–38.

Narver, J.C. and Slater, S.F. (1990). The effect of a market orientation on business profitability. *Journal of Marketing*, **54**(October): 20–35.

Nystrom, P. (ed.) (1949). *Marketing Handbook*. New York: Ronald Press.

Palamountain, J.C. (1955). *The Politics of Distribution*. Cambridge, MA: Harvard University Press.

Perlmutter, H.V. (1969). The tortuous evolution of the multinational corporation. *Columbia Journal of World Business*, **4**: 9–18.

Pettigrew, A.M. (1997). What is a processual analysis? *Scandinavian Journal of Management*, **13**(4): 337–348.

Phelps, D.M. and Westing, J.H. (1960). *Marketing Management*. Homewood, IL: Richard D. Irwin.

Rezvan, D.A. (1961). *Wholesaling in Marketing Organization*. New York: John Wiley & Sons.

Ritter, T., Wilkinson, I.F. and Johnston, W.J. (2002). Measuring network competence: Some international evidence. *Journal for Business and Industrial Marketing*, **17**(2/3): 119–138.

Robinson, P.J., Faris, C.W. and Wind, Y. (1967). *Industrial Buying and Creative Marketing*. New York: Allyn & Bacon.

Sharma, D.D. (1992). Experiential network knowledge in international consultancy. In: M. Forsgren and J. Johanson (eds), *Managing Networks in International Business* (pp. 126–137). Philadelphia: Gordon & Breach.

Sheth, J.N. (1973). A model of industrial buyer behaviour. *Journal of Marketing*, **37**: 50–56.

Simpson, C.L. and Kujawa, D. (1974). The export decision process: An empirical enquiry. *Journal of International Business Studies*, **5**(Spring/Summer): 107–117.

Stanton, W.J. and Buskirk, R.H. (1959). *Management of the Sales Force*. Homewood, IL: Richard D. Irwin.

Tookey, D. (1969). International business and political geography. *British Journal of Marketing*, **3**(3): 18–29.

Walter, A. (2003). Relationship-specific factors influencing supplier involvement in customer new product development. *Journal of Business Research*, **56**(9): 721–733.

Walter, A., Ritter, R. and Gemünden, H.G. (2001). Value-creation in buyer–seller relationships: Theoretical considerations and empirical results from the supplier's perspective. *Industrial Marketing Management*, **30**(4): 365–377.

Wilkinson, I.F. and Young, L. (1994). Business dancing: The nature and role of interfirm relations in business strategy. *Asia–Australia Marketing Journal*, **2**(1): 67–79.

A dynamic customer portfolio management perspective on marketing strategy

7

Fred Selnes and Michael D. Johnson

Introduction

Marketing strategy is a roadmap for how a company plans to allocate its resources to attract, keep and develop revenues from customers in order to create economic value (profit) and strengthen their competitive advantage. In a recent article we developed a typology of customer relationships and showed that economic value created in different types of relationships varies systematically over time with customer behaviour, supplier behaviour and industry characteristics (Johnson and Selnes, 2004). One important insight from this research is that for a given product the value created across relationships and over time differs substantially. As we will explore in this chapter, not only the amount of value will differ across relationships but also the type of value created will vary. The implication is that marketing strategy is less about allocating different amounts of resources and more about how to organize the resource allocation across relationships.

Our goal in this chapter is to provide a conceptual understanding of how value is created in exchange relationships which helps to understand and predict the consequences of dynamic changes and the strategic allocation of relationship resources. Our approach integrates the degree of continuity of a relationship with fundamentally different forms of value creation in relationships. The conceptual framework we develop will challenge the normative marketing concept that differentiated products always create more value than non-differentiated products. Rather, we suggest that marketers should ask when and for which customers is product differentiation likely to create more value than non-differentiated products.

We also challenge the relationship-marketing proposition that close collaboration with the customer and customization of product, service and/or communication will create more customer value, which implies that when the costs of customization are low enough relationship marketing will create more relationship value. We do not disagree that relationship marketing can be an optimal marketing strategy, but we do disagree that it will always be an optimal strategy. Rather, we should ask when and for which customers relationship marketing is a good strategy.

We will first define exchange relationship and present a typology of six fundamentally different forms of value creation. We will then relate this to how dynamic forces in the market affect the different forms of value creation and, thus, how companies should allocate and organize their resources to build customer relationships.

The exchange relationship as the unit of analysis

The fundamental phenomenon to be explained, predicted and controlled in the dynamics of the marketplace is the exchange relationship (Kotler, 1972; Bagozzi, 1975; Hunt, S.D., 1976; Hunt, D., 1983). The purpose of an exchange relationship is to connect a customer's needs with a supplier's resources and offering (Richardson, 1972). From a supplier's perspective, value creation is a process of understanding customer needs, developing products (goods and services) to fill those needs and matching customers to products through marketing activities in competition with other suppliers (Alderson, 1957, 1965). From a customer perspective it will be the supplier or suppliers who provide the highest expected benefits minus any associated costs and risk that will be chosen, where benefits encompass a bundle of qualities, processes and/or capabilities (Murphy and Enis, 1986).

An exchange relationship is a mechanism for creating value for both the supplier and the customer. At a basic level an exchange relationship serves its purpose when the customer has received the product and paid for it. However, relationships are formed because they create more value than would have been achieved through the market (price) mechanism (Coase, 1937; Richardson, 1972). Through information sharing, learning, socialization, collaboration or even commitment of resources, different forms of relationship value creation are formed. Following Johnson and Selnes (2004) we define an exchange relationship as a mechanism for creating value through co-ordination of production, consumption and related economic activities between a customer and a supplier. Our exchange relationship framework is presented in Figure 7.1. The central concept in the framework is the nature of the exchange relationship mechanism. The value created in an exchange relationship is a direct function of the customer's and supplier's capabilities and strategies, as well as exogenous industry and societal factors.

Customers in the market-matching process must decide when and where to problem-solve (Howard, 1977, 1983; Murphy and Enis, 1986; Spreng et al., 1996) in order to identify the supplier who is perceived as the best in terms of overall

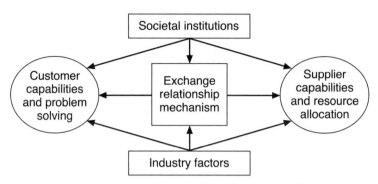

Figure 7.1—Exchange relationship framework.

benefits less the costs and risks involved. Customers' relationship goals are sometimes purely economic where the customer minimizes procurement costs or the lifetime cost of an investment. Sometimes, other types of goals, such as status, security, pleasure and comfort, are more dominant (Bagozzi and Dholakia, 1999).

This type of problem-solving has traditionally been linked to discrete product decisions (transactions). In our recent paper we conceptualize customer problem-solving more broadly to include implicit or explicit relationship decisions (Johnson and Selnes, 2004; see also Price and Arnould, 1999); that is, a customer evaluates both the expected benefits versus costs of a given relationship (versus the same relationship with other suppliers) as well as the benefits versus costs of alternative forms of that relationship. A customer's capability to evaluate these trade-offs affects their ability to either convert to a different form of relationship or change suppliers. Customers' motivation to problem-solve is a direct function of the homogeneity versus heterogeneity of demand (Alderson, 1965). The more hetero-geneous the demand the greater the benefit of finding an alternative that better fits customer needs relative to the costs and risks incurred.

Suppliers in the market-matching process organize resources and market offerings to match the needs of customers in order to create the best return on investment and a sustainable competitive advantage (Day, 1997; Dyer and Singh, 1998). The value for the seller is the profit generated over time in the relationship, directly or indirectly from the exchange, and thus the relationships that generate most profits are the most valuable. The objective for the supplier is to identify those relationships that have the highest profit potentials given the available resources and then develop sufficiently attractive offers (relative to competition) to create transactions. The challenge for marketing strategy is that there are significant ambiguities surrounding relationship portfolio decisions. Customer portfolios are not selected at a point in time; they take time to develop (Hunt, 2002).

A firm's and a customer's efforts to evaluate the relative value of different exchange relationships occur within a dynamic competitive environment in a state of constant change (Hayek, 1978; Day and Wensley, 1988; Dickson, 1992;

Hunt and Morgan, 1995). Exogenous factors naturally affect customer capabilities and problem-solving, supplier capabilities and resource allocation, and the exchange relationship mechanism directly. The direct effects of industry and societal factors capture the influence of an industry's or society's norms, customs, laws and "rules of competition" on exchange relationships. For example, as public service agencies, utilities are often required by law to serve segments of customers who are not profitable. The indirect effects capture those factors that influence customers' or suppliers' benefits, costs and risks of entering or maintaining a relationship.

By defining the exchange relationship as the fundamental unit of "explananda" we do not mean to say that competition is not important. Rather, our perspective is that competition is very important as it changes the way value is created in the market and, thus, the dynamics of formation, development and dissolution of exchange relationships. In addition to competitor dynamics, it is technology and customer needs that constitute the most important dynamics in the marketplace affecting value creation in individual relationships as well as the portfolio of relationships. We will return to these dynamic elements later in the chapter after we have defined six fundamental different forms of exchange relationship value creation.

Creating value in exchange relationships

In Figure 7.2 we present a typology of how exchange relationship value is created. The first dimension that differentiates relationships is the degree of customization of the value created as perceived by the customer. The second dimension is a

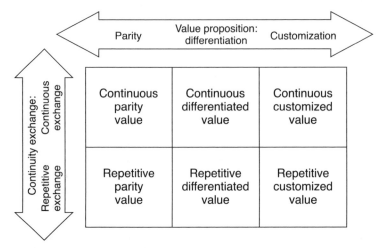

Figure 7.2—Typology of exchange relationship mechanisms.

distinction between repetitive and continuous exchange. In repetitive exchange the customer makes a new decision for each transaction, even if the decisions are routine (Howard, 1983). In continuous exchange the customer makes a commitment to exchange over a defined or open time period. This commitment may involve a formal payment plan (Bolton and Lemon, 1999) or idiosyncratic investments (Johanson et al., 1991) that are not required of repetitive transactions. We will now explicate how relationship value creation is fundamentally different across these types of relationships.

Repetitive parity value

From a customer perspective a product or brand is parity if the category is perceived to contain more or less similar products (brands), and the customer perceives low levels of risk in terms of selecting the wrong brand. The only relevant discriminating variable is price and effort required to buy the brands. If customers have gained positive experience with one of the brands it is very likely that they will repeat buying the brand, given that price and convenience perceptions of the alternatives remain more or less the same. For example, customers may be willing to walk to the next shop if they are dissatisfied with the first shop and satisfied with the second shop.

Thus, the reasons customers repeatedly buy a parity brand are rooted in convenience (less effort) of buying the brand, a level of satisfaction is achieved and a perception that the brand is not appreciably more expensive than alternatives. It is thus the perception of the customer that determines whether the product is creating a parity value or not.

To meet this type of buying behaviour, suppliers must provide their offering at a competitive price and with convenient access. By "convenient access" we mean the total time and cognitive effort expended by customers in the purchase process. As the customer is not willing to pay a price premium for additional quality or service, profit is achieved through volume and standardization which reduce costs. Customers are sensitive to price information and are likely to change behaviour to the degree a lower price exceeds additional effort. Customers are also sensitive to convenience improvements, especially if they are dissatisfied.

Repetitive differentiated value

From a customer perspective a product or brand is differentiated if the alternatives in the category are perceived to be different with respect to quality and/or functionality. There is a perceived risk associated with selecting the wrong brand, and thus a customer is motivated to find the best or most appropriate alternative. Price will be a trade-off between the perceived value of the different alternatives, and thus a customer is willing to pay a price premium if the value of additional quality or functionality is sufficiently high (given that the price is within budgetary limits).

Quality differences can in principle be assessed through experience or through inspection and evaluation of relevant objective information. However, as quality assessments usually are quite cognitively demanding, customers would rather come to trust suppliers' claims (Nelson, 1974; Wright and Lynch, 1995). As evaluating intrinsic quality is very difficult, customers often employ extrinsic cues like brand reputation as an indicator of quality (Zeithaml, 1988), and thus trust in a brand's reputation is a strong driver of repetitive purchasing behaviour (Selnes, 1993).

It is the customer's perception that classifies the product as parity or differentiated, and thus the same product (or brand) can by one customer be perceived as parity and by another as different. For example, one customer may perceive Dell personal computer as a parity product because a number of other brands (Compaq, IBM, HP, etc.) have similar quality and functionality, and thus the preference for Dell is rooted in convenience in acquisition and/or price. Another customer may perceive Dell as better in quality than the other brands (e.g., based on the value of Dell's direct sales model), and thus may be willing to pay a price premium for Dell relative to the competing brands.

Suppliers typically diversify their product portfolios to target customer segments with differentiated offerings (Buzzell, 1966) and superior value propositions (Best, 2000). Profit is a function of price premium relative to additional costs in advertising, product development and production. The key to creating value and profit is no longer just parity, standardization and repetitive operations. It is also convincing customers to pay a premium for superior performance. The strategy is to position the product in attractive segments with a sufficient number of customers and convince the customers in this segment to buy the product at a higher price when the need (and decision) arises on a repeated basis. Customers are sensitive to advertising about relevant product differences (product brand), relevant product improvements and capabilities of the supplier (corporate brand). Because quality is difficult to assess prior to buying the product, developing trust is key.

Repetitive customized value

When customers perceive that there are no available pre-manufactured products in the category that can satisfy their needs, they will appreciate that a brand can be designed and produced to their individual specifications. In the personal computer example, customers may prefer Dell because they can highly customize a personal computer. By definition, it is not possible to assess the quality of a customized product until after it is produced. Evaluating the relative quality or, that is, the quality received relative to what could have been achieved from a different supplier is even more difficult, even impossible (Darby and Karni, 1973). Thus, customers have to commit themselves to buying without knowing exactly the quality that will be delivered. Dell customers order a computer and commit themselves to paying when it is delivered. Thus, selecting a supplier requires trust and commitment, albeit transaction-based.

From a supplier perspective, production cannot start until the customer has delivered an order. Profit is primarily a function of capacity utilization and price, and in order to be competitive on delivery time the supplier must invest in capacity. Customers are sensitive to delivery time and, thus, prefer a supplier that can deliver quickly. However, the supplier must balance the advantages of available capacity and costs of unsold capacity. The primary element in marketing strategy is building brand reputation through advertising, networking and word of mouth.

Continuous parity value

The principal difference in our typology between continuous and repeated value creation is the time frame of the customer's decision. In repetitive relationships, customers make a new decision for every transaction whether highly deliberated or relatively routine and habitual. In continuous relationships, customers must decide to end one relationship before they can enter a new one, and there are costs associated with changing supplier (cognitive and/or financial). Continuous relationships are akin to the implementation of an ongoing system or process (such as online banking or cellphone services), and termination of a relationship requires disengaging from one system and implementing another.

The motivation to change from one brand to another is, as with repetitive parity value, better convenience and/or lower price. However, the expected advantage of a change has to exceed the costs of changing the system by which customer and supplier are integrated. Therefore, the alternative offer has to be substantially better in order to induce a change. In the personal computer example a continuous relationship exists when the customer has entered a contract to use Dell personal computers. Rather than paying for each transaction, the customer pays a monthly fee for having access to using the computer. Dell is preferred because it offers the most convenient service and/or the lowest fee.

To meet this type of buying behaviour the supplier must, as with repetitive exchange, offer and deliver parity value at a competitive price and with convenient access. As the customer is not willing to pay a price premium for additional quality or service, profit is achieved through volume and standardization. The core elements in the marketing strategy are price, convenience and loyalty incentives. Regarding the latter a number of suppliers employ monetary incentives like mileage points to stimulate loyalty. Here, loyalty is more likely to be "bought" rather than "earned" to increase the threshold required for the customer to switch. As with repetitive parity products, dissatisfied customers are sensitive to competitive offers with respect to price and convenience. Thus, suppliers have large incentives to keep their customers satisfied.

Continuous differentiated value

As with continuous parity value, continuous differentiated value relies on relationship commitment in the form of contracts and/or payment plans; and, as with differentiated repetitive value, a customer perceives the alternatives within the category as different in terms of quality and functionality. Customers associate risk with switching vendors and are thus initially motivated to continue as long as they are satisfied and trust that the quality received is worth the price paid (Bolton and Lemon, 1999). Thus, customers who are contracted to purchase and use Dell computer services will in this type of relationship trust Dell to be better in quality and/or functionality than other brands and for this reason be willing to pay a price premium for Dell.

Segmentation and positioning is different than for repetitive products as customers acquired in a segment at time t are likely to develop or move into different segments at time $t + 1$. Suppliers are thus faced with another type of heterogeneous and dynamic customer needs other than repetitive exchange. Negative disconfirmation at time $t + 1$ is likely unless the offer is continuously adjusted to the dynamic changes of customer desires and expectations (Spreng et al., 1996). Thus, positioning for continuous differentiated relationships is different from that for repetitive differentiated relationships.

With respect to the implications for marketing strategy, customers in a repetitive differentiated exchange self-select into that offering that provides more value from decision to decision and context to context. In contrast, customer–supplier interaction in a continuous differentiated exchange of value is more akin to an adaptive system.

In order to adjust to the heterogeneity within the customer portfolio the supplier is likely to offer menus with predefined alternatives. This form of adjustment is effective as long as production can be planned and organized in modules (Kahn, 1998). In order to adjust the product to the dynamic development of the individual customer's needs and desires (personalization), the supplier and the customer are motivated to share information and adjust their relationship accordingly. Customers benefit from suppliers whose customer knowledge and information systems allow them to deliver highly personalized offerings (Huffman and Kahn, 1998; Pine et al., 1995; Pine and Gilmore, 1998). This type of information sharing and learning requires trust in the other party (Morgan and Hunt, 1994). Thus, unless trust is present, the relationship is likely to deteriorate and customers become dissatisfied and motivated to change supplier. The core issue for marketing strategy is to adjust to the dynamics of relationships as they evolve and take different forms.

Continuous customized value

From a customer perspective there are no available parity or differentiated pre-manufactured products that meet the current needs and desires, and thus the product has to be customized. This form of value creation is a highly adaptive system that customizes goods and services to individual-level needs. The personal computer service (from Dell) is customized to the customers' needs and specifications. Imagine a system in which an individual's computer gets reordered automatically from Dell when ongoing feedback from customer to supplier indicates that the customer's current computer system is suboptimal. As this is a continuous relationship, customization is also a matter of matching closely complementary, but dissimilar activities that require different capabilities (Richardson, 1972). Over time the relationship may evolve through continuous adaptation and mutual commitment (Dwyer et al., 1987; Johanson et al., 1991) where the parties become increasingly interdependent.

Summary

The typology describes six distinct forms of exchange relationship value creation associated with different buyer and supplier behaviour and, therefore, different forms of value creation even for the same brand. Thus far, by adding the degree of continuity to an exchange relationship, two important conceptual distinctions to our understanding of how value is created in exchange relationships are observed. First, it highlights that marketers must distinguish between the continuity of a relationship and its strength. Using a simple label, such as "loyalty", to describe a customer's behaviour is inadequate. Strong relationships can be off again, on again, as in the case of repetitive customized value, while weak relationships can be continuous, as in the case of ongoing parity relationships. Second, it highlights the need to view some relationships as integrated systems, as when suppliers must adapt to changing customer needs in continuous exchange and others in the more traditional fashion of repeated decisions over time.

Another major observation is that marketing strategy should reflect the underlying type of value creation. From the descriptions provided of the different types of relationships, it should be obvious that we cannot claim that one type of relationship is creating more economic value than others and, thus, such claims as "differentiate or die" and "enterprise one to one" are misleading. Business practice shows that, depending on the various factors affecting the value of an exchange relationship, enormous economic value has been created in all six types of markets. For example, marketing strategies based on low price and standardization through an integrated IT-based supply chain has created enormous profits for some retail chains, such as Wal-Mart and Office Depot, which should not happen according to either the "differentiation" or the "one-to-one" schools of thinking. Rather, we suggest that effective marketing strategies are found when there is a good match with resource allocation and organization, and type of relationship value creation.

In the typology above we highlighted some of the dynamics within the different market forms. In addition to these within-dynamics there are also dynamics between market forms. Effective marketing strategies are not only well adjusted to the internal dynamics but also well adjusted to dynamics in the whole marketplace.

Dynamic forces in the market

A firm's efforts to affect the market occur within a dynamic competitive environment in a state of constant change (Hayek, 1978). A major tenant of dynamic theories of competition is that competitors are constantly trying to adapt to changing markets in customer needs, available technology and competitive moves (Alderson, 1965; Dickson, 1992; Hunt and Morgan, 1995). Related to the typology of exchange relationships, markets can change both within and between forms of value creation.

Customer needs dynamics

Customer needs are not constant, but tend to change over time. There are several factors affecting the speed and degree of change. One factor is related to changes in the product's purpose or goal due to changes in the individual customer's situation. For example, a consumer's need for a car changes with number and age of children, or, as a business customer grows from a small to a larger organization, its need for an IT system is likely to change. Another factor driving changes in customer needs is related to product innovation and the promotion of new and different product solutions in the marketplace. For example, the introduction of carving skis in the market has influenced customers' perception of the alpine ski category.

Changes in customer needs can change both within and between relationship forms. For example, in the category of repetitive parity value the norm for parity will change over time. What is considered convenient in retail shopping is clearly different today than 5 to 10 years ago. Retailers have adapted to longer opening hours, better parking convenience and larger product variety not to create a differential advantage, but more in order to remain consistent with expectations in the marketplace.

Customers' needs do not only change within but also between relationship forms. For example, most consumers would 10 years ago say that coffee is coffee and that there is really not much difference between the alternative brands. Although many consumers will still argue the same, there are a substantial number of consumers who argue that there are important quality differences. For example, Starbuck's Coffee is by many consumers perceived as different and better than alternative brands; this opens up a number of opportunities for competitive positioning, and as more suppliers of coffee enter the differentiated type of value creation this is likely to energize the development of the market (Dickson, 1992). The traditional coffee market has also developed into continuity value with the introduction of coffee machines distributed in a number of offices and cafeterias.

Technology dynamics

Technology is another major force driving market change. Related to the framework of exchange typologies we can distinguish between technologies that change value creation within a typology and technologies that change the form of value creation. An example of technology that changes value creation within is automated teller machines (ATMs). With this technology the customer receives a more convenient service with longer opening hours and availability at many more places than the traditional branch offices. This technology not only enhanced customer value but also supplier value as the technology replaced expensive manual labour.

A similar development is observed with EDI (electronic data interchange), a technology that has improved distribution systems. The customer (the distributor or the manufacturer) can with this system order products more easily and faster; this has reduced their need for inventory. In addition, both the supplier and the customer have reduced the need for manual tasks and, thus, reduced total costs in the system.

Technologies can move the type of relationship value creation in all directions within the framework. For example, new technology can reduce the costs of differentiating quality and functionality and, thus, lower the level of price premium required to cover differentiation costs. In the plastic food container business, most of the firms compete with limited, standardized offerings. Ultra Pack has adopted a different production technology with standardized components and flexible processes, and with the same level of costs and customer service they can deliver an assortment of several hundred offerings (Kahn, 1998).

It is important to note that technology can move relationship formation toward more parity products when justified by the increase in economies of scale (Johnson and Selnes, 2004). For example, the development in information technology has "forced" competitors to standardize their products. By adopting standardized components and standard software platforms a manufacturer takes advantage of the massive industry innovation in the industry and can thus achieve lower manu-facturing costs. As a consequence, personal computers are today far more similar than 15 years ago, with brands like MacIntosh, IBM, Compaq, Sperry, Toshiba and Facit, but with substantially lower prices for equivalent functionality and quality.

We have also seen technology that changes relationship forms from repetitive to continuous and vice versa. With the evolution of the Internet, customers can now subscribe for games like Lotto and interact directly with lottery suppliers (and not only through retailers). With new technology, mobile telephone users can now buy a package of call time in a retail store or through a vending machine (they do not have to form a payment contract with the supplier). Indeed, many consumers are using these repetitive transactions as a replacement for continuous long-distance service on their fixed phones.

This contradicts a prevailing perception about technology. If is often assumed that the principal effect of technology is to lower the costs of customizing a product or service and forming a continuous exchange relationship. Technology may also create economies of scale that facilitate profitable transaction-based relationships. An important consequence of new technology is that the nature of economies of scale is likely to change, either for the individual company or for the entire industry. For example, in order to automate services, companies have to invest in technology to set up a system of services (e.g., Internet banking). Clearly, the effect of accumulated volume is now larger than with manual operations.

Competitor dynamics

Competitor dynamics is the third force that brings about changes in how value is created in exchange relationships. Competitors innovate and imitate in order to develop and win markets (Dickson, 1992). Jaworski et al. (2000) suggest that competitors can change new market behaviour through introducing new product attributes (or concepts) and through reshaping the buying process. For example, Nokia introduced design as a key attribute for mobile telephones; this had far more appeal to the younger generation entering the mobile market in the late 1990s than Ericsson's functionality positioning.

IKEA, as another example, introduced a self-service concept as a new way of buying furniture that was different from the traditional furniture stores. Dell introduced and has been very successful with the "build to order" concept for personal computers. SAS introduced the "Businessman Airline" which changed the way business travellers chose airlines. As we see from these examples, innovation is not only about developing new products but is as much about creating new forms of relationship value.

Competitive forces are also about taking advantage of and developing compara-tive advantages (Day, 1994; Hunt and Morgan, 1995). Over time, competitors develop different comparative advantages (and disadvantages) through their system of activities (Porter, 1996). For example, IKEA has organized its system of activities in design, production (partnering), distribution and marketing in a way that is very different from competitors. Over time, IKEA continuously learns and improves its activities and, thus, continuously improves the value created for its customers.

Although a competitor can copy another competitor's activity, it is far more difficult and often impossible to copy their system of activities. Thus, the system of activities provides a sustainable comparative advantage. But, the system of interlinked activities is also a potential liability that may limit a company's options in changing the way customer value is created. Thus, if customer needs change dramatically the system of interlinked activities is no longer a sustainable competitive advantage but a sustainable competitive disadvantage, instead.

Some dynamic forces drive relationship value creation toward a more customized value, whereas other forces drive value creation toward a more parity value. Similarly, there are forces driving value creation toward continuous relationships, as well as forces driving value creation toward repetitive relationships. It is likely that the most successful companies have a better understanding of future development in these dynamic forces and, thus, are better able to take advantage of dynamics in the marketplace.

Customer portfolio lifetime value

Several authors in marketing have addressed differences among exchange relationship mechanisms and proposed typologies based, for example, on the differences between product and services (Shostack, 1977; Berry, 1980), the degree and form of collaboration (Heide, 1994; Day, 2000), industrial versus consumer markets (Webster, 1978) and the potential value of a firm's customer portfolio (Fiocca, 1982; Dickson, 1983; Krapfel et al., 1989). Based on our framework and discussion it is more parsimonious to focus on differences in how value is created; that is, the mechanism for co-ordination of production, consumption and related economic activities between a customer and a supplier.

It is important to keep in mind that the individual relationship is a building block for understanding the value created across an entire portfolio of customer relationships. Profit is systematically affected by both the firm's strategy and the dynamics in the market. Our goal is to link value creation at the level of individual relationships with value creation for the firm. How should firms allocate resources to attract customers and move relationships to other forms of value creation in order to maximize profits and develop a sustainable competitive advantage? Answering this question requires an understanding of value creation and the profitability of the different types of relationships.

The key elements in the analysis of customer portfolio lifetime value are customer revenues (base revenues and premiums from creating closer relationships), unit cost of production and distribution, customer acquisition and development costs (or investments) and the expected duration of the relationship.[1] If there is

---

[1] When the purpose is to assess the value of a single relationship at time t, the cash flow is discounted. However, when the purpose is to assess how the value of a portfolio of customers evolves over time, discounting the cash flow is not relevant.

only one type of customer in the portfolio with a similar expected lifetime and a similar form of value creation, then the value of the customer portfolio is the sum of the individual customer lifetime values. When there are different forms of value creation, aggregation is first done for each type of relationship.

Customer revenues

Price is a key variable in marketing. It has a strong effect on both demand and overall profit. The basic principle is that price will influence demand and, thus, volume produced, which again has a positive effect on unit costs through economies of scale mechanisms. A higher price will result in lower volume and, therefore, higher unit costs, and a lower price will result in higher volume and, therefore, lower unit costs. In parity relationships, price is the strongest variable that will attract new customers and competition tends to push prices downward. With lower prices, suppliers have to find ways to reduce their costs, such as standardization.

In differentiated relationships there is a price premium relative to parity value. Customers make trade-offs between incremental increases in quality (and functionality) and higher prices and are expected to buy products with the highest perceived value. For customized value, price is often an issue of negotiation. Customization implies that design and production will be different for each customer, and thus price is difficult to compare across different exchange relationships. Price will also reflect expected capacity utilization. In a situation where the supplier expects low-capacity utilization, prices will tend to come down.

Unit cost of production and distribution

Unit cost of production and distribution is a function of cost level and volume. Thus, a supplier can reduce unit costs through a lower cost level or through higher volume. Production and distribution for parity relationships will tend to be more standardized than differentiated and customized relationships. Standardization technologies tend to be disseminated throughout the market, meaning that standardization technologies are more or less easily available to all suppliers. Standardization reduces complexity, and thus cost levels can be lower. Also, standardization will enhance economies of scale potential, and therefore the effect of accumulated volume will be higher.

A differentiated value is more complex to produce and distribute, and thus levels of cost tend to be higher than for parity value. By definition, differentiated value implies that competitors have less in common, and thus available standardization technologies are less applicable. Thus, both the level of costs and the potential for economy of scale improvement will tend to be lower in differentiated market forms. Unit cost in production and distribution for customized value are likely to vary across customers; that is, two customers who buy the same volume of the product are likely to have different unit costs because production and distribution are organized differently.

Customer acquisition and development costs

Unit costs of customer acquisition and development are also different across the exchange relationship typologies. Moving from parity value to differentiated and customized values reflects a difference in the levels of customers' perceived risk; that is, customers perceive more differences among alternative brands in differentiated and in customized relationships than in parity relationships. The major function of advertising and sales is to reduce this risk and to build a preference based on trust.

Developing trust that a supplier can deliver a better differentiated or customized value than alternative suppliers will thus require an investment in the relationship. The pay-off from this investment will first of all take time to produce an effect, and, second, when the new level of trust is established the effect is expected to last for some time. Thus, it is reasonable to consider investments in customer acquisition and development as investment costs where the pay-offs are separated over time. It follows from the discussion above that customer acquisition and development costs increase from parity to differentiated and from differentiated to customized value creation.

As a result of continuous relationships requiring some form of commitment from the customer, it is likely to expect that customer acquisition and development costs will be higher than for repetitive relationships. For example, it is likely that a customer will think more thoroughly through a decision to sign a one-year contract for coffee supply than to buy one cup of coffee, and thus the needed investment in convincing this customer is likely to be higher. Regarding the costs of developing the relationship, moving from repetitive to continuous does not necessarily change unit costs but rather the media used. In continuous relationships the supplier and the customer are more likely to interact as part of an ongoing or integrated system that facilitates one-to-one communication between customer and supplier. In repetitive transactions, mass communication media are more applicable as customer interactions are irregular.

A major development over the past two decades in marketing is the recognition that satisfying customers to create closer and more continuous relationships can be very profitable, by assuring more continuous revenue streams and increasing profit per customer through cross-selling opportunities, decreased price sensitivity, lower service costs and greater word of mouth (Fornell et al., 1996; Reichheld, 1996). Here again, however, a portfolio view of customer relationships provides important insights into how to create value with closer relationships. In our research, focusing on creating more arm's length parity exchange is an important step toward building a large enough customer base from which closer relationships evolve (Johnson and Selnes, 2004). Those firms that focus only on building close relationships will end up with a smaller and less profitable portfolio. Put simply, the key to creating an entire portfolio of profitable relationships is to start by building a large, albeit "leaky bucket" of weak relationships.

Expected duration

The expected duration of a relationship is likely to increase as relationships move from parity to differentiated and customized value. Remember that customers will perceive more heterogeneity in supply with customized and differentiated value than for parity and, thus, there will be more uncertainty. Hoch and Deighton (1989) argue that as customers learn more about the focal brand they have a relationship with, the relative uncertainty of alternatives increases. Thus, as the potential for uncertainty is higher for differentiated and customized relationships, we expect the average duration of the relationships to grow.

We also expect continuous relationships to have longer duration than repetitive relationships; this is mainly because of the increase in cost of changing supplier but is also because customers in continuous relationships by definition are less likely to experiment with alternative suppliers and, thus, have less information about what they could have received. All in all we therefore expect repetitive parity products to have the shortest duration and the continuous customized products to have the longest duration.

Conclusions and implications for marketing strategy

Marketing strategy is a roadmap for how a company plans to allocate its resources to attract, keep and develop revenues from customers in order to create economic value (profit) and strengthen its competitive advantage. Our goal with this chapter was to provide conceptual understanding for how value is created in exchange relationships; this will help us to understand and predict the consequences of dynamic changes and the strategic allocation of resources.

We have developed a typology of exchange relationship mechanisms which illustrates fundamental differences in how value is created. An important conceptual contribution here is the distinction between the closeness of a relationship between a customer and supplier and the continuity of that relationship. Relationships can be continuous but may be weak or strong and involve intermittent transactions. Second, there are forces that drive companies to focus their marketing strategies toward closer relationships or weaker relationships or toward continuous or repetitive relationships, depending on the competitive forces at work. A major point is that the same product (or brand) can enter into one or more of the different forms of relationships. The challenge is to manage a portfolio of different relationships (with the same product or brand).

We assume that the overall objective is to create economic value and that the purpose of a marketing strategy is to choose a set of actions which is likely to attract and keep the type of customers the company can serve more effectively than other customers. The starting point for developing a marketing strategy should in our opinion be the customers the company serves today and decompose this down to a set of individual (or at least similar) exchange relationships. The next step is to estimate customer lifetime values for each customer and then aggregate across different forms of exchange relationships to a customer portfolio value. We then suggest that the marketing strategy should be directly connected to changes in the value of the customer portfolio.

References

Alderson, W. (1957). *Marketing Behavior and Executive Action: A Functionalist Approach to Marketing Theory*. Homewood, IL: Richard D. Irwin.

Alderson, W. (1965). *Dynamic Marketing Behavior: A Functionalist Theory of Marketing*. Homewood, IL: Richard D. Irwin.

Bagozzi, R.P. (1975). Marketing as exchange. *Journal of Marketing*, **39**(October): 32–39.

Bagozzi, R. and Dholakia, U. (1999). Goal setting and goal striving in consumer behavior. *Journal of Marketing*, **63**(Special issue): 19–32.

Berry, L.L. (1980). Services marketing is different. *Business*, **30**(May): 24–29.

Best, R.J. (2000). *Market-based Management: Strategies for Growing Customer Value and Profitability* (2nd edn). Upper Saddle River, NJ: Prentice Hall.

Bolton, R.N. and Lemon, K.N. (1999). A dynamic model of customers' usage of services: Usage as an antecedent and consequence of satisfaction. *Journal of Marketing Research*, **36**(May): 171–186.

Buzzell, R.D. (1966). Competitive behavior and product life cycles. In: J.S. Wright and J.L. Goldstucker (eds), *Proceedings of the American Marketing Association*. Chicago: American Marketing Association.

Coase, R.H. (1937). The nature of the firm. In: G.J. Stigler and K.E. Boulding (eds), *Readings in Price Theory* (pp. 331–351). Chicago: Richard D. Irwin.

Darby, M. and Karni, E. (1973). Free competition and the optimal extent of fraud. *Journal of Law and Economics.*, **16**(1): 67–88.

Day, G. (1994). The capabilities of market driven organisations. *Journal of Marketing*, **58**(October): 37–52.

Day, G. (1997). Maintaining the competitive edge: Creating and sustaining advantages in dynamic competitive environments. In: G.S. Day and D.J. Reibstein (eds), *Wharton on Dynamic Competitive Strategy* (pp. 48–75). New York: John Wiley & Sons.

Day, G. (2000). Managing market relationships. *Journal of the Academy of Marketing Science*, **28**(1): 24–30.

Day, G. and Wensley, R. (1988). Assessing advantage: A framework for diagnosing competitive superiority. *Journal of Marketing*, **52**(April): 1–20.

Dickson, P.R. (1983). Distributor portfolio analysis and the channel dependence matrix: New techniques for understanding and managing the channel. *Journal of Marketing*, **47**(Summer): 35–55.

Dickson, P.R. (1992). Toward a general theory of competitive rationality. *Journal of Marketing*, **56**(January): 69–83.

Dwyer, F.R., Schurr, P.H. and Oh, S. (1987). Developing buyer–seller relationships. *Journal of Marketing*, **51**(April): 11–27.

Dyer, J.H. and Singh, H. (1998). The relational view: Cooperative strategy and sources of inter-organisational competitive advantage. *Academy of Management Review*, **23**(4): 660–679.

Fiocca, R. (1982). Account portfolio analysis for strategy development. *Industrial Marketing Management*, **11**: 53–62.

Fornell, C., Johnson, M.D, Anderson, E.W., Cha, J. and Bryant, B.E. (1996). The American customer satisfaction index: Nature, purpose and findings. *Journal of Marketing*, **60**(October): 7–18.

Hayek, F.A. (1978). *New Studies in Philosophy, Politics, Economics and the History of Ideas* (Chapter 12). London: Routledge and Kegan Paul.

Heide, J.B. (1994). Inter-organisational governance in marketing channels. *Journal of Marketing*, **58**(January): 71–85.

Hoch, S. and Deighton, J. (1989). Managing what customers learn from experience. *Journal of Marketing*, **53**(April): 1–20.

Howard, J.A. (1977). *Consumer Behavior: Application of Theory*. New York: McGraw-Hill.

Howard, J.A. (1983). Marketing theory of the firm. *Journal of Marketing*, **47**(Fall): 90–100.

Huffman, C. and Kahn, B. (1998). Variety for sale: Mass customization or mass confusion? *Journal of Retailing*, **74**(Winter): 491–513.

Hunt, S.D. (1976). The nature and scope of marketing. *Journal of Marketing*, **40**(July): 17–28.

Hunt, D. (1983). General theories and the fundamental explananda of marketing. *Journal of Marketing*, **47**(Fall): 9–17.

Hunt, D. and Morgan, R.M. (1995). The comparative advantage theory of competition. *Journal of Marketing*, **59**(April): 1–15.

Hunt, S.D. (2002). *Foundations of Marketing Theory: Toward a General Theory of Marketing*. London: M.E. Sharpe.

Jaworski, B., Kohli, A.K. and Sahay, A. (2000). Market driven versus driving markets. *Journal of the Academy of Marketing Science*, **28**(1): 45–54.

Johanson, J., Hallén, L. and Seyed-Mohamed, N. (1991). Interfirm adaptation in business relationships. *Journal of Marketing*, **55**: 29–37.

Johnson, M.D. and Selnes, F. (2004). Customer portfolio management: Toward a dynamic theory of exchange relationships. *Journal of Marketing*, **68**(April): 1–17.

Kahn, B. (1998). Dynamic relationships with customers: High-variety strategies. *Journal of the Academy of Marketing Science*, **26**(1): 45–53.

Kotler, P. (1972). A generic concept of marketing. *Journal of Marketing*, **36**(April): 46–54.

Krapfel, R.E., Salmond, D. and Spekman, R. (1989). A strategic approach to managing buyer–seller relationships. *European Journal of Marketing*, **25**(9): 22–37.

Morgan, R.M. and Hunt, S.D. (1994). The commitment-trust theory of relationship marketing. *Journal of Marketing*, **58**(July): 20–38.

Murphy, P.E. and Enis, B.M. (1986). Classifying products strategically. *Journal of Marketing*, **50**(July): 24–42.

Nelson, P. (1974). Advertising and information. *Journal of Political Economy*, **81**: 729–754.

Pine, B.J. and Gilmore, J.H. (1998). Welcome to the experience economy. *Harvard Business Review*, **76**(July–August): 97–105.

Pine, B.J. II, Peppers, D. and Rogers, M. (1995). Do you want to keep your customers forever? *Harvard Business Review*, **73**(March–April): 103–114.

Porter, M.E. (1996). What is Strategy? *Harvard Business Review*, **73**(November–December): 61–78.

Price, L.L. and Arnould, E.J. (1999). Commercial friendships: Service provider–client relationships in context. *Journal of Marketing*, **63**(October): 38–56.

Reichheld, F.R. (1996). *The Loyalty Effect: The Hidden Force Behind Growth, Profits, and Lasting Value*. Boston: Harvard Business School Press.

Richardson, G.B. (1972). The organisation of industry. *Economic Journal*, **82**(September): 883–896.

Selnes, F. (1993). An examination of the effect of product performance on brand reputation, satisfaction and loyalty. *European Journal of Marketing*, **27**(9): 19–35.

Shostack, G.L. (1977). Breaking free from product marketing. *Journal of Marketing*, **41**(April): 73–80.

Spreng, R., Mackenzie, S. and Olshavsky, R. (1996). A re-examination of the determinants of consumer satisfaction. *Journal of Marketing*, **60**(July): 15–32.

Webster, F.E., Jr (1978). Management science in industrial marketing. *Journal of Marketing*, **42**(1): 21–27.

Wright, A. and Lynch, J.G., Jr. (1995). Communication effects of advertising versus direct experience when both search and experience attributes are present. *Journal of Consumer Research*, **21**(March): 708–718.

Zeithaml, V. (1988). Consumer perceptions of price, quality and value: A means-end model and synthesis of evidence. *Journal of Marketing*, **52**(July): 2–22.

From understanding to managing customer value in business markets

8

James C. Anderson

Overview

Customer value appears to be a well-known, venerable concept in business markets. After all, Anderson and Narus (1999, 2004) make it one of their four defining or guiding principles of business market management and even contend that customer value is the cornerstone of business market management. In this chapter, I revisit the conceptualization of customer value, its use in academic research to understand how customer managers make purchase decisions and its practical assessment in management practice research to examine just what we do know about customer value in business markets. This examination reveals that our understanding of this concept is not as clear or as complete as we might think. There is still much to learn about customer value in business markets, and a primary intent of this chapter is to stimulate further conceptualization and research to advance our knowledge of customer value.

In acquiring products and services, customer managers must decide which suppliers' market offerings will fulfill a set of requirements and preferences. When more than one supplier's market offering fulfills these requirements and preferences, customer managers then must decide which supplier's offering will deliver the greatest value to their firm. In many instances, customer managers make this decision intuitively: simply choosing the offering that they feel is best (or, alternatively, that has the lowest price). Little or no effort is given to specifically defining what each manager means by "value" and how it might be estimated in monetary terms. As an example, customer managers may feel that it is not worthwhile to conduct a formal value assessment to acquire repositionable sticky notes and, instead, simply purchase 3M Post-it® notes, even if the price for them is slightly higher than lesser known or generic brands. In other instances, though, customer managers consider it worthwhile to conduct a formal assessment, or *value analysis*, to enable them to make a better informed decision (Miles, 1989). Progressive suppliers may assist customer managers in these assessments or even provide their own assessments of how their offerings deliver superior customer value. I focus on these latter instances, where conceptualizing what exactly is meant by "value" and how to estimate it in practice are of principal interest.

An overview of the chapter is as follows. I first consider the various conceptualizations of customer value that have been put forth, what the differences between them mean, and the relationship between customer value and price. I next consider how customer managers appear to combine value and price to make purchase decisions in business markets. I end by considering the assessment of customer value in practice and briefly discuss a progressive, practical approach for accomplishing this.

What is customer value in business markets?

What is meant, specifically, by customer value in business markets? I first consider how others have defined customer value and then focus on the definition that Anderson and Narus (2004) advocate. I then take up the relationship between customer value and price.

Conceptualizing customer value in business markets

Various definitions of customer value have been offered. Considering them and contrasting them suggests the varying conceptualizations underlying this concept and the differences in what it means. It also suggests some gaps in our understanding of customer value.

According to Gale (1994, p. xiv, emphasis in original), "*Customer value* is market-perceived quality adjusted for the relative price of your product." Perhaps reflecting their interest in pricing, Dolan and Simon (1996, p. 9) state, "perceived value is the maximum price the customer will pay." Smith (2002, p. 36) contends that "Value = the benefits the customer receives relative to the price paid." Finally, Nagle and Holden (2002, p. 74, emphasis in original) state, "In common usage, the term *value* refers to the total savings or satisfaction that the customer receives from the product."

So, what is customer value? Is it adjusted market-perceived quality, maximum price, benefits relative to price, total savings or, even, satisfaction received? Each of these constituent components takes our understanding of the concept in a different direction. Given that customers will be more satisfied with paying a lower price, there would appear to be tension between customer value as maximum price and customer value as satisfaction received. Yet, the individuals providing these definitions do not go into much detail about what is meant by their definition nor do they discuss the conceptualization of customer value that their definitions suggest.

Another problematic aspect about customer value that has not been addressed is how disparate constituent elements defining value might be combined. As an instance of this, consider benefits in the preceding definition by Smith. To make this tangible, consider two benefits for titanium dioxide, which is a pigment that whitens, brightens and opacifies. Each is an improvement over a previous industry standard. *Dispersibility* improves by reducing from 30 minutes to 10 minutes the time required to reach 7 Hegman fineness units in a Cowles high-speed disperser, whereas *gloss* improves from 78 to 86 60° gloss units. How, specifically, a customer manager would directly combine Hegman fineness units and 60° gloss units is not at all clear. This example is typical of business markets, where benefits – desirable changes in performance – are expressed in precisely defined scientific, engineering and cost-accounting assessments.

We find a number of elements in the definitions of customer value: benefits, benefits expressed in monetary terms, costs, costs expressed in monetary terms and price. What is lacking is consideration of the *commensurability* of measurement units, which is essential to arrive at a meaning for customer value. Just as when we learn to combine fractions in school, we must first find a common denominator, convert the respective numerators to their units on this common denominator and then combine them to reach an answer. So, too, it would appear to be necessary in conceptualizing customer value. Of the elements given above, only three have direct commensurability: benefits expressed in monetary terms, costs expressed in monetary terms and price.

Anderson and Narus's conceptualization of customer value[1]

Anderson and Narus (2004, emphasis in original) provide a formal definition of customer value: "*value in business markets* is the worth in monetary terms of the economic, technical, service, and social benefits a customer firm receives in exchange for the price it pays for a market offering" (see also Anderson et al., 1993). They then elaborate on this definition to more fully delineate their conceptualization of customer value, which also considers what is *not* included in their conceptualization.

First, value is expressed in monetary terms, such as dollars per unit, euros per litre or Norwegian kronor per hour. Economists may care about "utils", but Anderson and Narus have never found managers who did.

Second, any market offering can be conceptually represented as a set of economic, technical, service and social benefits a customer firm receives. By benefits they mean *net* benefits, where any costs a customer incurs in obtaining the desired benefits, except for purchase price, are also included.

Third, value is what a customer firm gets in exchange for the price it pays.

[1] This section draws heavily from Anderson and Narus (2004, ch. 1).

Therefore, a market offering can be conceptually viewed as having two elemental characteristics: value and price. Whereas Anderson and Narus contend that it is best to keep price separate from value, in keeping with an exchange perspective, a related concept in purchasing does combine them. *Total cost of ownership* (TCO) refers to the purchase price plus all costs of acquiring, using and disposing of a market offering (Ellram, 1995). Even though price is a part of TCO, analysis focuses on the costs a customer firm incurs from a supplier's offering apart from its purchase price. A still broader purchasing concept, *total value of ownership* (TVO), captures total cost considerations in ownership of an acquired offering as well as any performance advantages the customer firm gains, to create value for its customers and to receive additional revenues and profits that it otherwise could not (Wouters et al., 2004). Simply put, we can view TVO as the sum of the Anderson and Narus conception of value plus purchase price.

Finally, considerations of value take place within some context. Even when no direct, in-kind offerings exist, there is always a competitive alternative. In business markets, one alternative may be that the customer firm decides to make the product itself rather than purchase it from outside suppliers.

The essence of the concepts in this definition of value can be captured in a *fundamental value equation*:

$$(\text{Value}_f - \text{Price}_f) > (\text{Value}_a - \text{Price}_a) \tag{8.1}$$

where Value_f and Price_f are the value and price of a particular firm's market offering (Offering$_f$), and Value_a and Price_a are the value and price of the next-best-alternative market offering (Offering$_a$).

Anderson and Narus do not specify a particular perspective in their definition of value, such as the customer firm's point of view, because they regard value in business markets as a construct, similar to market share. Because it is a construct, in practice we can only estimate value, just as we can only estimate market share. For example, the supplier may overestimate the value of a given market offering to a customer, while the customer may underestimate the value. The supplier may have a significantly different perception from the customer of the technical, economic, service and social benefits that the customer firm actually receives from a market offering or of what the specific benefits are actually worth in monetary terms to the customer.

Value changes occur in two fundamental ways (Miles, 1989). First, a market offering could provide the same functionality or performance while its cost to the customer changes. Remember, price is *not* considered in this cost. Thus, the technical, service and social benefits remain constant, while the economic benefits change. For example, one product has higher value than another product because it has lower conversion costs and has the same performance specifications. Second, value changes whenever the functionality or performance provided changes, while cost remains the same (again, price is not a part of this cost). For example, a redesigned component part now provides longer usage until failure for the customer's customer, yet its acquisition and conversion costs to the customer remain the same.

Even if functionality or performance of a product is lowered, it may still meet or even exceed a customer's specified minimum requirement. More is better for some, but not all, customer requirements. Exceeding minimum requirements continues to deliver benefits to the customer, even though the customer deems a lesser level to be acceptable. For example, lowering the melting point of a plastic resin beyond a specified temperature requirement continues to lower the customer's energy costs and to reduce the time it takes to convert the resin into a molded plastic part.

Finally, notice that in the Anderson and Narus definition, value is the expression in monetary terms of what the customer firm receives in exchange for the price it pays for a market offering. As a result of make versus buy decisions being possible in business markets the value provided must exceed the price paid. This difference between value and price is the *customer incentive to purchase*.[2] In this concept of value in business markets, raising or lowering the price of an offering does not change the value that offering provides to a customer firm; rather, it changes the customer's incentive to purchase that offering.

Relating customer value and price

How do customer value and price relate to one another? To motivate this discussion, please put yourself for a minute in the role of a customer manager and consider the following scenario, which might apply to the acquisition of an electronic component. Then, give your decision as to which product you would recommend that your firm purchase:

> Your firm needs to make a decision as to which of two alternative products to purchase: one offered by Supplier M and one offered by Supplier P. Based on two value analyses conducted by your firm, the value for Supplier M's product is found to be €4.00, while the value of Supplier P's product is found to be €6.00. The price of Supplier M's product is €1.00, while the price of Supplier P's product is €2.00.

Which supplier's product did you recommend: M or P? Taking two alternative perspectives would lead to a different decision. Under a ratio comparison, you would recommend Supplier M's product over Supplier P's:

$$\frac{Value_m}{Price_m} > \frac{Value_p}{Price_p}$$

$$\frac{€4.00}{€1.00} > \frac{€6.00}{€2.00}$$

(8.2)

[2] Economists refer to this difference as "consumer surplus" (cf. Pindyck and Rubinfeld, 1989); this is a doubly inapt expression in business markets because our focus is on customers, not consumers, and in our context this difference is not a "surplus" but an absolutely necessary inducement for customers to purchase a supplier's offering.

Such a ratio comparison has been stated as the way in which customer value and price would be related to one another. As Smith (2002, p. 36) asserts, "This almost always involves two dimensions of value: what the customer gets (benefits, savings, gains) and what the customer gives up (money, time, effort, opportunity cost). Most marketers combine these two dimensions in ratio form: Value = the benefits the customer receives relative to the price paid." Notice the overlooked commensurability issue in Smith's statements as well as his inclusion of price (indicated by "money") as part of value, both in contrast to the Anderson and Narus (2004) conceptualization.

Under a difference comparison, you would make the opposite decision, recommending Supplier P's product over Supplier M's:

$$\text{Value}_p - \text{Price}_p > \text{Value}_m - \text{Price}_m$$
$$\text{€}6.00 - \text{€}2.00 > \text{€}4.00 - \text{€}1.00$$

(8.3)

Although my sense of it is that Smith is probably correct that most marketers – at least marketing academics – embrace a ratio comparison, this thinking is misguided in two significant respects. First, qualitative research with customer managers suggests that individuals are much better difference processors than ratio processors. Although I have chosen the monetary amounts in my scenario to facilitate comprehension of the differences between the two kinds of comparisons, division remains a more difficult mathematical operation than subtraction. Pick four numbers a, b, c and d and try it for yourself, seeing how easy it is for you to divide a by b and c by d versus subtracting b from a and d from c.

Second, and more critically, difference comparisons are the way that businesses "keep score" on how they are doing: simply put, they subtract the total cost of doing business from the revenue produced from doing business to determine the profit for the business.

While the ratio comparison for the scenario that I presented leads to a decision to purchase Supplier M's product, would a customer firm indeed be better off by purchasing Supplier M's product versus Supplier P's product? Consider a situation where the customer has a purchase requirement of 1 million units. Even though Supplier P's product has a higher purchase price than Supplier M's product (€1.00), this is more than offset by the superior value that Supplier P's product delivers (€2.00). Thus, a customer firm would have €1 million of incremental profit by purchasing its requirement from Supplier P instead of Supplier M.

In many cases the values and prices for two competing offerings are such that the same decision would be made under either a ratio or a difference comparison. Nevertheless, as the scenario amply conveys, there are cases where they would lead to different decisions. The overarching point is that most researchers and authors have not sufficiently thought through how customer value and price are related to one another nor provided rationales to support their assertions. As we will see in the next section, though, even in adopting a difference comparison there are complications in understanding how customer managers combine value and price to make purchase decisions.

Combining value and price to make purchase decisions in business markets[3]

Nowadays people know the price of everything and the value of nothing
—Oscar Wilde, *The Picture of Dorian Gray*

When both customer value and price are expressed in monetary terms, combining them to make a purchase decision would seem to be a simple matter. Recent research (Anderson and Wynstra, 2003; Anderson et al., 2000) has found that understanding how customer managers combine value and price to make purchase decisions is not so simple. I first discuss value ambiguity as the posited conceptual explanation for this difficulty, then the effects of offering a monetary incentive to change and, finally, the search for non-monetary mechanisms to counter the effect of value ambiguity.[4]

Value ambiguity

Building on research in reference-dependent theory (Fox and Tversky, 1995; Kahneman and Tversky, 1979; Tversky and Kahneman, 1991), Anderson et al. (2000) have proposed value ambiguity as the conceptual mechanism underlying the difference in how customer managers regard value and price. Reference-dependent models have three distinguishing characteristics: reference dependence, loss aversion and diminishing sensitivity. *Reference dependence* means that individuals define alternatives that they consider as gains and losses relative to a reference point, rather than in an absolute sense. *Loss aversion* means that individuals will appraise differently alternatives that represent opposing deviations of the same magnitude from the reference point; the negative deviation will be regarded as more of a loss that the positive deviation will be regarded as a gain. Finally, *diminishing sensitivity* means that individuals will place smaller marginal values on same-size, incremental changes in prospects as those differences from the reference point become greater.

---

[3] This section draws heavily from Anderson et al. (2000) and Anderson and Wynstra (2003).
[4] This research stream has customer managers who make purchase decisions individually. It does not address the added complexity of many purchase decisions where a team is responsible for making the decision. Thus, the research cannot speak to group processes and their influence on how customer managers combine value and price to make purchase decisions.

Customer managers are more knowledgeable about price than value and they have more uncertainty about whether they will actually realize the estimated value of a market offering than the stated price of the offering. This difference in knowledge and uncertainty – *value ambiguity* relative to price – leads customer managers to differentially weight changes in value versus changes in price. This value ambiguity is conceptually captured by customer managers having similarly shaped, yet different utility functions for value versus price. Customer managers would rather have monetarily equivalent price decreases than value increases, both of which are regarded as gains from a reference offering, and they would also rather have monetarily equivalent value decreases than price increases, both of which are regarded as losses from the reference offering.

In their research, Anderson et al. (2000) found support for the value ambiguity explanation and separate underlying utility functions for value and price. One demonstration was especially persuasive. Under a single utility function a monetarily equivalent price decrease and value decrease from a reference offering should be regarded by customer managers as a loss relative to the reference offering, due to the loss aversion characteristic of reference-dependent models. Yet, Anderson et al. (2000) found that a significant proportion of purchasing managers did indeed view these kinds of offerings as gains, consistent with a separate-value-and-price-function model.

Monetary incentive to change

Anderson et al. (2000) and Anderson and Wynstra (2003) have found that giving incremental value to customer managers is one mechanism to counter the effects of value ambiguity. This incremental value, conceptualized as a percentage of the purchase price of the reference offering, provides customer managers with an *incentive to change*. Offering an incentive to change provides customer managers with a justification for purchasing higher value, higher price market offerings: even if their firm does not realize all of the stated value, it will likely realize enough to make it economically worthwhile; this allows the customer managers to take credit for any monetary gain realized, yet to avoid blame for any shortfall.

Anderson and Wynstra (2003) have found that incentive to change appears to work as a *threshold* phenomenon in value ambiguity reduction. While their research replicated the findings of Anderson et al. (2000) in offering an incentive to change of 7.5% of the price of the reference offering, they also found that offering a 2.5% incentive to change produced a significant increase in customer managers' purchase intentions for higher value, higher price offerings (relative to a 0% incentive-to-change condition). Of greater interest, in two experiments they found no significant difference in purchase intentions between the 7.5% and 2.5% incentive-to-change conditions.

Providing the incremental 5% monetary incentive from the 2.5% to the 7.5%

condition had virtually no effect on customer managers' purchase intentions. These findings (across two experiments) provide strong empirical support that incentive to change does work as a threshold phenomenon in ambiguity reduction, but that the threshold can be much lower than previously thought. The threshold level for maintenance, repair and operating (MRO) items, which Anderson and Wynstra (2003) studied, may be lower than that for offerings that become component parts of the customer's offering. Adopting a new MRO item has much less effect on the value that a customer's offerings deliver to its customers, making change less risky. The greater magnitude of the 5–7% incentive to change heuristic offered by Anderson and Narus (1999), who originally proposed this concept, may apply more to component offerings.

Non-monetary mechanisms to counter value ambiguity

To broaden our understanding of purchasing higher value, higher price offerings in business markets, we would like to find non-monetary mechanisms for reducing value ambiguity. Offering customer managers some sort of guarantee that they would receive the stated value of market offerings would seem to be one mechanism. However, despite studying variations over four experiments with purchasing managers, Anderson et al. (2000) were unable to find support for supplier value guarantees as a value ambiguity reduction mechanism. They offer two potential explanations for the lack of effects: first, customer managers have little experience with supplier value guarantees, so offering them may accentuate to purchasing managers their comparative ignorance of value relative to price (Fox and Tversky, 1995); and, second, providing a supplier guarantee of any sort may prime customer managers' loss aversion, negating any ambiguity reduction effects of the guarantee.

Anderson and Wynstra (2003) have proposed *value corroboration* as another manipulation of ambiguity about superior value that is non-monetary. Customer managers seek corroboration of the value estimate for a market offering from other sources. Seeking information from others who have experience with the offering is one way these managers can reduce their uncertainty (Cox, 1967). Anderson and Wynstra (2003) studied two value corroboration mechanisms: reference customers and pilot programs. *Reference customers* are respected competitors that are already using a market offering and are willing to share their experiences. *Pilot programs* enable a customer firm to discover on a small scale, at one of its plants, that the cost savings or greater value demonstrated in a value analysis actually is realized in practice.

Anderson and Wynstra (2003) found that customer managers in the reference customer and pilot program conditions had significantly higher purchase intentions for higher value, higher price offerings than in the no value corroboration condition (nothing stated). Further, they found no significant difference in purchase intentions for customer managers in the reference customer and pilot program conditions. This finding suggests that an internal versus external source does not matter as much as they hypothesized, so long as the customer managers find the source credible.

Customer value management[5]

Customer value management is a progressive, practical approach that, in its essence, has two basic goals:

- Deliver superior value to targeted market segments and customer firms.
- Get an equitable return on the value delivered.

Customer value management relies on customer value assessment to gain an understanding of customer requirements and preferences, and what it is worth in monetary terms to fulfil them. Although firms may be able to accomplish the first goal without any formal assessment of customer value, it is unlikely that they will be able to accomplish the second goal – getting an equitable return on the value delivered – without it. Simply put, to gain an equitable or fair return on the value their offerings deliver, suppliers must be able to persuasively demonstrate and document the value they provide customers relative to the next-best alternative for those customers. Box 8.1 shows how suppliers that do not spend the time and money on customer value management are unaware of how much *not* doing it is costing them.

An essential undertaking in customer value management is building *customer value models*, which are data-driven estimates of what a present or prospective market offering is worth in monetary terms to targeted customers relative to the next best alternative offering for those customers. Some suppliers have built what they regard as customer value models, but they have the character of being "data-light" and "assumption-heavy". Quite naturally, customers are sceptical of such models, claiming that they do not accurately reflect their businesses. In contrast, customer value management stresses building customer value models that are "data-heavy" and "assumption-light". Wherever possible, suppliers gather data to minimize the number of assumptions made and to ensure that the assumptions that are made are reasonable.

Drawing on experience in working with firms over the past several years, I briefly discuss customer value management. Anderson and Narus (2004) provide a more detailed discussion. I focus here on building customer value models in practice and creating value-based sales tools.

[5] This section draws heavily from Anderson and Narus (2004, ch. 2).

Box 8.1—Can suppliers afford not to build customer value models?

An electronics engineer was leading his firm's development effort for a next-generation, electronic control device, which was projected to have a total cost of about $7. An important component of this device was a power factor correction (PFC) integrated circuit (IC). This engineer had narrowed down the potential suppliers for these PFC ICs to two: Supplier *A*, which was quoting a price of 45 cents per IC, and Supplier *B*, which was quoting a price of 35 cents per IC. The firm anticipated purchasing 5 million of these PFC ICs for the new control devices.

This electronics engineer happened to be enrolled in a part-time, evening MBA program where he was taking a graduate course in business marketing. Having learned in this course that customer firms should focus on the total value of ownership rather than simply purchase price, he decided to build a customer value model, to fulfil part of his course requirements and to determine which of the two suppliers would provide the greater value to his firm.

Pulling together the data and building the customer value model the engineer estimated that Supplier *A*'s offering was worth 15.9 cents more per PFC IC than Supplier *B*'s. Two value elements emerged as the most critical points of difference between the two suppliers. Supplier *A* provided *earlier access to product samples*, which significantly shortened the time to market for the new devices. Because of the competitive nature of the customer firm's own market, getting to market earlier with new devices affected both the revenue and profit it earned. Supplier *A* also provided superior *technical engineering support*, which provided design expertise and was a supplementary engineering resource that the customer firm would otherwise have to supply itself. There were also several other points of difference that were of lesser monetary value.

Drawing on customer value model results the engineer's recommendation to purchasing was that, even though Supplier *A*'s price was 10 cents more expensive than Supplier *B*'s, the firm should purchase the PCF ICs from Supplier *A* because of the superior value that its offering provided. In delivering this report to the purchasing manager who was supporting his development project, the engineer related the outcome of his research to the purchasing manager. "That's interesting to learn," replied the purchasing manager with a smile, "But I think that you will be interested to learn that in the meantime, I have negotiated a price reduction with Supplier *A* from 45 cents to 35 cents per IC!"

Think for a moment about what occurred. By not standing firm on its price in the negotiation, how much incremental profit had Supplier *A* just given away? $500,000. On one transaction with one customer. Yet, Supplier *A*'s salesperson is not the culprit here; his firm is. Supplier *A* had done no customer value research, built no customer value models and constructed no value-based sales tools to enable the salesperson to persuasively demonstrate and document the superior value of his offering relative to Supplier *B*'s.

Interestingly, as part of his research the engineer interviewed the sales-persons from Supplier A and Supplier B and asked each of them what they thought was the source of their offering's superior value relative to the other. The salesperson from Supplier A did not name either of the two value elements that provided the greatest differential value. Apparently, he was unaware of the extent of the differences between his offering and Supplier B's on these elements. Instead, he stated that he believed that his offering was worth more, attributing it to his dedicated and superior servicing of the account. His superior service was worth something: 0.2 cents per IC in the engineer's customer value model!

Perhaps sensing that this superior service was not worth the 10-cent price difference between quotes, when push came to shove he reduced the price to match Supplier B's lower price. Now, even with a value-based sales tool that enabled him to persuasively demonstrate his offering's superior value, as part of the give and take of negotiation he might have reduced the price somewhat and perhaps even split the price difference with the purchasing manager. Even in this latter scenario, though, his firm still would have retained $250,000 in incremental profit.

This case study brings to life a choice that most often remains implicit for suppliers and, as such, one that they cannot fully know the consequences of implicitly making. They can spend the time and money upfront to persuasively demonstrate and document the superior value that their offerings deliver, and capture a more equitable portion of this delivered value, or they can choose not to and give value away unknowingly as price reductions, just as Supplier A did in this case study. Either way, suppliers are going to pay. As this case study amply reveals, can suppliers afford *not* to build customer value models?

Building customer value models

Working in a cross-functional team, supplier managers begin by listing all the value elements for the market offering under consideration. Value elements define in a comprehensive and elemental way how the offering reduces customer costs or adds value to what the customer is trying to accomplish. They also capture the technical, economic, service and social benefits that customers receive from the offering. Teams generally find it easier, first of all, to consider the value elements for the core product or service and, then, the value elements for the supplementary services, programs and systems that augment the core offering. A fundamental consideration here is to be *comprehensive* and *elemental*.

Leaving out elements, particularly if they are unfavourable for the supplier's market offering relative to the next best alternative offering, compromises the effort and undermines its credibility with customers that detect the missing elements. By being as elemental as possible the supplier firm is able to more accurately gauge the differences in functionality and performance its offering provides relative to the next best alternative. Customer managers may find it easier to answer broadly stated questions, such as the cost of an hour of downtime in the customer's plant. However, their answers often will leave out some effects on the customer's business, producing less valid estimates of worth.

Teams are advised to write out this list of the value elements, which can be lengthy, in relatively quick fashion, drawing on their collective experience. Each team next hypothesizes what kinds of customers would receive the greatest value from the offering and what kinds of customers would receive the least value. Team members determine what customer characteristics, such as application or customer capabilities, best capture these hypothesized differences in value received and could be used to segment (or further segment) the market. The team uses these customer descriptors to define two market (sub) segments that would be of most interest to study in the customer value research.

Each team next considers what would be the next best alternative offering in the minds of customers in each segment. The team selects the next best alternative offering and the firm providing it for each segment (the next best alternative offering may vary between selected segments and, on rare occasions, teams may choose to study two next best alternative offerings within a segment). The team then revisits its list of value elements, with this next best alternative in mind.

While firms are doing many wonderful things for their customers the reality in most business markets is that so, too, are the competitors supplying the next best alternative offering doing many wonderful things. So, to focus the customer value research and make it more manageable, we take advantage of a rearrangement of the preceding fundamental value equation from:

$$(\text{Value}_f - \text{Price}_f) > (\text{Value}_a - \text{Price}_a) \qquad (8.4)$$

$$(\text{Value}_f - \text{Value}_a) > (\text{Price}_f - \text{Price}_a) \qquad (8.5)$$

$$\Delta\,\text{Value}_{f,a} > (\text{Price}_f - \text{Price}_a) \qquad (8.6)$$

where Value_f and Price_f are the value and price of the focal firm's market offering (Offering_f), Value_a and Price_a are the value and price of the next best alternative market offering (Offering_a) and Δ denotes the difference in value between Offering_f and Offering_a. Thus, what really matters is not the value of each offering but the *differences* in value between the two offerings relative to the difference in their prices.

For each value element on its list, the team decides whether there is a difference on its offering's functionality or performance on that element relative to the next best alternative. Teams are encouraged to be candid in their appraisals. If the team is honest with itself, out of a lengthy list the team typically will decide that only a handful of value elements are differences between offerings. Most of these differences will be in favour of the team's offering, yet some will be differences favouring the next best alternative offering. Value elements on which the team believes that there are no differences between the two offerings are termed *points of parity*. Value elements on which the team believes that there are differences are termed *points of difference*. The team constructs an initial *word equation* for each point of difference, which expresses in words how to assess the differences in functionality and performance on the element and what those differences are worth in monetary terms. Accompanying each word equation are the assumptions that the team is making about the value element and how its monetary value can be assessed. It is crucial to be explicit in all assumptions made.

The teams focus their customer value research on the points of difference, setting the points of parity aside.[6] In initial meetings to invite customers to participate in the customer value research, team members relate the list of value elements and which of them they regard as points of parity and points of difference. Team members then share the initial word equations for the hypothesized points of difference. If the team has been honest with itself the customers will largely agree with them. Inevitably, though, on some value elements they will disagree with the team's assessment. For example, the customer might regard a point of parity as a point of difference favouring the the next best alternative. Value elements on which disagreements occur are termed *points of contention*. Such disagreements should not be regarded as bad because they provide further motivation to the customers to participate in research and gather data to resolve the point of contention. I elaborate on points of difference, points of contention and word equations in Box 8.2.

Following customer value research, where the data are gathered the team analyses them to estimate what each value element that is a point of difference or a point of contention is worth in monetary terms. The team next collects these value element results in a value summary – the *customer value model*. The team should be certain to list any assumptions made in assigning monetary amounts to each element. To gain a deeper understanding of the results the team performs sensitivity analyses, using the information on the variances around each element. It considers what characteristics might drive the variation in value and whether that variation warrants a new segmentation approach. It identifies which customers are the most attractive prospects.

The team finally considers the *value placeholders*, which are value elements where measurement is either too difficult or too costly. Relying on customer perception, what is each qualitatively worth? How might proxy estimates be obtained? When there is no other source than customer perception, framing the worth of the element in the customer's mind is critical. What seems reasonable?

---

[6] Once in a while a team might pursue a point of difference that represents a nuisance to customers. Nuisances are points of parity at which could a supplier make a difference, it would have a significant effect on the value the customers receive and it would also deliver a social benefit of ending or reducing the "pain" customers experience.

Box 8.2—Points of difference, points of contention and word equations

Customer value research focuses on the points of difference and points of contention between the studied market offering and the next best alternative offering. Together, these capture the prospective differences in value between offerings and what they are worth in monetary terms. The intent of the supplier is to demonstrate and document these differences so that customer managers can easily grasp them, understand precisely how the supplier has assessed them and find the results persuasive. To assist in accomplishing this, we have created the concept of word equations.

A *word equation* expresses in words precisely how to assess the differences in functionality and performance between the studied offerings for a value element and how those differences are converted into worth in monetary terms. One is constructed for each point of difference and point of contention, where the value element, expressed as either cost savings or incremental profit, is on the left side of the equals sign and the components defining the differences in functionality or performance and what these are worth are on the right side. Word equations were invented to counter a rampant problem in business markets, "spreadsheet mania". By spreadsheet mania we mean the construction of overly complicated, difficult-to-understand spreadsheets. In many businesses, technically minded individuals take pride in their capabilities with spreadsheet software, such as Microsoft Excel®. This unfortunately often manifests itself as densely packed, number-laden spreadsheets with minimal to non-existent explanations of what the numbers mean. When questioned about their contents, even their creators sometimes have difficulty reconstructing what is meant.

In contrast, customer value research teams first construct a word equation for each point of difference and point of contention. These word equations make clear to the teams and the customers participating in the research what data need to be gathered and how they will be combined to provide value estimates. After the data have been gathered, each word equation is the first item presented in the presentations of the results. Then, the data are substituted in each equation to calculate the estimate in monetary terms for each value element. These results are then collected in a value summary, which we refer to as the *customer value model*. As an example, a point of difference between two large-format document reproduction systems (denoted as B and next best alternative A) was the number of paper jams a customer would experience each day. The word equation for this was expressed as:

$$\text{Paper jam cost savings}_{B,A} = [(\text{Paper jams per day} \times \text{Minutes to fix jam})_A$$
$$- \text{Paper jams per day} \times \text{Minutes to fix jam})_B]$$
$$\div 60 \text{ minutes per hour} \times \text{Operator wages per}$$
$$\times \text{Annual work days}$$

Substituting in the gathered data, an estimate for this value element then was calculated as:

$$\text{Paper jam cost savings}_{B,A} = [(3 \times 10)_A - (1 \times 10)_B]/60 \times €31.82 \times 240$$

$$= €2545.60$$

Thus, the estimate for this value element was €2,545.60 annually for system B relative to system A.

Accompanying each word equation are the assumptions that the team is making about the value element and how its monetary value is assessed. In all customer value research, some assumptions will be needed to complete the analysis. The assumptions might be about the functionality or performance the market offering actually provides in the customer's specific setting, particularly for aspects that are extraordinarily difficult or costly to measure. Alternatively, assumptions might be made in assigning worth in monetary terms to measured differences in performance an offering provides in the customer's setting. Continuing with the example an explicit assumption made was that if operator hours could be reduced, the Engineering Department would reassign him or her to other value-adding tasks.

It is crucial that the supplier be *explicit* in the assumptions it makes. When a customer firm catches the supplier in one or more implicit assumptions, particularly ones that are dubious, it has a devastating effect on the credibility of the whole analysis. In contrast, when all assumptions are made explicit, customer management simply can disagree with them. When this happens, the astute supplier invites customer managers to share the rationales underlying their alternative assumptions. Depending on how plausible their rationales seem, the supplier can either adopt the alternative assumptions for the analysis or suggest that the supplier and customer engage in some joint research to mutually discover the most appropriate assumptions for the customer's specific setting.

Although QUALCOMM assigns no monetary amounts to some less tangible elements, it still includes them in its analysis as value placeholders. In this way QUALCOMM conveys that it believes those elements are worth something to the customer and leaves open the possibility that some specific amount might be ascertained in the future.

Value-based sales tools

Suppliers not only use customer value models to inform and guide their own decision making, they also use them to create value-based sales tools that better enable their salesforces to persuasively convey the superior value their firms' offerings provide. These tools tend to take one of two forms: value case histories or value assessment as a value-adding, consultative selling tool. Whichever form a supplier employs, it is critical that the salesperson presents the results to customer managers having responsibility for the areas where the greatest cost savings or added value will occur. Although value-based sales tools provide an integrating function to help customer managers appreciate how a supplier's offering delivers value in various areas within their firm, customer managers nonetheless are most willing to be persuaded and push for a supplier's offering when they personally stand to gain the most.

Value case histories are written accounts that document the cost savings or added value a customer firm actually received from its use of a supplier's market offering. Sonoco Product Company's Protective Packaging Division (SPPD), for example, audits actual cost savings that implementation of its total packaging solution proposals produce. At the end of the first year, SPPD constructs a cost of use case study and reports the findings to customer management. SPPD maintains a database of these cost of use case studies, which SPPD salespersons draw on when making proposals to other prospects. These case studies persuasively convey the cost savings that the prospects themselves would likely realize.

Value assessment itself can become a value-adding service that suppliers offer as part of a consultative selling approach. They develop customer value assessment tools, which we term *value calculators*, as spreadsheet software applications that salespeople or value specialists conduct on laptop computers to demonstrate the value that customers would receive from their offerings. Although these value calculators are typically quite user-friendly, they may require input data that the customer does not have readily available. To facilitate gathering the required input the supplier may develop a worksheet that pulls together the necessary input data. The BT Compass Logistics Planning System that BT Products AB of Sweden (which is a member of Toyota Industries Corporation) has developed serves as an outstanding example. A case example of how BT Compass is used as part of a value-adding, consultative approach to selling appears in Box 8.3.

Suppliers that practice customer value management understand that they must not only demonstrate the value that their offerings would deliver to customers but that they must also document the cost savings and/or incremental profits their offerings actually deliver to customers purchasing them. Thus, they work with customers to define the measures on which they will track the cost savings or incremental profit produced and, then after a suitable period of time, work with customer managers to document what the actual results have been. They use these tools, which we term *value documenters*, to further refine their customer value models, create value case histories, enable the customer managers to turn "grey" money into "green" money and enhance the credibility of the demonstrated value of their offerings, because customer managers know that the supplier is willing to return to document the actual value received. W.W. Grainger's practice of customer value management with Pharma Labs (a disguised name) provides an outstanding case of the significant benefits to each firm, which I relate in Box 8.4.

Box 8.3—BT Compass's logistics planning system

BT Lifters, a Division of BT Products AB, based in Sweden, has created *BT Compass*, which is a logistics planning system, to help customers make a significant difference in the profitability of their businesses through lowering the total cost of the handling process. The BT Compass system is an advanced software package that provides:

- A full analysis of the customer's operational requirements.
- A fast comparison of different pallet-handling and order-picking solutions.
- Optimum warehouse layout.
- Accurate calculations of handling capacities.
- A complete analysis of projected life cycle costs.

The BT Compass system has been developed to work in seven languages, and all inputs and outputs can be translated to any language with a single keystroke. It displays different layout options by using high-quality colour graphics, and all plans can be printed quickly using a printer or plotter.

BT Lifters uses Compass when a customer is contemplating a change in materials handling or is adding a new facility. About 75% of the applications are for making changes in existing facilities, with about 25% of the applications for new facilities or "greenfield" sites. Compass is used about 50% of the time for new customers and 50% for existing customers. Compass provides BT Lifters a means of demonstrating its expertise as a materials-handling solutions supplier to new customers.

Compass provides a layout of the warehouse. It optimizes interactions, such as aisle width, with the dimensional requirements for a counterbalance truck. It calculates the layout and equipment requirements to meet peak hour needs in pallets per hour. The calculations include performance specifications, such as the number of 90° turns. BT Lifters measures the actual performance of its competitor's equipment, often buying the equipment to test it. Thus, it knows the actual performance on critical measures that customers use to judge lift trucks. A detailed, accurate understanding of the customer's usage system is also critical. A number of customers provide functional specifications and ask the lift truck suppliers to respond with the number and type of trucks required to provide the functional performance. If the performance is not met, the selected supplier has to provide additional trucks at no cost!

The data required as input for using Compass requires some competence on the customer's part. Some customers know the required data very well, others do not. BT Lifter's most senior salespeople serve as internal materials-handling champions for the customers and work with them in using Compass and doing the analysis. They will even provide "hands-on" data collection as needed at the customer's facility.

Although some customers use logistics consultants to help them in facilities planning, the advantage of working with BT Lifters and using Compass is that it provides a combination of planning the warehouse and specification of the kind and number of trucks needed to optimize warehouse performance. A recent case example illustrates this. Birkenstock, a German manufacturer of health shoes, decided to build a new warehouse in Asbach, Germany. An in-house consultant responsible for the procurement process for this new warehouse had made a layout that indicated three lift trucks would be necessary to handle the pallet movements per hour. By using Compass, BT Lifters was able to demonstrate how an alternative layout in conjunction with its high-performance trucks required only two trucks – one less truck and also one less operator. According to BT Lifter's management, without Compass they would never have been to find this new solution and see the detailed performance results for their trucks. In addition, they believed that they would not have been able to convince Birkenstock management that their solution was correct.

Box 8.4—Customer value management benefits Grainger and its customers

Pharma Labs (a disguised name) is a rapidly growing pharmaceuticals manu-facturer. At one of its largest plants – a facility with 380 employees – purchasing managers were questioning whether to outsource their MRO procurement and inventory management processes. During a routine sales call the W.W. Grainger account manager learned of the managers' concerns and arranged a half-day meeting with the vice president of operations, the purchasing manager and the maintenance manager at that facility. He asked two Grainger Consulting Services (GCS) managers to attend this meeting, thinking that GCS might be of assistance.

Following the meeting, GCS proposed that it perform what it calls a *baseline assessment*, which documents the total costs of MRO supplies management and then, following that assessment, offer Pharma managers some strategic recom-mendations about how they could improve their operations. GCS told Pharma Labs that the assessment and the strategy development would take 6 to 12 weeks to complete and would cost $45,000. Pharma Labs management agreed to the proposal, hiring GCS in January 1997.

To begin, GCS put together a case team, which consisted of a consulting manager, a consultant and a business analyst. Pharma Labs formed a steering committee and a project team. The steering committee comprised the relevant department heads, such as maintenance, purchasing, manufacturing, inventory management, management information systems and finance, and was responsible for project oversight and strategy development. The project team was a cross-functional group with representatives from each of the departments on the steering committee and was responsible for working with the GCS case team.

Generally, GCS looks for the elements of its customer value models in four primary areas: processes (from how the need for items is identified to payment of invoices), products (product price, usage factors, brand standardization and application), inventory (on-hand value and carrying costs) and suppliers (performance, consolidation and value-adding services provided). In each area, GCS defines value and cost-saving elements (such as freight and courier charges and the cost of overtime), specifies the measures for the elements (such as procurement cost per purchase order, number of suppliers and inventory accuracy), collects the data and analyses them and specifies measures for monitoring performance. At Pharma Labs the measures for monitoring performance included supply expenditures, number of suppliers and transaction volume.

In a baseline assessment, GCS uses process mapping and activity-based costing to build customer value models, drawing on proprietary databases that the company has built from its findings in past engagements. At Pharma Labs, GCS applied an activity-based costing approach to identify procurement costs across all typical functional areas: purchasing, maintenance, receiving and accounts payable. These identified costs were generally in line with costs tracked in the GCS databases.

In any analysis, GCS attempts to use the customer's electronic data whenever possible. The team usually attempts to get one year's worth of data. Early on, the case team makes a site visit to examine the customer's data and to assess how accurate and complete they are. In the case of Pharma Labs, GCS analysed two years' worth of purchasing and accounts payable data, as well as six months of procurement card data. The data provided GCS and Pharma with insights about the potential for consolidating the number of products Pharma purchased regularly from various suppliers. It also suggested how Pharma might consolidate its purchases in return for lower prices and greater value-adding services from its remaining services.

At Pharma Labs, as in most GCS engagements, the case team also had to do an invoice analysis – actually inspecting past invoices to gather usable data – to validate the electronic data and to provide additional line item product detail when available. The level of detail that the customer has is usually not adequate. The customer's system may contain only aggregated purchase order information, showing only how much was paid in total. Complicating the task further, invoices themselves often have incomplete item descriptions that make it difficult to determine exactly what was purchased.

The GCS team also found from its inventory analysis that Pharma Labs had no records of the amount of inventory on hand or its usage. Inventory levels were extremely high – the team later found that Pharma had more then $1 million worth of slow-moving inventory – but no actual record of this inventory was maintained in a system to track and manage its items.

The GCS case team supplemented its analyses by interviewing the Pharma project team members. In these interviews, GCS shared its preliminary findings, tried to uncover anything that they might have overlooked and learned what the Pharma managers themselves perceived to be potential areas of improvement. The interviews were in fact fruitful, alerting GCS and Pharma managers to at least one significant finding in the procurement area. It turned out that Pharma lab technicians played an unusually large role in the procurement process, handling some routine purchasing, maintaining detailed, handwritten logs of all transactions, receiving the items into inventory and managing that inventory. The GCS value model showed that Pharma Labs was spending 30% of its procurement costs – or the equivalent of nearly three full-time positions – on lab technicians who could be redeployed from this purchasing function to more value-adding activities in their intended function. Pharma Labs eventually signed a supply agreement with another company, which in return put one of its people on site to manage this procurement process.

After GCS completes a baseline assessment, it then tries to specify improvements that the customer can make in 6 to 12 months. It also works with the customer to formulate changes in the MRO supplies management strategy.

At Pharma Labs, GCS identified at least $327,000 in total cost savings on the $6.1 million Pharma Labs was spending yearly on MRO supplies, including the costs of acquiring and managing them. These projected cost savings came about through consolidation of suppliers and product-spending reductions ($165,000), inventory reduction ($72,000) and process improvements ($90,000). For example, GCS recommended that Pharma Labs dramatically consolidate its MRO supplies purchases. Pharma Labs agreed and initiated a national account agreement with Grainger in June 1997. In return, Grainger provided Pharma Labs with an on-site Grainger representative to manage the purchase and inventory processes at the company. This allowed a Pharma Labs maintenance technician who had been spending 100% of his time purchasing MRO supplies to return to performing value-adding maintenance activities.

What were the ultimate results of Grainger's work with Pharma Labs? In December 1997, GCS and Pharma Labs jointly conducted an audit of achieved cost savings, which were found to be $387,000 during the first 6 months. What's more, for the whole of 1997, W.W. Grainger sales to Pharma Labs increased sevenfold, from $50,000 to $350,000. The next year, sales nearly doubled, to $650,000. Clearly, a better understating of value created substantial benefits for each company.

Adapted from Anderson and Narus (1998).

Conclusions

This chapter has attempted to persuasively communicate that customer value in business markets is deserving of much greater work. Refining its conceptualization is critical for theory-building research as well as specifying an operational definition to guide its assessment in practice. More academic research is needed to better understand customer value and the factors that significantly affect how customer managers regard it, particularly with respect to price. Finding effective non-monetary mechanisms to counter the greater ambiguity that customer managers apparently have for value relative to price can make an enormous contribution.

Giving value away in business markets is easy to do and requires no particular skill. It is the responsibility of marketing and sales, though, to get an equitable return on the value that their firm's offerings deliver in business markets. When an offering delivers superior value relative to the incumbent or next best alternative offering, a supplier firm most often would seek to claim a portion of this superior value by asking for a higher price relative to that of the incumbent or next best alternative. Nearly 30 years ago, Håkansson and Wootz (1975) found that purchasing managers were most often unwilling to select bids for higher quality (i.e., higher value) offerings when they had to pay a higher price, even though: "The price they had to pay for this extra quality was trifling, at most 0.4%" (p. 49). Today, we still have only rudimentary ideas on how we might overcome this reluctance.

The time for a change is now. Scholars in business marketing should be strongly motivated and encouraged to take up research in understanding how suppliers can better create, communicate and equitably share value with customers. Building conceptual frameworks to understand this and providing managerial guidance to practitioners ought to be vital and principal pursuits of academic business marketing. After all, what topic is calling out more for and is more deserving of a *Zeitgeist* among business marketing academics than customer value?

References

Anderson, J.C. and Narus, J.A. (1998). Business marketing: Understand what customers value. *Harvard Business Review*, November/December: 53–65.

Anderson, J.C. and Narus, J.A. (1999). *Business Market Management: Understanding, Creating, and Delivering Value*. Upper Saddle River, NJ: Prentice Hall.

Anderson, J.C. and Narus, J.A. (2004). *Business Market Management: Understanding, Creating, and Delivering Value* (2nd edn). Upper Saddle River, NJ: Pearson Prentice Hall.

Anderson, J.C. and Wynstra, F. (2003). Purchasing higher-value, higher-price offerings in business markets. Unpublished working paper, Kellogg School of Management, Northwestern University, Evanston, IL.

Anderson, J.C., Jain, D. and Chintagunta, P. (1993). Customer value assessment in business markets: A state-of-practice study. *Journal of Business-to-Business Marketing*, **1**(1): 3–29.

Anderson, J.C., Thomson, J.B.L. and Wynstra, F. (2000). Combining value and price to make purchase decisions in business markets. *International Journal of Research in Marketing*, **17**(December): 307–329.

Cox, D.F. (1967). Risk taking and information handling in consumer behaviour. In: D.F. Cox (ed.), *Risk Taking and Information Handling in Consumer Behaviour* (pp. 604–639). Boston: Division of Research, Harvard Business School.

Dolan, R.J. and Simon, H. (1996). *Power Pricing: How Managing Pricing Transforms the Bottom Line*. New York: Free Press.

Ellram, L.M. (1995). Total cost of ownership: An analysis approach for purchasing. *International Journal of Physical Distribution and Logistics*, **25**(8): 4–23.

Fox, C. and Tversky, A. (1995). Ambiguity aversion and comparative ignorance. *Quarterly Journal of Economics*, **110**(3): 585–603.

Gale, B.T. (1994). *Managing Customer Value*. New York: Free Press.

Håkansson, H. and Wootz, B. (1975). Supplier selection in an international environment: An experimental study. *Journal of Marketing Research*, **12**(February): 46–51.

Kahneman, D. and Tversky, A. (1979). Prospect theory: An analysis of decision under risk.*Econometrica*, **47**(2): 263–291.

Miles, L.D. (1989). *Techniques of Value Analysis* (3rd edn). Washington, DC: Lawrence D. Miles Value Foundation.

Nagle, T.T. and Holden, R.K. (2002). *The Strategy and Tactics of Pricing* (3rd edn). Upper Saddle River, NJ: Prentice Hall.

Pindyck, R.S. and Rubinfeld, D.L. (1989). *Microeconomics*. New York: Macmillan.

Smith, G.E. (2002). Segmenting B2B markets with economic value analysis. *Marketing Management*, March: 35–39.

Tversky, A. and Kahneman, D. (1991). Loss aversion in riskless choice: A reference-Dependent Model.*Quarterly Journal of Economics*, **106**(4): 1039–1061.

Wouters, M., Anderson, J.C. and Wynstra, F. (2004). The adoption of total cost of ownership for sourcing decisions: A structural equations analysis. *Accounting, Organizations and Society* (forthcoming).

Developments on the supply side of companies

9

Lars-Erik Gadde and Gøran Persson

Introduction

A review of publications in purchasing after 1990 indicates that major changes have taken place on the buying side of companies. This development is sometimes characterized as a "revolution in purchasing" (see, e.g., van Weele and Rozemeijer, 1996). There seems to be a common perception that this reorientation involves four significant changes in relation to purchasing and suppliers.

First, the view of *purchasing efficiency* has shifted from a focus on single transactions to performance improvements in series of transactions; this is mainly expressed as a change from price chasing to a total cost perspective. A second change relates to the *role of purchasing* in the company. From being considered a clerical/administrative function it has now become repositioned as a strategic function for the company; this is because the costs of purchased goods and services tend to account for an ever-increasing part of the total costs of a company.

Third, when purchasing becomes more significant and the view of efficiency is modified the perception of the *role of suppliers* is affected as well. It is, in fact, the potential contribution from suppliers that is the point of departure for the reconsideration of purchasing efficiency, because these suppliers are important tools in a purchasing department's involvement in the rationalization and development efforts of the company. Finally, reaping these potential benefits from suppliers calls for a revised perception of what kinds of *relationships with suppliers* are appropriate. Traditional recommendations of "arm's length" relationships have now been supplemented with arguments strongly favouring interaction and involvement with suppliers.

There is no clear causality among these changes. Above, it was formulated in the sequence "the view of efficiency – the role of purchasing – the role of suppliers – the nature of relationships". However, the actual sequence might well go in the opposite direction. By reconsidering the nature of its relationships with suppliers a company may be led in the direction of exploring what the role of suppliers could actually be, which may in turn affect the view of what role purchasing might eventually have, thus impacting on the perspective of efficiency. In fact, the development of purchasing is a complex interplay among these interconnected changes.

Aim and scope of the chapter

Our assignment is to present an overview of the developments on the buying side of companies, with a particular focus on the two latest decades. We begin by illustrating the main changes of purchasing in this period as they are mirrored in purchasing textbooks and international journals. We continue by analysing the shifts over time in the conceptualizations of buying and how this is related to the supplier side. Then, we explore the consequences of these changes for three significant issues in purchasing: the changing view of purchasing efficiency and effectiveness is discussed first; the second theme relates to the role of purchasing and suppliers in the overall corporate strategy; and third, we analyse the strategic options for purchasing and the supply side of companies and how they have developed over time. The chapter closes with a concluding discussion.

Changes as illustrated in the literature

Purchasing in refereed journals

The analysis of the issues covered in refereed journals departs from a review published in 1987 in the *Journal of Purchasing and Materials Management* (*JPMM*). This review (Williams and Oumlil, 1987) covers the period beginning in 1965, when the journal was established. During this period the journal was the most prominent one in the purchasing field and should therefore provide a re-presentative view of what purchasing issues were considered relevant by researchers. For a comparison with this picture we also made a brief review of the articles in the same journal 2000–2002. Its name is now the *Journal of Supply Chain Management* (*JSCM*), which in itself signals a change. To increase the sample we made a similar review of the *European Journal of Purchasing and Supply Management* (*EJPSM*), which was established in 1994 and is a respected journal today. Table 9.1 shows the findings from these reviews. For the first period we also found a survey of US dissertations (Williams, 1986), giving a complementary view of what issues attracted researchers at the time.

There are three significant shifts to be observed in these figures. The first concerns what issues in the materials flow was focused on by researchers. In the period 1965–1987 inventory management was a highly prioritized area. In fact, this was the dominant issue overall, represented by 11% of the articles and no less than 13 out of 35 dissertations. In the first few years of the 21st century this area has been virtually neglected. Instead, attention concerning materials flow shifted toward various aspects of supply chains, accounting for 12% of the papers.

Table 9.1—Purchasing issues in the literature 1965–1987 and 2000–2002

Purchasing issue	1965–1987		2000–2002
	Ia* (%)	Ib**	II*** (%)
Inventory management	11	13	1.5
Supply chains (management and principles)	—	—	12
Planning, organization and budgeting	13	4	6.5
Supplier selection, processes and criteria	6	7	4
Purchasing performance and evaluation	9	2	6.5
Price and pricing issues	7	1	—
Costs in purchasing, target costing and accounting	—	—	6.5
Information technology and purchasing	4	4	5
Legal and ethical aspects	6.5	1	1.5
Sourcing (strategic and international)	4.5	2	6
Make or buy	1.5	—	—
Outsourcing	—	—	4
Negotiation and bargaining processes	2	1	—
Customer–supplier relationships	—	—	13.5
Disposables, waste and environmental concerns	0.5	—	1.5
Purchasing and product development	—	—	5

* Ia = percentage of all articles in *JPMM* 1965–1987.
** Ib = number of US dissertations 1973–1982.
*** II = percentage of all articles in *JSCM* and *EJPSM* 2000–2002.

The second change is the increasing significance of interaction and customer–supplier relationships. In the first period there were few studies of interaction, and the existing ones focused on negotiations between buyer and supplier. In the recent period issues concerning relationships among customers and suppliers has been the single most researched area, including 13.5% of all the articles.

The third change relates to financial and economic aspects. In the first study period, prices and pricing appeared quite frequently in the journal, while there has been no observation of this issue in the second period. The interest seems to have shifted to costs rather than price, and the articles deal with, for example, target costing (which actually is pricing from the buyer's side) and the connection between purchasing and accounting.

Other areas seem to have roughly the same significance in the two periods; for example, supplier selection, purchasing performance, strategic sourcing and (surprisingly) information technology and purchasing. "Make or buy" has changed labelling to "Outsourcing" and occurs more frequently than before. "Organization and planning" is less significant than it was in the earlier period, while "Purchasing and product development" accounted for 5% of the publications in the second period, an increase from no representation at all in the first period.

Purchasing in textbooks

Purchasing Principles and Techniques has long been one of the leading textbooks in the field of purchasing and supply. Written by Peter Baily and David Farmer at the request of the Institute of Purchasing and Supply, it was first published in 1968 with new editions following in 1974, 1977, 1981, 1987 and 1990. Beginning with the 7th edition from 1994 and continuing in the 1998 edition, David Jessop and David Jones were included as co-authors. We have chosen to compare three versions of the book: the 2nd edition (Baily and Farmer, 1974), the 5th edition (Baily and Farmer, 1987) and the 8th edition (Baily et al., 1998).

Looking at the three editions, we observe both similarities and differences. All versions cover the basic purchasing issues, such as the purchasing process, the organization of the purchasing function, performance measurement and efficiency in purchasing, make or buy decisions, subcontracting and negotiation. In terms of differences, many of the more general techniques are the subject of separate chapters in the early editions, while they are integrated into other chapters in later editions (e.g., critical path method, operations research and value analysis). The major changes in the book, however, concern four specific reorientations.

First, purchasing strategy and strategic issues related to purchasing are expanded and elaborated on in later editions. These issues are not mentioned at all in the 1974 version, while the edition from 1987 includes a chapter recognizing the need for purchasing management to be involved in corporate planning, as well as some of the strategic alternatives for the purchasing function. In the 1998 version several chapters cover various strategic issues related to purchasing and supply, such as the strategic role of purchasing, the development of purchasing strategy and strategic options available.

Second, the book becomes more and more context-specific with successive editions, in the sense that it addresses particular purchasing situations characterized by different purchasing processes. For example, procurement of commodities, services and capital goods represent different purchasing contexts, each one imposing particular challenges and problems for purchasing personnel. These conditions are increasingly focused in later editions.

Third, the 1987 version expands on several issues related to internal relationships and internal connections. These include materials planning and the interdependencies between production and purchasing, the role of specifications and its relation to product design and engineering, as well as sourcing and its relationship to strategy. The co-ordination of purchasing activities in larger corporations is also discussed in terms of concepts, such as lead buyer, as are organizational concepts, such as decision-making units to handle internal interdependencies. Such interdependencies between the purchasing function and other functions are increasingly recognized and elaborated on.

Fourth, compared with previous editions of the book the 1998 version covers an array of topics concerning supplier relationships. The authors describe a shift from a transactional view of purchasing where the buyer's primary objective is "finding a supplier who is willing to exchange the goods or services required for an agreed sum of money" (Baily et al., p. 8). This simplistic view is supplemented with an analysis of mutual buyer–supplier relationships, where "the benefits of doing business together arise from ideas of *sharing* as well as *exchanging*" (Bailey et al., p. 8). Other contemporary issues dealt with in this edition are organization of suppliers in tiers, outsourcing principles and their consequences.

The conclusion is that all editions cover some general purchasing issues at the same time as they deal with specific issues, which change over time. Increasingly, purchasing strategy and strategic issues related to purchasing are elaborated on and integrated into the discussion. Furthermore, the impact of different contexts and applications is taken into consideration. Two main changes concerning interdependencies and relationships can be observed: the first is the focus on internal interdependencies and the co-ordination and collaboration of internal functions in the 1980s; and, second, in the 1990s the perspective shifted toward interorganizational interdependencies and the exploitation of such interdependencies through, for instance, partnerships and collaboration.

Changing conceptualizations of purchasing

The sections above illuminate the changes in terms of what aspects and issues of purchasing have been focused on in research and in textbooks. In this section we analyse in greater detail how purchasing has been conceptualized by researchers. The point of departure for this analysis is the view of purchasing as an act of buying, involving exchange with a particular supplier. In the "clerical and administrative era" a representative title of a book could have been "Handbook of Purchasing". This type of literature was concerned mainly with issues related to purchasing procedures: how to make enquiries, how to handle tenders, calculation of optimum order quantities and so on. The literature was dominated by suggestions for improving purchasing efficiency through well-developed purchasing routines (see, e.g., Westing et al., 1969). Over time the scope of these conceptualizations and models expanded. The unit of analysis was extended beyond the single transaction. Our review of this broadened scope includes conceptualizations of customer–supplier interaction, supply chains and supply networks, respectively.

Transaction orientation

In the late 1960s the first models of organizational buying behaviour were launched; these applied the logic of rational decision-making models to acquisition processes and identified a number of stages from the buying company's "need recognition" to its selection of supplier(s) and order routines. Depending on the type of purchase, the resources of the company and various situational conditions these processes were assumed to follow different patterns. By applying such models the researchers aimed at improving the understanding of the decision-making process in the buying company in order to identify the factors determining the final selection of product and supplier.

The first important contribution in this respect was Robinson et al. (1967), who discussed the distinction between "straight re-buy", "modified re-buy" and "new task". Another useful concept in these models was the "buying centre", indicating that purchasing decisions are influenced by several functions in the buying company (Webster and Wind, 1972). In general, these models reinforced the view that purchasing efficiency is secured through rational purchasing procedures. This procedure, in turn, is concerned with the rationality of single purchases, thus promoting the transaction-oriented approach. Sometimes, these models seem to have been developed mainly as tools for recommendations concerning the marketing activities of selling firms (e.g., Sheth, 1973). In this way these models also reinforced the perception that marketing in one firm and purchasing in another are antagonistic counterparts involved in zero-sum contests.

Kraljic (1982) presented an analytical toolbox that has been very helpful for purchasing managers in dealing with transactions and exchange with suppliers. Kraljic's matrix is useful for allocation of the scarce resources in the purchasing department to the procurement tasks where they are most needed, depending on the "type of purchase and situational conditions" mentioned above. By using Kraljic's 2×2 matrix with the two axes "complexity of supply market" and "importance of purchasing", the buyer can group the items to be procured into the four cells of the matrix. Each cell is then characterized by its particular features when it comes to sourcing behaviour and resource input. Kraljic's portfolio approach has been extensively used by purchasers. There are some important assumptions to be observed as underlying its recommendations: it takes the product as the point of departure for analysis, and this product is perceived as being more or less given.

Customer–supplier interaction

When the transaction-oriented approach is applied, suppliers are seen as an aggregate. A number of alternative vendors are assumed to exist in a "supplier market", and the issue for purchasing is to select the best offer in each situation. Two developments changed these perceptions: the first was the view that purchasing has an important strategic role (e.g., Kraljic, 1982; Axelsson and Håkansson, 1984; Spekman, 1988); and the second stems from the increasing insight into the benefits associated with close interaction and mutual adaptations in relationships observed, for example, in the first study by the IMP Group (Håkansson, 1982).

One of the early studies of buyer–seller dyads based on the IMP (industrial marketing and purchasing) interaction model was presented by Campbell (1985). He argues that previous studies tended to emphasize the role of the buying company, to focus on discrete transactions and to deal mainly with "new buy" situations. The main contribution of Campbell's article is that the dyadic approach is applied and that the frequency of transactions is taken into account. "Interaction" is used in the title of the paper, but the interaction actually dealt with is only marginally related to the actual involvement among the firms. The focus of the paper is to analyse under what conditions the purchasing strategy of a buying firm and the marketing strategy of a selling firm actually match – or fail to match. There is still quite a distance between the two parties, and the applicability of the various buying strategies is discussed in relation to the conditions of different types of "markets".

Over the years an enormous number of studies of customer–supplier relationships emerged. As the review of journal contributions revealed, this is the issue that has been most frequently dealt with by researchers in the early 21st century. It would be an impossible task to give a representative overview of the research that has been published in this area. However, it is obvious that the exploration of the substance and function of business relationships in general (Håkansson and Snehota, 1995) has been of the main sources of inspiration for the analysis of buyer–supplier relationships. Examples of publications dealing with interaction and relationships are: Carlisle and Parker (1989), Lamming (1993), Nishiguchi (1994), Cox (1996), Ellram and Edis (1996), Dyer and Singh (1998), Gadde and Snehota (2000) and Ford (2002). One of the main findings in these studies is that what goes on in a relationship affects (and is affected by) what goes on in other relationships; this calls for extension of the relationship scope. Below we discuss two such extensions: supply chains and supply networks.

The increasing attention to relationships affects the view and the significance of purchasing issues. One example of reconsideration in this respect concerns the evaluation of supplier performance. What a supplier can actually do for a customer is strongly dependent on the customer's actions. Therefore, the relevant unit of evaluation should be the relationship rather than the supplier. Lamming et al. (1996) present a relationship assessment model (RAP), suggesting criteria for the evaluation of the supplier, the customer and the relationship. Araujo et al. (1999) explore the consequences for the utilization of the suppliers' resources, depending on the type of interface between buyer and supplier. Further, they argue that in close relationships the object of exchange is developed over time through joint activities. Therefore, the approach of purchasing portfolio models, taking the product as a given, needs to be reinterpreted (see, e.g., Dubois and Pedersen, 2002; Gelderman and van Weele, 2001).

Supply chains

The most obvious connections to the link between a customer and a supplier are the customer's customer and the supplier's supplier. The attempts to link these connections and those further downstream and upstream have been at the top of the agenda under the label "supply chain management" (SCM).

The notion of supply chain management appears to have been established in the early 1980s (Dubois et al., 2003). The perspective on supply chains originated from logistics and had an intra-organizational orientation. At the time, logistics focused primarily on the firm's internal supply chain and how different functions, such as purchasing, manufacturing, distribution and sales, could be integrated in order to smooth out the materials flow within the company. This view is to some extent derived from the value chain concept, where the firm is seen as "a collection of activities that are performed to design, produce, market, deliver and support its products" (Porter, 1985, p. 36). However, although Porter recognizes the inter-dependence with activities undertaken by other firms, his main emphasis is on the value chain of the individual firm. This orientation is partly explained by the situation in practice where "key measures and systems were, in most cases, inwardly focused and few individuals or organisations were concerned or focused on chains of suppliers for their products" (Morgan, 1999, p. 85).

From this intra-organizational focus the scope of the analysis of the value chain was later extended beyond the activities of the individual firm to include "upstream production chains" and "downstream distribution channels" (Lamming et al., 2000). In the beginning this broadened scope seems to have been primarily associated with attempts to better control the flow of materials (Harland, 1996). Over time, supply chain issues increasingly evolved toward managerial issues concerning the relationships among the actors involved in the supply chain processes. This shift is illustrated by the considerable attention to supply chain management identified as "the management of multiple relationships across the supply chain" (Lambert and Cooper, 2000, p. 65).

The performance measures for evaluation have become increasingly advanced as the view of supply chains has been developed and extended; this is illustrated in a study by Spekman et al. (1999), where the authors explore the connection between supply chain performance and the sourcing and supply management practices of buying firms. This article includes an alternative conceptualization of purchasing portfolios. Rather than categorizing products in the spirit of Kraljic the authors classify supplier relationships in terms of their technical and commercial complexity.

Supply networks

The models and conceptualizations within the supply chain paradigm are important for the development and understanding of the changes on the buying side of companies. The increasing reliance on an activity structure characterized by interdependencies spanning the boundaries of firms is an important aspect of the changes that have taken place.

However, understanding the developments in purchasing requires an even more extended scope than a chain. Advocates of the supply chain approach tend to argue that the objective of SCM is the "linkage and co-ordination between processes of other entities in the pipe-line, i.e. suppliers and customers, and the organisation itself" (Christopher, 1992, p. 14). It is therefore claimed "real competition is not company against company but rather supply chain against supply chain" (Christopher, 1992, p. 17).

We do not share this view. First, we would like to tone down the focus on competition and, instead, emphasize the efforts to achieve efficiency improvements as the main driving force. The strategic actions taken are related primarily to customers and suppliers in the chain – not to competitors. Second, different supply chains are both competing and co-operating. The efficiency and effectiveness of a specific supply chain is, in fact, strongly contingent on how it relates to other supply chains. The sharing of resources with others is what improves performance of the operations in the individual supply chain, thus creating economies of scale. Analysing the consequences of the connections among supply chains clearly requires a network perspective (Gadde and Håkansson, 2001).

Economizing in supply chains is thus about taking into account the embeddedness of chains. The same is true when customer–supplier relationships are analysed in a wider scope. With a network view the connections of the specific dyad to relationships upstream and downstream in the supply chain are crucial to both parties where it comes to process integration. Furthermore, the connections among different customers and different suppliers set the conditions for the utilization of resources.

Changes in three central purchasing issues

Above we have identified the main tendencies in what has been written about purchasing in terms of changing areas of focus and conceptualizations. In this section we analyse the development over time of three central issues related to purchasing:

- The view of purchasing efficiency and effectiveness.
- The role of purchasing and suppliers in the overall corporate strategy.
- The strategic options on the supply side and how they have developed.

The view of purchasing efficiency and effectiveness

For a long time the recognized procedure for efficient purchasing was the optimization of single transactions. This approach builds on the assumption that overall performance is maximized when each individual purchase is conducted in the most appropriate way. As shown above, this transaction-oriented view of efficiency is rooted in models of rational decision processes, including various stages from "need recognition" to "selection of an order routine". The company is supposed to secure adequate performance in its operations by following a predetermined procedure. The evaluation of tenders from a number of competing suppliers is of particular significance in this process. The competitive struggle among these suppliers is considered to favour improvements from which the buying firm can benefit; for example, in terms of reduced price or innovative solutions.

According to this criterion of efficiency, purchasing should focus on achieving the lowest price, on the basis of the assumption that there is no difference in the value of the offerings of various suppliers. Furthermore, the costs of dealing with suppliers are supposed to be identical, irrespective of which vendor is used. Obviously, these conditions are not at hand in all situations, which makes a complementary view of efficiency necessary.

Most transactions are not isolated. On the contrary, for the buying firm a single transaction is always part of a series of transactions over time – often with one and the same supplier. Furthermore, it is related to other transactions undertaken at the same time. Therefore, rather than conducting the individual transaction in a way that minimizes price it sometimes makes sense to consider a wider scope of costs and benefits associated with a transaction. In this discussion we refer to Figure 9.1, which is an attempt to grasp the financial impact of a transaction by distinguishing between costs and revenues on both sides of the transaction and, in turn, divided into primary and secondary effects (Gadde et al., 2002).

Every business transaction is characterized by a price (i.e., what the buyer pays). The amount paid by the buyer and the revenue received by the supplier, however, represents only one dimension of the financial conditions and effects of a single transaction. For the buyer the price paid is one of the "primary" costs that are directly associated with the transaction. There are other primary costs as well; for example, costs of transportation, insurance and other expenses, and costs of handling the relationship with the supplier. However, the total financial effects of a single transaction have a much wider scope.

For the buyer there are also "secondary" costs to be taken into consideration. Any transaction with one supplier impacts on and is affected by transactions with other suppliers, with customers and with the buyer's internal operations. Furthermore, the main reason for the buyer to be involved in the transaction is

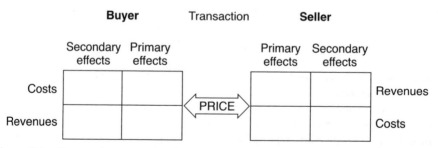

Figure 9.1—Costs and revenues in a business transaction. From Gadde et al. (2002, p. 324).

that it is a prerequisite for future revenues, when what is delivered by the supplier is used by the buyer; this means that the analysis of the economic effects of a transaction for the customer should also include the revenues on the buying side. "Primary" revenues on the buying side are directly associated with the value of the product or service delivered by the supplier, while "secondary" revenues stem from increased revenues or decreased costs in other relationships.

Figure 9.1 indicates quite a complex pattern of the effects on costs and revenues associated with a transaction. Once the scope of efficiency is extended beyond the single transaction a major demarcation problem arises. It is often argued that the buying firm should adopt a "total cost" perspective. As the above discussion illustrates it is an onerous task (i) to identify and (ii) to evaluate, what the total cost actually is. Furthermore, the revenues associated with the transaction with the supplier in some way need to be taken into account. Ferrin and Plank (2002) explored the actual use and the role of total ownership cost models and found that companies are increasingly applying these models. The authors argue, however, that developing "generic" models of total ownership costs is not appropriate because the effects on costs are completely contingent on contextual conditions.

The buying task takes quite different forms depending on which view of efficiency is applied. When the transaction-oriented model is used the buying firm avoids becoming overly involved with individual vendors. The dependence accompanying increasing involvement is assumed to delimit the freedom of the buyer to behave rationally in each transaction. The main task is then to secure opportunities for playing the market by keeping the exchange object standardized, thus allowing for competitive tendering.

The transaction-oriented purchasing approach, however, makes it difficult to utilize the specific capabilities of the various suppliers; this is because they are asked to offer a predetermined solution, which, by necessity, is standardized. It is therefore not possible for the supplier to suggest a solution that makes the best use of its own resources. The main concern is the ability to compete in terms of price. In such contexts, purchasing remains much of a clerical and administrative function. The primary responsibility of purchasing is to handle the tendering procedure and, through market research on supplier markets, to identify potential vendors.

When the complementary interpretation of efficiency is applied the attention shifts from focusing on price in a single transaction to economizing on a wider scope, including sets of connected transactions. Once this perspective is applied it changes the purchasing agenda from seeing the object of exchange as a given. A buying firm may affect its supply conditions considerably by adapting its requirements to the solution of a specific supplier. In these cases both costs and revenues are clearly contingent on the nature of the interaction between customer and supplier.

In such situations the buyer's main mission is to exploit the resources of suppliers. In order to utilize the resources of other firms the buying company must have substantial knowledge of these resources. Furthermore, it must be able to relate its internal resources to those accessed through relationships and to combine them in creative ways. Basically, the rationale of this approach stems from adaptations in relation to individual counterparts. These adaptations take various forms, such as the smoothing out of material flows, more efficient exchange of information and innovative use of technological resources.

In this context the tasks of the buying company involve efforts to motivate and mobilize suppliers to enter into the co-operative relationships that are necessary to gain the benefits associated with an extended scope of efficiency. As Figure 9.1 indicates, the supplier also envisages both revenues and costs (primary and secondary) from a transaction. Adaptations are always resource-intensive for both parties. Therefore, the buying firm must try to develop the content of the relationship in a way that is also favourable for the supplier. Similarly, the buying firm must continuously monitor and evaluate the financial effects of the way transactions with suppliers are conducted. Adaptations are always costly, and they can only be motivated in situations where the benefits outweigh the costs. In some situations the primary cost (i.e., mainly price) is still the most appropriate view of efficiency for the buying company.

The roles of purchasing and suppliers in corporate strategy

The question of whether or not purchasing is strategic has long been debated. In a review of the long-term development of purchasing the situation 100 years ago was described as "not exactly a prestige position" (Morgan, 1999, p. 73). The position and image of a company function tends to be a mirror of its perceived importance. The view of purchasing as a fairly passive function long remained prevalent. For example, Ammer (1969) described the role of purchasing as reactive rather than proactive, both with regard to internal demands and to external situations. In the same vein, Ansoff (1965) characterized purchasing as an administrative function rather than a strategic.

Farmer (1978) criticized this view and argued that any company that ignores potential supply strategies of a creative rather than a defensive nature is foregoing sources of competitive advantage. Three years later he wrote that the argument that purchasing should be involved in the management of strategy in manufacturing firms is almost refutable. Despite the "apparent obviousness of the argument there appear to be few organisations in which the purchasing function makes a significant contribution to strategy development" (Farmer, 1981, p. 20). Over time this position gradually improved, as what was going on at the supply side of companies was seen as increasingly important.

The developments in industrial operations brought the interfaces with other companies into focus; for example, through just-in-time deliveries and concurrent engineering spanning buyer–supplier boundaries. However, this process of reconsideration of the importance of purchasing was quite long, as illustrated by a purchasing director at IBM who described the company's purchasing reorientation in the late 1990s, arguing that "in the past when you could do nothing else at IBM we made you a buyer" and indicated that the past was "not so long ago" (Carbone, 1999, p. 42). Even in more recent years the position of purchasing in this respect has been questioned. For example, Ramsay (2001, p. 257) concluded that "purchasing typically has no significant strategic role to play", mainly because purchasing is responsible for supplying resources that have been outsourced and for that reason are considered non-core and, thus, not strategic. Mol (2003) criticizes this view and argues that strategic advantage not only resides within the firm but also between the firm and its partners. In fact, purchasing can even be said "to have become more relevant in recent years as firms have outsourced more activities and increasingly look towards suppliers to create added value" (Mol, p. 7).

One consequence of these developments in companies is that the competitiveness and performance of any firm is highly dependent on its capacity to handle the supply side. There is a direct effect on financial outcome because purchasing takes up a substantial portion of the total costs of a company. There is also a major indirect impact owing to the fact that the buying company's internal costs are greatly affected by what is going on at the interface with suppliers. Moreover, most companies are dependent on suppliers for technology provision.

As a result of enhanced technological diversification it is difficult for firms to be at the cutting edge of all the various technologies on which they rely. There is thus a strong connection between the role of purchasing and the role of suppliers. When purchasing is important, suppliers are important as well. The increasing significance of the supply side of companies has made purchasing a strategic function and made a reconsideration of the role of suppliers necessary. In this section we draw together these changes because they are closely intertwined.

Axelsson and Håkansson (1984) identify three strategic roles of purchasing: the rationalization role, the development role and the structural role. The role of rationalization involves activities concerned with the company's need to carry out its day-to-day operations as efficiently and economically as possible. These efforts include systematic influences on design, manufacturing, logistics and administrative operations. Purchasing impacts considerably on the outcome of these attempts through its co-operation with internal company functions, such as production, logistics, etc., and its awareness of the capacity and capability of suppliers. In these rationalization efforts the single most important issue is to develop effective routines for dealing with a large number of purchases (Ford et al., 2003). Thus, rather than trying to optimize single transactions, buying firms need to consider series of transactions in their rationalization efforts.

The second strategic role of purchasing where suppliers can contribute is the development role; this is where the problem-solving ability of the supplier is important. The reason for its significance is that suppliers can be important resource providers for the technical development of the customer firm. The development role has been enhanced owing to the increasing specialization of the actors in industrial networks. Most firms today make use of products and services based on a variety of technologies. Over time it has become increasingly difficult for a firm to develop and maintain its own capability in each specific area of technology relevant to its operations. Therefore, buying firms rely more and more on suppliers as sources of technical development and product design (e.g., Wynstra, 1998).

One important mission for the purchasing function, then, is to become involved as early as possible in the R&D process, mainly in order to bring in suppliers. Early supplier involvement makes it possible to fully utilize vendor capabilities in design, as well as being a means of shortening lead times in the development of new products. On the other hand, when the transaction-oriented approach governs the operations of the buying company, supplier involvement in product development is not recommended. On the contrary, such involvement is considered a problem because it reduces short-term opportunities to change from one supplier to another and is perceived as risky owing to potential long-term "lock-in" effects.

Finally, purchasing has a structural role because procurement activities affect supplier markets. By spreading its purchases among a number of vendors a large-volume buyer can secure the long-term availability of a dispersed supplier structure. On the other hand, by concentrating its purchases on one supplier the large-volume buyer strengthens this vendor, but can erode the business conditions for others. It is possible for a supplier to actively encourage this role of purchasing.

Recently, one issue at the top of the purchasing agenda has been "consolidation". In other words, to reduce the number of suppliers by focusing purchases of a specific item on one supplier and to have one and the same vendor to supply various items. The significance of such actions is illustrated by Dubois (2003) in a case study of a chemical manufacturer. Such efforts are expressions of the rationalization role, but have obvious structural impacts as well. A supplier can encourage these efforts by actively offering buyers assistance in these attempts.

Purchasing is a cross-border function because it is an important link between the suppliers and the other functions in the buying company. To be able to function as an effective interface in this respect, purchasing must have the ability to interact both internally and externally. The opportunities for interaction and co-operation are mainly contingent on the position and status of purchasing and the organizational structure of the buying company. The enhanced role of purchasing imposes increasing requirements on the skills and capabilities of purchasing staff. The clerical and administrative competence needs to be complemented with engineering and technical knowledge.

When suppliers increasingly contribute to innovation and product development, purchasing must involve people with technical backgrounds. The entrance of technicians into the purchasing function provides other advantages as well. First, since people with a background in engineering have become involved in purchasing the status and image of the function is positively affected. Second, since engineers have become involved in purchasing, production and design the conditions for interaction among these functions have been considerably improved.

Over time, the internal interactions between purchasing and technical functions have become increasingly important, because purchasing has become more complex. Components, materials and systems are more technically sophisticated today than they used to be in the past, and, thus, even more interaction in the buying company is necessary; this is because the causes of (and the solutions to) many problems span the borders of different corporate functions, thus requiring the combined efforts of cross-functional teams. Successful outcomes of these change efforts have required the active involvement of suppliers and "more and more sourcing teams began working with preferred suppliers to assure the quality of purchased parts and systems" (Morgan, 1999, p. 90). In turn, the strategic options for purchasing had to be reinterpreted.

Strategic options for purchasing

The developments on the supply side of a company have made suppliers increasingly important to company performance and made buying firms reconsider their strategies concerning the relationship with their suppliers. Therefore, the first issue to discuss in this section is the company's strategy with regard to individual suppliers. As mentioned in previous sections, however, the relationship with each specific supplier has to be considered in its network context, which emphasizes strategies for supplier networks as the second issue.

Supplier relationships

A review of the purchasing literature clearly illustrates a shift in the view of what is perceived as the most preferred type of relationship. Historically, customers were recommended to avoid becoming dependent on individual sources. By having a number of alternative suppliers the buying firm would (i) reduce uncertainty in transactions, (ii) avoid becoming "locked in" to the technical solution of one supplier and (iii) encourage competition among different vendors. Applying this strategy leads to what has been identified as "arm's length" relationships; these are inexpensive to operate, impose little interdependence and make it possible for the buying company to switch supplier when better conditions are offered elsewhere. Investments in this type of relationships are limited, making it appropriate to identify this as a "low-involvement" approach toward suppliers (Gadde and Snehota, 2000).

According to this strategic view, suppliers are considered more or less efficient providers of identical input. It is thus rooted in the transaction-oriented approach, neglecting the effects of secondary costs and the potential effects on the revenue side. It is an appropriate approach when the customer's problems are clear and unquestioned and there are a number of suitable suppliers available, offering standardized solutions. Low-involvement relationships are handled with limited co-ordination, adaptations and interaction. On the other hand, the buyer must adapt its internal activities and resources to fit with what suppliers have to offer, which leads to increasing costs.

High-involvement relationships based on close co-operation in terms of substantial activity links, resource ties and interaction among people show a very different pattern. The main rationale for high involvement is based on opportunities to affect the revenue side of the customer and the approach is thus concerned with the development role of purchasing. Through enhanced involvement it may be possible for the buyer to take advantage of supplier skills and capabilities to improve the quality of its own products and services. Furthermore, internal costs in production processes and material flows may be reduced through mutual adaptations of various kinds.

High-involvement relationships are the most important ones to any company. They are based on an alternative view of purchasing efficiency, a different perspective on the role of suppliers, and the nature of relationships. Increasingly, companies rely on the resources of outside suppliers and this means that the activities of the buyer must be co-ordinated with those of its suppliers, which in turn requires investments in dedicated resources. These adaptations create inter-dependencies, and in these situations it is not possible for a buyer to switch suppliers frequently. Furthermore, high-involvement relationships are resource-intensive in terms of costs of adaptation and interaction among people; this means that a high-involvement relationship follows investment logic and makes sense only when the increasing costs are more than offset by relationship benefits.

On the basis of these conditions there are clearly good arguments for a buyer to develop relationships of various types. Depending on the level of involvement, suppliers offer different contributions in terms of benefits and sacrifices. Therefore, it is common to argue that a firm needs a portfolio of supplier relationships with different contents (e.g., Dyer et al., 1998; Bensaou, 1999). The strategic choice when it comes to supplier relationships is to determine the appropriate level of involvement with individual vendors; this is an onerous task because it is difficult to evaluate the primary and secondary costs and revenues associated with different levels of involvement. There are problems for the buyer associated both with identifying and evaluating these effects.

The customer cannot decide the level of involvement in isolation – it takes two to tango. Sometimes, the customer may find it difficult to induce the supplier to make reciprocal efforts to develop a close relationship. Being highly involved may not suit a large supplier because of the relative small scale of the buyer in question or the perceived absence of potential benefits in technology development. But, the main efforts of the supplier may also be directed elsewhere, making it impossible to be highly involved with this specific customer.

Managing in relationships with suppliers

The discussion above revealed that both high and low-involvement relationships have their pros and cons and there is no such thing as a "universally best" type of relationship. However, irrespective of the level of involvement it is important to handle the relationship appropriately. Bensaou (1999) analysed the performance of relationships that were characterized by different levels of supplier and customer-specific investments. The conclusion of the author is that no one type of relationship is superior to any other. The various combinations of involvement all "contained low and high-performing relationships, suggesting that each type of relationship can be well or poorly managed" (Bensaou, p. 37). Obviously, principles of managing do matter.

Managing in relation to suppliers can take various forms. In many cases the improvement efforts of the customer lead to the establishment of various programs for supplier development (see, e.g., Hahn et al., 1990; Krause and Ellram, 1997). These programs usually aim at directing the operations of the supplier to fit better with those of the buying firm. In many cases the role of the supplier is then decided mainly from the internal perspective of the buying firm. There might be good reasons for a customer to support the development of its suppliers in this way, but there is a danger in pushing these efforts too far; for example, Quinn (1999) discusses problems that might evolve from too strong control and security ambitions of the buying firm. If the customer specifies how to do the job in too much detail "it will kill innovation and vitiate the supplier's real advantage" (Quinn, p. 19). The author concludes that one crucial step for the customer is to shift the outlook to managing *what* result is desired, rather than managing *how* the result is to be produced.

The actions taken by the buyer in this respect will have direct implications for what the supplier can do. The directions given affect the extent to which the customer gains access to the resources of the supplier. In particular, too much specification can prevent the supplier from making the best use of its own network. The higher the involvement in the relationship the more likely it is that buyer and seller can together identify the most appropriate solution by considering their joint set of resources.

Managing in relationships takes place in an atmosphere characterized by both co-operation and conflict. These conditions prevail simultaneously because the parties have both contradictory and shared interests. In a short-term and transaction-oriented perspective the price paid by the buyer is the income of the supplier, making financial aspects a conflicting issue. When a longer term view is applied the two parties may have differing opinions of what is the most appropriate direction for technical development and joint projects.

In general, there is a tendency to portray arm's length relationships as con-flictual, while partnerships are assumed to be more friendly and co-operative. In our view, however, this is a misconception; instead, all relationships are character-ized by a mixture of conflict and co-operation. In fact, the absence of conflict in a high-involvement relationship indicates that the two parties have not really "clinched" and have not tried hard enough to explore the full potential for collaborative action.

High-involvement relationships, therefore, normally involve more conflict than low-involvement relationships. In the latter type of arrangements there may be frequent discussions concerning prices and delivery times, but on the whole there is not much more to debate because exchange is fairly standardized. If conflict in relation to a supplier escalates it is possible to change counterpart, even in the short run. On the other hand, in high-involvement relationships, joint investments, product adaptations, and other strategic issues require the buyer and the supplier to agree on a common approach, in spite of the fact that their views might differ considerably in other respects.

Thus, the higher the involvement between companies the greater the interdependence and the more pronounced the potential for conflict. The mutual interdependence between the two companies implies that conflicting issues must be "managed" before they escalate to confrontation; this does not mean, however, that conflicts should be avoided. On the contrary, diversity of goals and convictions are prerequisites for innovation and dynamics.

Another dimension of the relationship atmosphere that impacts on managing in relationships is related to power and dependence. Recent changes in purchasing strategy and behaviour have affected the power balance between buyer and seller. Buyers have deliberately entered into situations where they become dependent on suppliers. They do so because this approach is the way to make the best use of supplier resources and capabilities. Thus, rather than avoiding dependence the focus of the efforts of buying firms has shifted toward finding mechanisms to handle dependence; this does not mean, however, that power is a less important aspect than in arm's length relationships. Instead, the reciprocal dependence characterizing firms in high-involvement relationships is used in constructive ways (Gadde and Håkansson, 2001).

Supplier networks

The issues discussed above have profound implications for the supplier base of a company. In recent decades, most companies have reduced their number of suppliers considerably. When low involvement is the recommended strategy, buying companies tend to rely on multiple sourcing, because this approach helps in dealing with the negative consequences related to dependence on individual suppliers. Once the view concerning the potential contribution from individual suppliers changed, the size of the supplier base was affected. High-involvement relationships are resource-intensive and a buying company cannot handle too many of them; this means that a high-involvement strategy is often accompanied by single sourcing, which reduces the supplier base.

In terms of low-involvement relationships, buyers have become increasingly aware of the substantial costs associated with handling a large supplier base.

Therefore, the costs for securing competition among a number of potential suppliers can easily outweigh the benefits (Hahn et al., 1986); this means that a buyer may stay with the same supplier for a long time without ever entering into a high-involvement relationship. Such relationships have been identified as "durable arm's length relationships" (Dyer et al., 1998).

Even more important to the size of the supplier base is the increasing attention to system sourcing and consolidation. System sourcing is one way for a company to reduce supplier-handling costs. For example, instead of having five suppliers delivering one component each the buyer assigns one of them to supply a system consisting of these five components assembled to form a system. The advantages related to this approach were initially discovered in the automotive industry and later spread as kind of "best practice" to other industries. However, the gains in relationship handling costs have to be balanced against some problems associated with system sourcing. In particular, complex situations arise when both production and development of components and systems are outsourced – sometimes to different suppliers (Gadde and Jellbo, 2002).

Consolidation of the supply base has been a strong driving force for reduction of the number of suppliers. In particular, companies with a multitude of operations may gain substantial benefits in terms of economies of scale by centralizing their buying efforts. Furthermore, using one and the same supplier for different operative units is favourable in terms of quality consistency. Even for a single firm, consolidation might be advantageous. For example, appointing one supplier as a single source should make the buying firm a more interesting business partner in the eyes of the supplier. A further step in this direction is when the supplier takes on other manufacturers' products in its assortment to cover the whole need of a specific customer (e.g., Dubois, 2003).

Above, we have explored the changes when it comes to the number of suppliers and the need for variety in the supplier base and discussed the potential benefits from high involvement in relationships with individual suppliers. However, if a company is to make the best use of its suppliers, the network context must be taken into consideration. A customer can achieve considerable benefits through active co-ordination of what is going on between different suppliers and through adapting its internal operations to networks of embedded suppliers, rather than simply to individual vendors (Ford et al., 2003).

For example, the assembly operations of an automobile manufacturer would be difficult to conduct efficiently if each supplier delivered in its particular way. In this case the customer can improve performance considerably by organizing the supplier network so all suppliers deliver in a co-ordinated fashion. However, again the buyer must be careful about not giving too much direction to suppliers. Since most suppliers have other customers it would cause problems if each buyer demanded the supplier adapt to their specific requirements. In the end, the costs of these adaptations have to be borne by the buying firm.

Applying a network perspective to the strategic actions on the supply side is a most complex task. One of the fundamental assumptions in network analysis is

that any action undertaken by one actor impacts on others in various ways. Therefore, it is difficult to analyse the overall consequences of various strategic options.
Any change has some direct effects as well as a number of indirect effects on other
firms, which in turn impact on the performance of the first actor. Particular
problems are associated with evaluating the overall efficiency of various operations. The view of efficient behaviour depends on the perspective applied by the
buying firm. Gadde and Håkansson (2001) argue that a buying firm's ambitions to
act in accordance with a network view have to consider three dimensions simultaneously: efficiency in a single transaction; efficiency in a series of transactions
with a specific supplier; and efficiency in the transactions with all suppliers.

Effective supply strategies must handle all three types of efficiency at the same
time, which is problematic because they are often contradictory – at least to some
extent. As argued above, network efficiency is not necessarily maximized by
conducting each transaction as efficiently as possible. Similarly, too strong a relationship focus will result in suboptimization at the expense of totality. Any
network of business relationships contains a huge number of dimensions, all of
which are important from an efficiency point of view. Therefore, an actor aiming at
developing its supply side must be able to combine a number of efficiency criteria
and find ways of compromising among them. It goes without saying that these
characteristics make the supply side crucial to the overall strategy of the
corporation.

Concluding discussion

We began the chapter with the objective of describing and analysing the developments of purchasing. Our main conclusion is that the status, tasks and behaviour
of the purchasing function and the purchasing department have been subject to
major modifications over time. The significance of purchasing has been enhanced
considerably, and purchasing is now considered strategically important. This
changing position in turn is related to modifications of the view of purchasing
efficiency and reorientation of purchasing strategies, particularly concerning the
extent of involvement with individual suppliers.

The interesting question is why these changes have occurred. Should they be
regarded as outcomes of the ambition over many years to improve the position of
purchasing and give it the strategic role it deserves? Purchasing representatives
have long claimed that their actual potential has been underexploited and worked
intensively to change these conditions. We think that this effort is one reason for
the progress, but it is our conviction that the main explanation is to be found
elsewhere.

Morgan (1999) reports on a historical review of purchasing over the last hundred
years. His review provides two main implications for our analysis. First, the
common perception of a revolution in purchasing beginning around 1980 is a

somewhat misleading characterization of what has actually taken place. According to Morgan, the significance of purchasing and purchasing issues has varied over time. Purchasing operations have been a top priority in some periods (sometimes handled by top management), followed by periods when other functions received greater strategic attention.

Second (and more importantly for our analysis), further exploration shows that the role of purchasing is mainly determined by the "general business conditions" of companies; this means that in order to understand the developments in purchasing in the two recent decades we need to relate them to some overall business reorientations. In our opinion two particular changes in general conditions help to explain the developments on the supply side of companies: one is the increasing specialization of companies and the other the subsequent need for the co-ordination of activities and resources across the boundaries of firms.

The first factor to consider is the enhanced specialization of industry (e.g., Miles and Snow, 1986). The individual company increasingly tends to focus on a limited part of the total activity structure in which it is involved. Morgan (1999) comments on this change in his review and argues that outsourcing makes possible the "conserving of corporate resources for use where they are most effective" (p. 90). In this way a company may improve its skills and capabilities by concentrating on a narrow range of activities and relying on its business partners for other tasks. The main benefit of such resource sharing has been expressed as giving the company access to other firms' "investments, innovations and specialized professional capabilities that would be prohibitively expensive, or even impossible, to duplicate internally" (Quinn and Hilmer, 1994, p. 43).

Such perceptions indicate significant reorientation of the image of an efficient and effective company. In fact, they represent the dismantling of the modern business enterprise (MBE). Chandler (1977) uses the notion of the MBE to illustrate the role of the "visible hand" in an analysis of the development of US industry in the early 20th century. The MBE (represented, e.g., by Ford, General Motors and General Electric) assembled within their corporate boundaries all resources that were crucial to operations, because ownership control was considered the most appropriate means of securing access to these resources. Over time it became increasingly difficult for the individual company to retain this control. In particular, problems with vertical integration become manifest when the technological frontier expands rapidly (Langlois, 1988). Similarly, Piore and Sabel (1984) argue that consolidation within one firm can lead to problems when resources get more and more specialized.

Once buying firms reconsidered the need for resource control through ownership, the relations to other actors had to be modified as well. The MBE was characterized by strong interdependencies among its internal activities, while the interfaces with suppliers were standardized owing to the prevailing low-involvement approach. When some of the internally integrated activities were outsourced it became necessary to maintain co-ordination in relation to the remaining in-house activities of the buying firm. Business process integration and resource sharing across corporate boundaries were required to handle these inter-dependencies.

It is probable that the effects obtained from these inter-organizational efforts made buying companies reconsider their definition of an appropriate relationship with a supplier. This reinterpretation in turn contributed to the other changes discussed above. When buying companies realized the benefits that might be captured from high-involvement relationships, a general reorientation of the view of supplier relationships occurred.

These findings support the conclusion of Morgan (1999) that the role of purchasing is determined by the general business conditions in which companies work. The combined effects emanating from enhanced integration of business processes and outsourcing of activities to suppliers significantly strengthened the position of purchasing. Owing to these changes, purchasing accounts for an increasing portion of the total costs of the company. Furthermore, purchasing represents the main interface with the suppliers' resources, which have become crucial to any company. The impact of these changes is probably far more significant to the developments in purchasing than the ambitions of purchasers to improve the position of the function by improving its capabilities and extending the scope of its operations. The most important determinant of this reorientation and restructuring is the increasing understanding of the way in which purchasing is embedded in its context. The main cause of the revolution on the supply side of companies is thus the changes in the purchasing context.

A corollary to this conclusion is that the future role of purchasing is far from given. The fact that purchasing has become more important in recent decades does not necessarily imply that this role will be further improved nor does it guarantee that purchasing will retain its current position. In recent years the changes in the context have strengthened the position of purchasing in the company, but future developments may well move in the opposite direction; for example, outsourcing may have reached a stage at which its advantages are outweighed by its disadvantages.

Specialization in some part of an activity structure calls for integration in others (Piore, 1992). Therefore, benefits from further specialization in some cases are outweighed by increasing demands for co-ordination across the boundaries of firms. Consequently, previously quite one-sided arguments favouring outsourcing are now being supplemented with recommendations for insourcing (Gadde and Håkansson, 2001). Such reinterpretations will have an impact both on the importance of the supply side and on the role of purchasing. In cases where central activities and crucial resources are reinstated in-house, we can expect the strategic role of purchasing to be reduced.

In other cases, however, it is likely that the role of suppliers will become increasingly important, because it has been shown to be problematic to re-insource activities once they have been outsourced. At first glance a development in this direction may seem to support further strengthening of the position of purchasing. However, the historical exposé of Morgan (1999) illustrates that acquisition of the most critical resources in large corporations were once in the hands of top management, owing to its strategic significance. According to Farmer (1997) the same conditions seem to apply in small companies, because "when a one-man business develops, the last key task that is delegated by the entrepreneur is the control of major purchases" (p. 5). It is possible, therefore, that increasing significance of suppliers might lead to situations where the supply side of companies becomes too important to be handled by purchasing.

Acknowledgements

This chapter draws heavily on previous work conducted together with other people. We gratefully acknowledge these co-operative efforts with, in particular, Håkan Håkansson, David Ford, Ivan Snehota, Anna Dubois, Lars-Gunnar Mattsson and Luis Araujo.

References

Ammer, D. (1969). Materials management as a profit center. *Harvard Business Review,* **47**(1): 234–256.

Ansoff, I. (1965). *Corporate Strategy.* New York: McGraw-Hill.

Araujo, L., Dubois, A. and Gadde, L-E. (1999). Managing interfaces with suppliers. *Industrial Marketing Management,* **28**: 497–506.

Axelsson, B. and Håkansson, H. (1984). *Inköp för konkurrenskraft.* Stockholm: Liber [in Swedish].

Baily, P. and Farmer, D. (1974). *Purchasing Principles and Techniques* (2nd edn). London: Pitman Publishing/Institute of Purchasing and Supply.

Baily, P. and Farmer, D. (1987). *Purchasing Principles and Management* (5th edn). London: Pitman Publishing/Institute of Purchasing and Supply.

Baily, P., Farmer, D., Jessop, D. and Jones, D. (1998). *Purchasing Principles and Management* (8th edn). London: Pitman Publishing/Financial Times.

Bensaou, M. (1999). Portfolios of buyer–supplier relationships. *Sloan Management Review,* Summer: 35–44.

Campbell, N. (1985). An interaction approach to organisational buying behaviour. *Journal of Business Research,* **13**: 35–48.

Carbone, J. (1999). Reinventing purchasing wins the medal for Big Blue. *Purchasing,* **16**: 38–62.

Carlisle, J. and Parker, R. (1989). *Beyond Negotiation: Redeeming Customer–supplier Relationships.* Chichester, UK: John Wiley & Sons.

Chandler, A. (1977). *The Visible Hand: The Managerial Revolution in American Business.* Cambridge, MA: Harvard University Press.

Christopher, M. (1992). *Logistics and Supply Chain Management.* London: Pitman.

Cox, A. (1996). Relational competence and strategic procurement management. *European Journal of Purchasing and Supply Management,* **2**(1): 57–70.

Dubois, A. (2003). Strategic cost management across boundaries of firms. *Industrial Marketing Management*, **32**: 365–374.

Dubois, A. and Pedersen, A-C. (2002). Why relationships do not fit into purchasing portfolio models. *European Journal of Purchasing and Supply Management*, **8**(1): 35–42.

Dubois, A., Hulthén, K. and Pedersen, A-C. (2003). Interdependence within and among "supply chains". *Proceedings of the 12th International IPSERA Conference, Budapest, 14–16 April*.

Dyer, J. and Singh, H. (1998). The relational vew: Cooperative strategies and sources of interorganizational competitive advantage. *Academy of Management Review*, **23**(4): 660–679.

Dyer, J., Cho, D. and Chu, W. (1998). Strategic supplier segmentation: The next "best practice" in supply chain management. *California Management Review*, **40**(2): 57–76.

Ellram, L. and Edis, O. (1996). A case study of successful partnering implementation. *International Journal of Purchasing and Materials Management*, **32**(Fall): 20–28.

Farmer, D. (1978). Developing purchasing strategies. *Journal of Purchasing and Materials Management*, **14**(Fall): 6–11.

Farmer, D. (1981). Seeking strategic involvement. *Journal of Purchasing and Materials Management*, **17**(Fall): 20–24.

Farmer, D. (1997). Perspective: Purchasing myopia – Revisited. *European Journal of Purchasing and Supply Management*, **3**(1): 1–8.

Ferrin, B. and Plank, R. (2002). Total cost of ownership models: An exploratory study. *Journal of Supply Chain Management: A Global Review of Purchasing and Supply*, **38**(2): 18–29.

Ford, D. (ed.) (2002). *Understanding Business Marketing and Purchasing*. High Holborn: Thomson Learning.

Ford, D., Gadde, L.-E., Håkansson, H. and Snehota, I. (2003). *Managing Business Relationships*. Chichester, UK: John Wiley & Sons.

Gadde, L-E. and Håkansson, H. (2001). *Supply Network Strategies*. Chichester, UK: John Wiley & Sons.

Gadde, L.-E. and Jellbo, O. (2002). System sourcing: Opportunities and problems. *European Journal of Purchasing and Supply Management*, **8**(1): 43–51.

Gadde, L.-E. and Snehota, I. (2000). Making the most of supplier relationships. *Industrial Marketing Management*, **29**: 305–316.

Gadde, L-E., Håkansson, H. and Harrison, D. (2002). Price in a relational context. *Journal of Customer Behaviour*, **1**(3): 317–334.

Gelderman, K. and van Weele, A. (2001). Advancements in the use of a purchasing portfolio approach: A case study. *Proceedings of the 10th International Annual IPSERA Conference, Jönköping International Business School* (pp. 403–415).

Hahn, C., Kim, K. and Kim, J. (1986). Costs of competition: Implications for purchasing strategy. *Journal of Purchasing and Materials Management*, **22**(4): 2–7.

Hahn, C., Watts, C. and Kim, K. (1990). The supplier development program: A conceptual model. *International Journal of Purchasing and Materials Management*, **26**(2): 2–7.

Håkansson, H. (ed.) (1982). *International Marketing and Purchasing of Industrial Goods: An Interaction Approach*. New York: John Wiley & Sons.

Håkansson, H. and Snehota, I. (1995). *Developing Relationships in Business Networks*. London: Routledge.

Harland, C. (1996). Supply chain management: Relationships, chains and networks. *British Journal of Management*, **7**(Special issue): S63–S80.

Kraljic, P. (1982). Purchasing must become supply management. *Harvard Business Review*, **60**(September/October): 109–117.

Krause, D. and Ellram, L. (1997). Critical elements of supplier development. *European Journal of Purchasing and Supply Management*, **3**(1): 21–31.

Lambert, D. and Cooper, M. (2000). Issues in supply chain management. *Industrial Marketing Management*, **29**: 65–83.

Lamming, R. (1993). *Beyond Partnership: Strategies for Innovation and Lean Supply*. Hemel Hempstead, UK: Prentice Hall.

Lamming, R., Cousins, P. and Notman, D. (1996). Beyond vendor assessment: Relationship assessment programs. *European Journal of Purchasing and Supply Management*, **2**(4): 173–181.

Lamming, R., Johnsen, T., Zheng, J. and Harland, C. (2000). An initial classification of supply networks. *International Journal of Operations and Production Management*, **20**(6): 675–691.

Langlois, R. (2003). The vanishing hand: The changing dynamics of industrial capitalism. *Industrial and Corporate Change*, **12**(2): 351–385.

Miles, R. and Snow, C. (1986). Organizations: New concepts for new forms. *California Management Review*, **28**(3): 62–73.

Mol, M. (2003). Purchasing's strategic relevance. *Journal of Purchasing and Supply Management*, **9**(1): 43–50.

Morgan, J. (1999). Purchasing at 100: Where it's been, where it's headed. *Purchasing*, **18**(November): 72–94.

Nishiguchi, T. (1994). *Strategic Industrial Sourcing: The Japanese Advantage*. New York: Oxford University Press.

Piore, M. (1992). Fragments of a cognitive theory of technological change and organizational structures. In: N. Nohria and R. Eccles (eds), *Networks and Organizations: Structure, Form and Action*. Boston: Harvard Business School.

Piore, M. and Sabel, C. (1984). *The Second Industrial Divide*. New York: Basic Books.

Porter, M. (1985). *Competitive Advantage*. New York: Free Press.

Quinn, J. (1999). Strategic outsourcing: Leveraging knowledge capabilities. *Sloan Management Review*, **40**(Summer): 9–21.

Quinn, J. and Hilmer, F. (1994). Strategic outsourcing. *Sloan Management Review*, **35**(4): 43–55.

Ramsay, J. (2001). Purchasing's strategic irrelevance. *European Journal of Purchasing & Supply Management*, **7**(4): 257–263.

Robinson, P., Faris, C. and Wind, Y. (1967). *Industrial Buying and Creative Marketing*. Boston: Allyn & Bacon.

Sheth, J. (1973). A model of industrial buyer behaviour. *Journal of Marketing*, **37**(4): 50–56.

Spekman, R. (1988). Strategic supplier selection: Understanding long-term buyer relationships. *Business Horizons*, **31**(4): 75–81.

Spekman, R., Kamauff, J. and Spear, J. (1999). Towards more effective sourcing and supplier management. *European Journal of Purchasing and Supply Management*, **5**(2): 67–116.

van Weele, A. and Rozemeijer, F. (1996). *Revolution in Purchasing: Building Competitive Power through Pro-active Purchasing.* Eindhoven, The Netherlands: Eindhoven University of Technology.

Webster, F. and Wind, Y. (1972). *Organizational Buying Behaviour.* Englewood Cliffs, NJ: Prentice Hall.

Westing, J., Fine, I. and Zenz, G. (1969). *Purchasing Management: Materials in Motion.* New York: John Wiley & Sons.

Williams, A. (1986). Doctoral research in purchasing and materials management: An assessment. *Journal of Purchasing and Materials Management,* **22**(1): 13–16.

Williams, A. and Oumlil, B. (1987). A classification and analysis of JPMM articles. *Journal of Purchasing and Materials Management,* **23**(3): 24–28.

Wynstra, F. (1998). Purchasing involvement in product development. Dissertation, Eindhoven Centre for Innovation Studies, Eindhoven University, The Netherlands.

Part Three
Scientific approaches

A third prerequisite for investigating the role of marketing when market exchange is characterized by interaction concerning heterogeneous resources is to develop appropriate research tools or scientific approaches.

Scientific approaches can be considered at a variety of levels of analysis. The term is often conflated to include epistemology, research strategies and research methods. At the most basic level we can think of the practical tools used to approach a theoretical problem (e.g., an experiment or an interview guide). However, whether or not the researcher is aware of it, any scientific approach incorporates a view of what the world is and how it operates. Whether narrative or conceptualized, a scientific approach includes both demands of the contemporary research fields (the understanding of what is good research) and personal preferences. Thus, as Burke (1992) and others argue, any scientific approach colours the outcome of research.

The following three chapters (Chapters 10–12) all consider different aspects of scientific approaches. Each chapter touches on the multiplicities of understanding research methods and the questions and challenges that arise. In Chapter 10, Geir Gripsrud makes a general assessment of the scientific approaches used in the current research of distribution by putting it into a 100-year perspective. He demonstrates how the scientific approach has varied over time due to the background of the researchers as well as the research context. The author demonstrates how the current way to approach distribution problems has become very narrow due to the dominating theoretical approach. The conclusion is that distribution research should reclaim some of the territory lost to other research areas by widening the theoretical base.

In Chapter 11, Anna Dubois and Luis Araujo relates two central research issues to the use of a special research method – case research. As described in Chapter 1, time and boundaries are central for the understanding of marketing. Time is clearly connected to all development issues, and fuzzy boundaries are consequences of the intricate way companies are currently related to each other. Over the last few decades the use of case study research has developed in order to grasp and analyse these dimensions. The authors use an example of a doctorial thesis conducted in the IMP (industrial marketing and purchasing) research tradition to illustrate how the dimension of time and unclear boundaries can be handled empirically. Furthermore, the authors also argue that the handling of time and boundaries is as much a theoretical question as an empirical one.

In Chapter 12, Sigurd Troye and Roy Howell provide an analysis of the discipline of marketing rather than a particular method. They start from a variety of criticisms of marketing as a discipline (e.g., "attentional", "theoretical" and "methodological"). Examples of a lack of interplay among marketing theory, research methods used by marketing researchers and marketing phenomena are provided. The authors go on to identify four domains of interrelated activities and processes: the substantive, theoretical, managerial and methodological domains. By combining them the authors argue that each domain influences and is influenced by the other three. Troye and Howell use this analysis to suggest how marketing research overall might change in order to diminish the challenges raised by both theoretical and methodological criticisms.

The common picture emerging from these contributions is that their research tools influence both researchers and their products. Any scientific approach allows us to grasp certain aspects, but it also excludes others; this is not unique for social sciences, but is, as Galison (1997) argues, also characterizing science. Thus, if we want to grasp and examine new aspects of any subject, we have to develop our scientific approaches and have to construct new theoretical research tools. The aim of the final section is to take some first steps on this route.

References

Burke, P. (1992). *History and Social Theory*. Cambridge, UK: Polity Press.

Galison, P. (1997). *Image and Logic: A Material Culture of Microphysics*. Chicago: The University of Chicago Press.

The marketing discipline and distribution research: Time to regain lost territory?

10   *Geir Gripsrud*

Introduction

Marketing as an academic discipline is coming of age. The first marketing courses were taught and the first explicit marketing studies undertaken close to a century ago. The analysis of how the distribution of specific products was carried out was at the centre of attention in the emerging new discipline (Jones and Monieson, 1990). There is a lesser focus on distribution today, as an inspection of any modern marketing textbook clearly demonstrates. Distribution is now generally treated as one of the four P components of the marketing mix (*place*). It is typically described in a fairly short chapter on "how to manage" marketing channels (Kotler et al., 2002).

This approach to distribution builds on the "managerial approach" to the marketing discipline, which developed through the 1950s and first appeared on the textbook scene with *Basic Marketing* authored by McCarthy (1960). The four Ps are actually integrated in the present definition of marketing endorsed by the American Marketing Association: "Marketing is the process of planning and executing the conception, pricing, promotion, and distribution of ideas, goods, and services to create exchanges that satisfy individual and organizational goals" (Bennett, 1995).

In the first 50 years of its history, marketing had a more societal approach to its topic. It is interesting to note that in the latest edition of his very influential textbook *Marketing Management*, Philip Kotler states, "we can distinguish between a social and a managerial definition of marketing" (Kotler, 2003, p. 8). While the definition cited above is the managerial one, he offers the following *social* definition: "Marketing is a social process by which individuals and groups obtain what they need and want through creating, offering, and freely exchanging products and services of value with others" (p. 9).

These definitions may be compared with official definitions of the marketing discipline before the managerial approach became dominant. One of the earliest attempts to propose a formal definition of marketing was made by the Committee on Definitions of the American Marketing Association in 1935: "Marketing is a series of activities which are involved in the flow of goods from production to consumption." In 1948 the same committee published a proposal for another definition of marketing in the *Journal of Marketing*: "Marketing is the performance of business activities that direct the flow of goods and services from producer to consumer or user" (Holbæk-Hanssen, 1958, p. 101). The importance of distribution is evident in both definitions.

Mainstream marketing has a problem when it comes to fully appreciate and integrate the importance of the distributive sector today. The managerial approach usually focuses on the manufacturer and, traditionally, only looks forward toward the consumer or user. The marketing – or distribution – channel is conceived to start with the manufacturing company, which usually is also considered to be the "channel captain"; this means that the supply of raw materials and other inputs to the manufacturer receives limited or no attention. Similarly, the importance of the large retailers in many industries seems to escape the attention it deserves. Large retailers design products and/or outsource production to manufacturers who compete to gain orders for private brand production. In many cases, manufacturers also have to pay large amounts in slotting allowances/listing fees just to gain access to the shelves of large retailers for their manufacturer brands (Corstjens and Corstjens, 1995).

As the managerial approach became dominant in marketing, both purchasing and the supply of inputs to the manufacturer increasingly became the domain of a new academic discipline – *logistics*. This functional *spin-off* from the marketing discipline has contributed to making mainstream marketing today less relevant for analysing and understanding the supply and net chains that are increasingly dominating in the distribution literature (Lazzarini et al., 2001). The marketing discipline has during the last decades mainly focused on analysing dyadic relationships, initially in terms of power and conflict relations and later from a transaction cost and agency theory perspective. In this literature, specific distribution issues are typically not addressed. Marketing focuses on the legal and psychological aspects of exchange, while physical distribution and the related costs receive limited attention, if any.

The aim of this chapter is twofold. First, the role of distribution and channels research in the marketing discipline is explored in a historical context and the changing theoretical basis of this research is underlined. Based on this historical review the second aim of the chapter is to contribute to a reorientation of channels research in the future. It is argued that channels research in marketing has become extremely narrow and needs to be broadened in several ways.

In the next section we give a short description of the early history of marketing and the approaches that dominated the discipline during the first 50 years. As noted above, distribution of products was at the core of marketing in this period. After the managerial approach became dominant, interest in distribution channels reduced. However, the level of research interest and the favoured theoretical approach have varied over the last decades. In the third section we give a brief overview of how research on distribution channels has evolved since the 1960s up to today in mainstream marketing.

In an early attempt to disentangle the various approaches to distribution research, Gattorna (1978) maintained that as many as six different "schools" could be discerned at that time. Actually, national differences in distribution channels research are clearly also present, as can be seen from the reviews of research in different European countries published in Falk and Julander (1983). To simplify we will not discuss such differences here, as we follow "mainstream marketing", which may be loosely defined as research published in the *Journal of Marketing* (*JM*) and the *Journal of Marketing Research* (*JMR*). Moreover, in line with the tradition in marketing the literature dealing with retailing and retail marketing (Mulhern, 1997) is also not included.

In the fourth and last section of the chapter we compare the conceptualization of a marketing channel with the concept of a supply chain or supply network. The notion of supply chain management was coined approximately 20 years ago and has recently become very popular in business as well as academia. We discuss the relevance of channels research in marketing for analysing supply chains and supply networks. We argue that the received frame of reference in marketing may be inadequate and suggest some changes that may make channels research in marketing more relevant.

Marketing and distribution: the first decades

Marketing emerged as an academic discipline in the early 20th century in the USA. According to Jones and Monieson (1990), economists trained in Germany were instrumental in the new discipline. In Germany the Historical School of Economics had emerged as a reaction to classical economics and presented an alternative to the mathematics-oriented and the deductive approach of neoclassical economics. The Historical School was known for its historical, statistical methodology and its pragmatism rather than for theoretical or conceptual ideas. It focused on solving real economic problems and favoured an inductive approach to research as opposed to neoclassical economics.

Richard T. Ely led a group of German-trained economists in founding the American Economic Association in 1885 and the German Historical School had a strong influence on economists in the USA at that time. The universities of Wisconsin and Harvard were the primary centres of influence on early marketing thought (Bartels, 1962). In both places, economists trained in Germany spearheaded the development that gave rise to marketing as a separate discipline. At Wisconsin, Richard T. Ely became the first director of the School of Economics in 1892 and invited John R. Commons to join the faculty in 1904. Commons later became one of the most important institutional economists. Graduate research was historical and descriptive with a focus on the distribution of agricultural products. A former student of economics at Wisconsin, Edward David Jones, offered the first official course in marketing at an American university when in 1902 he taught "The Distributive and Regulative Industries of the United States" at the University of Michigan.

Samuel Sparling, in his book *Introduction to Business Organization*, classified in 1906 all business activity as extractive, manufacturing or distributive. Distribution was divided into marketing activities that facilitate exchange. Marketing proper was defined as "those commercial processes that are concerned with the distribution of raw materials of production and the finished output of the factory ... Their function is to give additional value to these commodities through exchange (cited from Jones and Monieson, 1990, p. 105). It is worth noting that marketing was conceived to cover the whole "supply chain" in today's terminology and did not start at the manufacturer stage.

Edwin Francis Gay became the first dean of the Harvard Business School, founded in 1908. Gay divided business into "two fundamental functions of industrial management (production) and commercial organization or marketing" (cited from Jones and Monieson, 1990, p. 107). When the School opened in 1908 there were three required courses: Principles of Accounting, Commercial Contracts and Economic Resources of the United States. Gay developed the general idea for the latter course based on his interest in economic history and marketing methods. The course was taught by Paul Cherington and by 1914 had developed into the course entitled *Marketing*.

Arch W. Shaw, a former student of Gay at Harvard, is usually credited with writing the first scholarly article that signified the start of the marketing discipline. His article "Some problems in market distribution", published in the *Quarterly Journal of Economics* in 1912, introduced the concept of *marketing functions*, which has been described as contributing most to the development of the science of marketing (Hunt and Goolsby, 1988, p. 35). Shaw was particularly interested in distributors, which he called "middlemen". He used the term "functions" to refer to the useful acts or services historically performed by middlemen, but pointed out that "functional middlemen" have taken over many of these services, as exemplified by banks in the case of financing.

Another influential author in the introductory period of marketing was L.D.H. Weld, who was an economist with a particular interest in agriculture. He defined seven marketing functions in his article entitled "Marketing functions and mercantile organization" (Weld, 1917). He defined marketing functions in general as "the services that must be performed in getting commodities from producer to consumer" (p. 317). Hunt and Goolsby (1988) conclude that the originators of the *functional* approach to marketing focused on distribution for a number of reasons: economists had ignored the topic, distribution problems were important, changes took place in the distributive institutions and the usefulness of marketing institutions in distributing goods and services should be recognized.

In the marketing textbooks that appeared in the 1920s onward, three different ways of organizing the presentation can be discerned: the *commodity*, the *institu-*

Table 10.1—Marketing functions (from Clark, 1923)

A. *Functions of exchange*
   1. Demand creation (selling)
   2. Assembly (buying)

B. *Functions of physical supply*
   3. Transportation
   4. Storage

C. *Auxiliary or facilitating functions*
   5. Financing
   6. Risk-taking
   7. Standardization

tional and the *functional* approach. In the first case the different types of commodities play a vital role in organizing the text, while the different types of companies (institutions) are the most important in the institutional approach. The functional approach became the favoured approach for organizing and studying the subject. According to Hunt and Goolsby the functional approach to the study of marketing dominated for five decades.

Principles of Marketing, authored by Fred E. Clark (1923), was one of three best-selling textbooks (with later revisions) that used the functional approach. Clark lists seven marketing functions divided into three main types and acknowledges that he closely follows the functions suggested by Weld (1917). The seven marketing functions are listed in Table 10.1.

In his discussion of the marketing functions, Clark makes it clear that he considers marketing to cover the stages both before and after manufacture. Marketing also includes purchasing (assembly) as well as demand creation. According to Clark there are three ways of creating demand: (i) through the satisfaction derived from the article itself, (ii) through personal solicitation by salesmen and (iii) through the use of advertising (Falkenberg, 1994).

An important feature of the functional approach is that the marketing functions are all considered useful functions from a societal point of view. The "four-utilities" concept was adopted by early marketing academics to substantiate this claim. The four-utilities concept maintains that the economic value of a product to a consumer is explained by the creation of four types of utility: first, *form utility* is created by making materials into a product that is wanted; second, *place utility* is created by making the product available where it is wanted; third, *time utility* is created by making the product available at the time it is wanted; and last, *possession utility* is created by transferring ownership. The last three utilities were traditionally used to explain how middlemen (distributors) and marketing contribute to welfare (Shaw, 1994).

The four-utilities concept was conceived by institutional economists and used to argue that merchants contributed value, just like farmers and manufacturers. Traditionally, economists distinguished between productive and unproductive labour. The physiocrats in 18th century France maintained that only farming could produce a net product and provided value. Classical economists (e.g., Ricardo and Smith) who subscribed to the labour theory of value extended the value-creating activity to include manufacturing, but merchants and service providers were excluded.

The emphasis on analysing the whole marketing system with its various functions was the hallmark of the functional approach to marketing. The distributive sector was centre stage during this period. Alderson (1957) used *A Functionalist Approach to Marketing Theory* as a subtitle to his book *Marketing Behavior and Executive Action*. According to him, "functionalism is that approach to science which begins by identifying some system of action, and then tries to determine how and why it works as it does. Functionalism stresses the whole system and undertakes to interpret the parts in terms of how they serve the system" (p. 16). He considered the "trade channel" as one such system, even if the companies involved may have no consciousness of group membership.

Distribution research after the managerial approach

The introduction of the managerial approach in marketing is usually associated with the publication of the textbook *Basic Marketing: A Managerial Approach* by McCarthy (1960). Actually, the whole period 1950–1970 represents a transitional period where the emerging managerial approach coexisted with the declining popularity and impact of the functionalist approach. The focus in the period gradually shifted to the problems of the marketing manager, and the marketing system at large received less attention. The particular manager that took the centre stage in the textbooks was the marketing manager in a large manufacturing company that produces goods for consumers.

In the managerial approach the management of a manufacturing company is the starting point and the task is to explore the parameters that are available to achieve the goals of the company. These parameters are usually referred to as the four Ps: product, price, promotion and place. It is interesting to note that this approach is very similar to earlier developments in neoclassical microeconomic theory in the 1930s. In particular, the theory of monopolistic competition put forward by Chamberlin (1933) is based on the acknowledgment that companies have other parameters in addition to the price of the product (e.g., advertising and product differentiation). While the economists were occupied with exploring the characteristics of the market solution that would arise given an extended set of parameters, the societal aspect was not given priority in the managerial approach to marketing.

Neoclassical microeconomic theory had been applied to the analysis of vertical price relations in marketing channels as early as 1950 in an effort to develop marketing theory further (Hawkins, 1950). However, this approach did not attract many followers at that time. Many marketing researchers outside the USA were closer to the neoclassical tradition of economics. In particular, at the Copenhagen School of Economics and Business, several researchers in the marketing department were inspired by the theories of monopolistic and imperfect competition developed in the 1930s (Kjær-Hansen, 1966).

The research aiming at the development of a general theory of parameters is probably best presented and summarized in Rasmussen (1955). While mainstream marketing applying the new "managerial approach" was less mathematically oriented, the basic frame of reference was shared with the new developments in neoclassical economics and the Copenhagen School. It is worth noting that marketing at this stage turns to neoclassical economics as its main source of inspiration, while the discipline originally evolved from the competing German Historical School and institutional economics.

With the new frame of reference, distribution research in marketing slowly turned from a systemwide perspective to a focus on how the channel captain should behave to secure an efficient distribution of his products. However, the new managerial perspective did not immediately result in much research in distribution, apart from general discussions of distribution strategies (intensive, selective and exclusive) which only related to the optimal *availability* of the products.

During the 1960s a broad-based functionalist approach still had some impact. Important contributions regarding the structure of distribution channels were made by Bucklin (1965, 1966). In particular, Bucklin in his 1965 article developed further the principle of *postponement*, originally introduced by Alderson in 1950, and extended it to the *postponement-speculation* principle. This principle concerns the shifting of risk and uncertainty between different institutions in a channel and is instrumental in analysing any given channel structure.

Baligh and Richartz (1967) developed a mathematical model of the channel of distribution, which also can be considered as a refinement of the functionalist approach. In this model a fundamental premise is that exchanges or transactions are not costless, and, therefore, the possibility exists that these costs can be reduced. The attempt to model this was later to become the key dimension in transaction cost economics (Williamson, 1975), although the types of costs differ somewhat.

The many competing perspectives on distribution research in the 1960s are evident in the book *Vertical Marketing Systems* edited by Bucklin (1970). The book was based on the papers presented at a seminar in 1968, and it is interesting because so many different approaches are reported. The papers analyse the vertical system as a whole (functionalist) and the micro-issues facing the individual managers (managerial). The theoretical basis of the papers includes microeconomics, game theory and social psychology.

Participants at the conference included J.L. Heskett, Professor in Business Logistics, and Donald J. Bowersox, an Associate Professor of Marketing at the time but later an influential person in logistics. It is particularly interesting that the paper which most clearly used a social science approach to power issues was co-authored by J.L. Heskett, L.W. Stern and F.J. Beier (1970). Thus, the logistics professor J.L. Heskett and the primary spokesman for the new behavioural approach to channels research L.W. Stern joined forces.

The publication of *Distribution Channels: Behavioral Dimensions*, edited by Stern in 1969, introduced a new era in channels research. The academic inspiration now turned away from economics and its conception of economic actors as "economic men" and focused on social sciences like sociology (role theory), political science (power) and social psychology (conflict). Attempts to analyse such issues – in particular, conflicts between actors at different levels – had been made earlier (e.g., Palamountain, 1955; Mallen, 1963) but not with an explicit behavioural science basis. It was now acknowledged that distribution channels – as a rule conceived to be governed by manufacturers – consisted of human beings with particular roles to play. Empirical research was typically restricted to two adjacent levels in the channel (i.e., *dyads*). A dyad could consist of a manufacturer and a wholesaler that interacted or it could be a wholesaler–retailer relationship. In this way the whole channel was broken down into smaller parts. It is important to note that the approach is still managerial, it is only the means available to the manager and the problems typically faced by him that have changed.

Conflicts between the interacting partners in a dyad could arise due to goal incompatibility, domain dissensus and differences in perceptions of reality among channel members (Rosenberg and Stern, 1971). While a low level of conflict might be productive in a channel context, a high level of conflict could become destructive. Power and the various bases of power became an important topic in channels research, particularly since the roles of the players had to be determined by the channel leader (El-Ansary and Stern, 1972). This behavioural approach to channels research dominated in mainstream marketing in the 1970s. Gaski (1984) published a thorough review of the strengths and weaknesses of power-related channels research, and after that time this approach to channels research has been limited. In particular, very little attention has been given to analysing conflicts between the parties involved.

A major weakness in the behavioural approach to distribution channels was that economic aspects were neglected. In an attempt to integrate the economic and the behavioural aspects, Stern and Reve (1980) suggested a framework for analysing channels that incorporated both. This "political economy" framework analysed the structure of a channel in terms of an "internal economic structure" and an "internal socio-political structure". Corresponding to these structures were internal economic processes and internal socio-political processes, respectively. It was argued that all aspects should be taken into account in order to be able to fully comprehend and analyse a distribution channel. The "political economy" framework, with its focus on the total system, resembles previous attempts to analyse relevant aspects of the "marketing system". In particular, Mattson (1969) analysed efficiency in such systems and its relationship to integration at the *institutional* level, integration in terms of *decisions* and integration in terms of *execution* of decisions.

The political economy model was appealing in the sense that it pointed out the complexity of a distribution channel, yet made an attempt to classify and structure the various parts of the phenomenon. The framework became a standard reference in channels research for several years, yet it is not a separate theoretical approach. In discussing the internal economy of a channel, Stern and Reve (1980) explicitly refer to the theory of transaction costs put forward by Williamson (1975). Broadly speaking, from the early 1980s transaction cost analysis (TCA) gradually came to dominate channels research (Rindfleisch and Heide, 1997).

Transaction cost economics (TCE) regards the firm as a *governance structure* as opposed to standard microeconomic theory, where the firm is a *production function*. The basic issue we attempt to analyse is how transactions (transfers) between separate technical units should be organized most effectively. The approach is still managerial, but the problems faced and the means available to the manager have changed once more.

In his original formulation, Williamson (1975) argued that the choice of governance structure was a dichotomy as one either had to choose a market or a firm (hierarchy). In analysing the governance problem, Williamson makes two important assumptions regarding human nature: first, he is assuming that the decision makers are characterized by *bounded rationality* (this means that there are constraints on their cognitive capability and limits to their rationality), and second, he assumes that the people involved are *opportunistic*. Opportunism is defined as "self-seeking behaviour with guile", meaning that people pursue their self-interest, but may try to conceal their real intentions and behaviour (Wathne and Heide, 2000). It is hard to determine in advance who is trustworthy and who is not. A third behavioural assumption is *risk neutrality*, but this assumption is less important and has received limited attention in channels research.

The transactions that have to be governed in one way or the other differ in a number of ways. Three aspects of transactions were originally considered central to the governance problem: first, to what extent are *specific assets* involved in the transactions?; second, to what extent is *uncertainty* (environmental and/or behavioural) important in the specific context?; and, third, the *frequency* of transactions was considered important in early research, but has received less attention in later studies. Early contributions analysed vertical integration decisions (Anderson, 1985; John and Weitz, 1988), but the type of research problems have recently changed somewhat. As pointed out by Williamson (1985), any problem that can be formulated as a contracting problem can be investigated using transaction cost terms.

The initial focus in TCA studies was on the problems created by specific assets or assets with limited value outside the focal relationship, when opportunism is

Table 10.2—A classification of distribution research in mainstream marketing literature during the last century

Time period	Approach	Dominant theory	Focus	Unit of analysis
1900–1950	Functionalist	Historical School of Economics	Functions and flows	Whole system
1950–1970	Functionalist/ Managerial	Neoclassical economics	Costs	System/Company
1970–1985	Managerial	Social psychology and political science	Power and conflict	Dyad
1985–Present	Managerial	Transaction cost economics	Governance	Dyad

present. For instance, a manufacturer will hesitate to invest in training a distributor if the distributor can easily withdraw from the relationship and make his investment useless. Specific assets create *safeguarding problems*, which may be solved in various ways.

Recently, the effects of uncertainty – given the inescapable bounded rationality of the decision makers – seem to have attracted more interest. The two types of uncertainty that are considered are *environmental* and *behavioural*. Environmental uncertainty gives rise to an *adaptation problem*, as changing circumstances may require a change in the original agreement with a partner in the distribution channel. Since a comprehensive contract that takes into account all contingencies hardly ever can be written, changes in the environment can lead to considerable renegotiation costs. Behavioural uncertainty leads to a performance evaluation problem; this means that the channel captain may have a problem in determining whether a distributor actually behaves in the way the contract specifies. The latter type of problem – *information asymmetry* – is one problem typically associated with "agency" theory (Mishra et al., 1998), and recent TCA research and principal–agent theory are very much related.

Table 10.2 summarizes the dominant approach, theoretical basis, focus and unit of analysis in distribution research in marketing in different periods. Starting out with descriptive analyses of how the various distribution functions and activities were performed in society, the focus was on the vertical system as a whole for a very long time.

The emerging, new managerial approach to marketing meant that distribution became just one of the four Ps, while previously it had been at the core of the discipline. In the period 1950–1970 competing approaches to distribution research are clearly present and the theoretical basis differed, even through neoclassical microeconomics was the main theoretical underpinning of the theory of parameters (the four Ps). Since then, two distinct periods of managerial approaches may be discerned. The first was the *behavioural* type of research that dominated in the 1970s; this introduced the "dyad" as the theoretical unit of analysis, but much empirical work was still undertaken at the firm level.

The second type of research, which remains dominant, is preoccupied with how incentives for particular types of conduct may be most efficiently established. It may be argued that this research does not give much guidance when it comes to understanding and explaining the comprehensive changes that take place in distribution today.

One weakness associated with the present channels research is that the "dyad" still is the unit of analysis in most cases. It is interesting to note that this seems to be the case, even though the "transaction" is the relevant unit of analysis from a theoretical point of view. The total supply chain or distribution network from raw materials to end-customer is hardly ever analysed in marketing journals. As an indication, using the search word "supply chain" in the ABI Database covering the period 1987–2002 produced only two articles in the *Journal of Marketing* and none in the *Journal of Marketing Research*.

Marketing channels and supply chain management

A century ago, marketing emerged as an academic discipline from economics. Centre stage in the new discipline was occupied by empirical studies of how distributive functions were carried out in different industries. The quest for increased scientific status implied that "acceptable" research topics became more narrowly defined. As we pointed out earlier, the favourite research topics have also changed over time. The distributive sector is now mainly an empirical context for testing general theories, be it power relations or governance structures, rather than an area that deserves in-depth analysis by itself. The recent preoccupation with incentive schemes and ownership issues, for instance, does not tell us much about how supplies to the manufacturers are procured and how the final goods are delivered to end-users.

To gain a better understanding of how issues in distribution are regarded and treated in mainstream marketing, it seems reasonable to consult the most influential textbook in the area. The fifth edition of *Marketing Channels* by Stern, El-Ansary and Coughlan (1996) states that "marketing channels can be viewed as sets of interdependent organizations involved in the process of making a product or service available for consumption or use" (p. 1). Thus, the "marketing channel" concept is defined by the *organizations* involved. With regard to the process of making a product or service available, the textbook refers to eight marketing flows and each "flow is a set of functions performed in sequence by the channel members" (p. 10). The eight functions are illustrated in Figure 10.1, which shows a typical situation with four levels of organization involved in the channels.

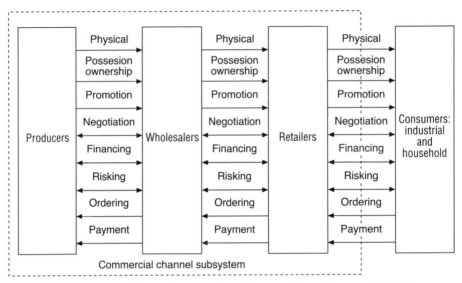

Figure 10.1—Marketing flows in channels according to Stern et al. (1996).

Two aspects of this figure are worth noting. First, the starting point of the channel is the *producer* of the relevant goods. As we pointed out earlier, the tendency in marketing is to regard the manufacturer as the starting point of the channel. Still, it is argued in the textbook that different channel institutions are involved in the various flows, and for some flows (title flow, physical flow, promotion flow and payment flow) suppliers are typically members of the channel. The result is a rather confusing picture of the institutions that are involved in the marketing channel.

Second, physical distribution (possession) is treated as just one of eight flows. The image conveyed is that physical distribution is of limited importance in a marketing channel, and in the textbook it is discussed in a single chapter almost as a necessary evil. As we pointed out earlier, the focus in distribution research in marketing is now on transaction cost analysis, which mainly means the "ownership" flow. To some extent we may argue that "negotiation" and "risking" flows are also relevant in a transaction cost context.

Two vital questions are "does it make sense to treat the eight 'flows' as equally important marketing flows?" and "to what extent does it make sense to examine them separately?" The basic task of a marketing channel is to deliver goods at the point and time of consumption in the most efficient way. In order to achieve this, flows of goods and information are clearly the most fundamental. Given a market system with different institutions involved, a flow of money is also necessary to govern the process. When analysing the working of a channel in more detail, the remaining functions, such as ordering, risking, promotion and negotiation, are second-order functions related to the three basic flows. As mentioned before, the different nature of the various functions (flows) had already been pointed out by Clark (1923).

In earlier editions of the *Marketing Channels* textbook the authors pointed out that our Figure 10.1 was adapted from the book *Marketing in the American Economy* (Vaile et al., 1952). When consulting the original reference (p. 113), it turns out that the first level in the channel was "producers of raw materials", while the second was named "processors and manufacturers" and the third was entitled "consumers (business and individual)". The middlemen (i.e., the wholesalers and retailers) were not specified in the original version of the figure. The reason was that a detailed presentation of many different types of middlemen followed when the channels for different flows were discussed in detail. Still, it is worth noting that the channels of distribution in general originated at the raw materials level in the early 1950s.

During the 1950s the physical distribution aspect of marketing became the domain of a new academic discipline, usually called *physical distribution*, or *logistics*. The first textbook in this area was published in 1961 according to Stock and Lambert (2001). Bartels (1988) talks, on the one hand, about the social aspects of exchange (traditional marketing) and, on the other hand, about the physical aspects of exchange (logistics). This dichotomy – referred to as the two halves of marketing by Converse (1958) – has since become the established "division of labour" between the two disciplines. Several researchers have explored whether there is any tendency to reintegrate the two disciplines, but the conclusion drawn by Rosen and Manrodt (1995) was that the evidence at that time did not support such a reintegration.

The concept *supply chain management* was coined in the early 1980s by consultants working in logistics (Oliver and Webber, 1982). During the last decade this concept has attracted a lot of interest. In their original formulation the authors underlined that the supply chain must be viewed as a single entity and that strategic decision making at the top level is needed to manage the chain. This viewpoint is shared by channel theorists in marketing, but the two disciplines still operate independently. A number of different definitions of supply chain management have been offered since the concept was introduced. Svensson (2003) concludes his review of the various definitions by stating that "Supply Chain Management might be seen as a management philosophy that strives to integrate the dependent activities, actors, and resources into marketing channels between point-of-origin and the point-of-final-consumption" (p. 306).

While the concept was originally tied to the physical distribution aspect the tendency now seems to be toward a broadening of the concept. Examples include Lambert et al. (1998), who maintain "Supply chain management is the integration of key business processes from end user through original suppliers that provide products, services, and information that add value for customers and other stakeholders" (p. 1).

Figure 10.2 gives an overview of the different types of business processes with the focal company as the key actor. The supply chain in this case has three

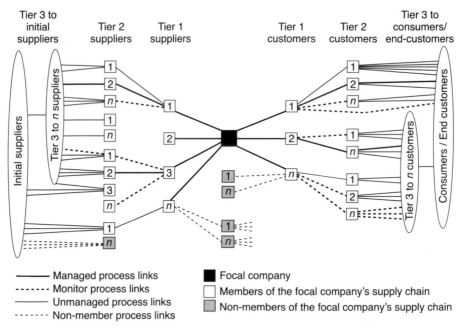

Figure 10.2—Different types of inter-company business process links in a supply chain. From Lambert et al. (1998, p. 7).

levels of suppliers and three levels of customers, and the focal company strives to manage some of the processes and monitor others. Other business process links are explicitly defined as not critical enough to try to manage or even monitor.

While supply chain management originally was considered a part of logistics, it now seems to aspire to become a separate discipline. Much research on supply chains and supply networks is published in new journals, such as *Supply Chain Management: An International Journal* and *Journal on Chain and Network Science*. In these and other journals we can find detailed descriptions of, for instance, how the supply chains of large retailers are structured and function. The willingness to empirically investigate and analyse how distribution is carried out in different industries was the hallmark of marketing in the beginning. In mainstream marketing today this is no longer the case.

In his assessment of the changes that have taken place during the period he has served as editor of the *Journal of Marketing*, Stewart (2002) found five articles dealing with channels of distribution in the period 1996–1998, while there was not one in the period 2000–2002. He comments that "work that once focused exclusively on channels of distribution has largely been replaced with work that focuses on broader strategic issues of design of value delivery systems and inter-organisational governance" (p. 2).

It seems that the marketing discipline has come to a crossroads and should make a choice: does it want to regain distribution channels as a topic of central importance or should it leave the area to logistics and supply chain management? The empirical evidence is mixed when it comes to what actually is happening. The decreasing interest in specific channels studies referred to above indicates that marketing scholars are more attracted to study general strategic issues. Faced by a growing community of strategic management scholars defending their turf, it is probably going to be an uphill struggle to carve a niche for the marketing discipline in that particular direction. Given the competition between the various management disciplines to deliver something useful to managers, it seems more appealing to revitalize an area of research that initially served as the *raison d'être* of the discipline. Scattered attempts to move in that direction exist. In their forthcoming study, Wathne and Heide (2004) argue that it is necessary to broaden the focus in channels research from the dyad to a network. They analyse strategies that can be used to manage supply chain relationships. Even if the network in their study is rather narrow, consisting of a three-level channel, it is indeed a step in the right direction.

If marketing is to regain the lost territory of distribution channels, it is necessary to once more conduct case studies of how distribution, both before and after the manufacturing stage, is carried out. The framework and insights developed in supply chain management may be a useful starting point, but the concepts developed in marketing studies will aid in understanding processes as well as in designing strategies for "channel captains", be they retailers or manufacturers. Physical distribution and legal/social issues should not be separated at the outset, and the working of the distribution system/network is not properly understood if only dyads are analysed.

An alternative paradigm may be needed if the development of distribution systems as a whole is to be analysed. The so-called "network approach" was long ago promoted as an alternative to the transaction cost approach (Johanson and Mattsson, 1987). The supply chain may be interpreted as a network consisting of business relationships, which may be described in terms of activity links, actor bonds and resource ties (Håkansson and Snehota, 1995). If, for example, the fundamental changes that have taken place in the system of grocery distribution in Norway during the last 25 years were to be analysed, such a framework may prove useful.

Distribution channels may once again become an important research area in the marketing discipline. However, the approach, theory base, focus and unit of analysis in present channels research in marketing all need to be scrutinized if a revitalization of distribution research is to be achieved. The challenge is to develop a framework and a theoretical basis that can bring marketing back in the forefront in this area.

Acknowledgements

Helpful comments to an earlier version of this chapter from Jan Heide, Håkan Håkansson, Lars-Gunnar Mattson and Torger Reve are appreciated.

References

Alderson, W. (1957). *Marketing Behavior and Executive Action*. Chicago: Richard D. Irwin.

Anderson, E. (1985). The salesperson as outside agent or employee: A transaction cost analysis. *Marketing Science*, **4**(Summer): 234–254.

Baligh, H.H. and Richartz, L.E. (1967). *Vertical Market Structures*. Boston: Allyn & Bacon.

Bartels, R. (1962). *The Development of Marketing Thought*. Homewood, IL: Richard D. Irwin.

Bartels, R. (1988). *The History of Marketing Thought*. Columbus, OH: Publishing Horizons.

Bennett, P.D. (1995). *Dictionary of Marketing Terms*. Chicago, IL: American Marketing Association.

Bucklin, L.P. (1965). Postponement, speculation and the structure of distribution channels. *Journal of Marketing Research*, **2**(February): 26–31.

Bucklin, L.P. (1966). *A Theory of Distribution Channel Structure*. Berkeley, CA: IBER Special Publications.

Bucklin, L.P. (ed.) (1970). *Vertical Marketing Systems*. Glenview, IL: Scott, Foresman & Co.

Chamberlin, E.H. (1933). *The Theory of Monopolistic Competition*. Cambridge, MA: Harvard University Press.

Clark, F.E. (1923). *Principles of Marketing*. New York: Macmillan.

Converse, P.D. (1958). The other half of marketing. In: A.E. Seeyle (ed.), *Marketing in Transition* (pp. 114–121). New York: Harper & Row.

Corstjens, J. and Corstjens, M. (1995). *Store Wars: The Battle for Mindspace and Shelfspace*. New York: John Wiley & Sons.

El-Ansary, A.I. and Stern, L.W. (1972). Power measurement in the distribution channel. *Journal of Marketing Research*, **9**: 47–52.

Falk, T. and Julander, C.R. (eds) (1983). Current trends in distribution research. *International Journal of Physical Distribution & Materials Management*, **13**(5/6) (a special edition).

Falkenberg, A. (ed.) (1994). *Marketing Perspectives: A Book of Readings*. Bergen, Norway: Fagbokforlaget.

Gaski, J.F. (1984). The theory of power and conflict in channels of distribution. *Journal of Marketing*, **48**(Summer): 9–29.

Gattorna, J. (1978). Channels of distribution conceptualizations: A state-of-the-art review. *European Journal of Marketing*, **12**(7): 471–512.

Håkansson, H. and Snehota, I. (1995). *Developing Relationships in Business Networks*. London: Routledge.

Hawkins, E.R. (1950). Vertical price relationships. In: R. Cox and W. Alderson (eds), *Theory in Marketing* (pp. 179–191). Chicago: Richard D. Irwin.

Heskett, J.L., Stern, L.W. and Beier, F.J. (1970). Bases and uses of power in interorganization relations. In: L.P. Bucklin (ed.), *Vertical Marketing Systems* (pp. 75–93). Glenview, IL: Scott, Foresman & Co.

Holbæk-Hanssen, L. (1958). *Contributions to a Theory in Marketing* (mimeo). Bergen, Norway: Norwegian School of Economics and Business Administration.

Hunt, S.D. and Goolsby, J. (1988). The rise and fall of the functional approach to marketing: A paradigm displacement perspective. In: T. Nevett and R.A. Fullerton (eds), *Historical Perspectives in Marketing* (pp. 35–51). Lexington, MA: Lexington Books/D.C. Heath & Co.

Johanson, J. and Mattson, L-G. (1987). Inter-organizational relations in industrial systems: A network approach compared with the transaction-cost approach. *International Studies of Management and Organization*, **17**(1): 34–48.

John, G. and Weitz, B.A. (1988). Forward integration into distribution: An empirical test of transaction cost analysis. *Journal of Law, Economics and Organization*, **4**(Fall): 121–139.

Jones, D.G.B. and Monieson, D.D. (1990). Early development of the philosophy of marketing thought. *Journal of Marketing*, **54**(January): 102–113.

Kjaer-Hansen, M. (1966). Main features in Danish research in marketing. In: *Readings in Danish Theory of Marketing*. Copenhagen: Einar Harcks Forlag. Reprinted in Hollander S.C. and Rassuli, K.M. (1993), *The International Library of Critical Writings in Business History: Marketing* (Vol. 1, pp. 73–85). Aldershot, UK: Edward Elgar.

Kotler, P. (2003). *Marketing Management* (11th edn). Upper Saddle River, NJ: Prentice Hall.

Kotler, P., Armstrong, G., Saunders, J. and Wong, V. (2002). *Principles of Marketing* (3rd European edn). Harlow, UK: Prentice Hall.

Lambert, D.M., Cooper, M.C. and Pagh, J.D. (1998). Supply chain management: Implementation issues and research opportunities. *International Journal of Logistics Management*, **9**(2): 1–18.

Lazzarini, S.G., Chaddad, F.R. and Cook, M.L. (2001). Integrating supply chain and network analyses: The study of netchains. *Journal on Chain and Network Science*, **1**(1): 7–22.

Mallen, B. (1963). A theory of retailer supplier conflict, control and cooperation. *Journal of Retailing*, **39**: 24–32 and 51–52.

Mattson, L-G. (1969). *Integration and Efficiency in Marketing Systems*. Stockholm: Economic Research Institute.

McCarthy, E.J. (1960). *Basic Marketing: A Managerial Approach*. Homewood, IL: Richard D. Irwin.

Mishra, D.P., Heide, J.B. and Cort, S.G. (1998). Information asymmetry and levels of agency relationships. *Journal of Marketing Research*, **35**(August): 277–295.

Mulhern, F.J. (1997). Retail marketing: From distribution to integration. *International Journal of Research in Marketing*, **14**: 103–124.

Oliver, R.K. and Webber, M.D. (1982). Supply-chain management: Logistics catches up with strategy. In: M. Christopher (ed.), *Logistics: The Strategic Issues* (pp. 63–75). London: Chapman & Hall.

Palamountain J.C., Jr (1955). *The Politics of Distribution*. Cambridge, MA: Harvard University Press.

Rasmussen, A. (1955). *Pristeori eller parameterteori*. Copenhagen: Einar Harcks Forlag [in Danish].

Rindfleisch, A. and Heide, J.B. (1997). Transaction cost analysis: Past, present, and future applications. *Journal of Marketing*, **61**(October): 30–54.

Rosen, D. and Manrodt, K.B. (1995). Marketing and logistics: A tale of two disciplines. Paper given at *Breakthrough Thinking in Logistics: Proceedings of the 24th Annual Transportation and Logistics Educators Conference, The Ohio State University.*

Rosenberg, L.J. and Stern, L.W. (1971). Conflict measurement in the distribution channel. *Journal of Marketing Research*, **8**: 437–442.

Shaw, A.W. (1912). Some problems in market distribution. *Quarterly Journal of Economics*, **26**: 703–765.

Shaw, E.H. (1994). The utility of the four utilities concept. In: R.H. Fullerton (ed.), *Explorations in the History of Marketing, Research in Marketing* (Suppl. 6, pp. 47–66). Greenwich, CT: JAI Press.

Sparling, S.E. (1906). *Introduction to Business Organization.* New York: Macmillan.

Stern, L.W. (ed.) (1969). *Distribution Channels: Behavioral Dimensions.* Boston: Houghton-Mifflin.

Stern, L.W. and Reve, T. (1980). Distribution channels as political economies: A framework for comparative analysis. *Journal of Marketing*, **44**(Summer): 52–64.

Stern, L.W., El-Ansary, A.I. and Coughlan, A.T. (1996). *Marketing Channels* (5th edn). Upper Saddle River, NJ: Prentice Hall International.

Stewart, D.W. (2002). Getting published: Reflections of an old editor. *Journal of Marketing*, **66**(October): 1–6.

Stock, J.R. and Lambert, D.M. (2001). *Strategic Logistics Management* (4th edn). New York: McGraw-Hill.

Svensson, G. (2003). Holistic and cross-disciplinary deficiencies in the theory generation of supply chain management. *Supply Chain Management: An International Journal*, **8**(4): 303–316.

Vaile, R.S., Grether, E.T. and Cox, R. (1952). *Marketing in the American Economy.* New York: The Ronald Press.

Wathne, K.H. and Heide, J.B. (2000). Opportunism in interfirm relationships: Forms, outcomes, and solutions. *Journal of Marketing*, **64**(October): 36–51.

Wathne, K.H. and Heide, J.B. (2004). Relationship governance in a supply chain network. *Journal of Marketing* (forthcoming).

Weld, L.D.H. (1917). Marketing functions and mercantile organization. *American Economic Review*, **2**(May): 196–213.

Williamson, O.E. (1975). *Markets and Hierarchies: Analysis and Antitrust Implications.* New York: Free Press.

Williamson, O.E. (1985). *The Economic Institutions of Capitalism.* New York: Free Press.

Research methods in industrial marketing studies

11

Anna Dubois and Luis Araujo

Introduction

The purpose of this chapter is to examine the interaction between theory, research methods and empirical work in the development of the interaction and industrial network approaches. Although we do not claim that these approaches have been mono-method the focus of this chapter is on one particular research method: the case research or case study method.[1] Case research has undoubtedly played a key role in the development of these theoretical approaches and, for many researchers operating within the industrial networks paradigm, it continues to be the methodology of choice (Easton, 1995).

Contrary to those who assume that case research is a method best employed in a discovery or exploratory mode and, thus, appropriate to the early stages of the development of a paradigm, this method has continued to be fruitfully applied in industrial networks studies. Easton (1995, p. 480) attributes the predilection for case research among industrial networks researchers to attributes of the method and the phenomena: "Because of the richness of the picture produced by case research, the approach is suitable to handle the complexity of network links amongst actors and can be used to trace the development of network changes over time."

The reason for the widespread adherence to the case method will be explored in more detail later in this chapter. For the moment it is sufficient to say that there have been solid reasons to persist with the case method as the primary tool to develop and illustrate concepts within the industrial networks research programme.

In this chapter we will focus on two aspects of case-based research and their relationships with industrial networks: (i) time and the temporal frames within which we conduct network studies and (ii) the delineation of boundaries in network studies. Both time and boundaries are problematic aspects in industrial networks research. There are no hard and fast rules specifying what temporal

---

[1] Structural equation modelling (namely, LISREL-based studies) have also played a role in the development of these approaches (see Hallén et al., 1991).

frames or set of interdependent elements should be included in a particular network study. In both cases, researchers are required to make and justify contestable decisions. A key argument of this chapter is that the strength of the case method is that it allows these decisions to emerge in the course of the research process as the nature of the phenomenon and its context become clearer.

The structure of this chapter is as follows. In the first section, we will look briefly at the characteristics of case research and present an argument as to why case research is particularly suited to industrial marketing studies in the interaction and industrial networks traditions. In the second section we will present a brief historical sketch of the development of the case method in the interaction and industrial network approaches. In the third section we will examine one doctoral project as an illustrative example of case research in the industrial networks tradition. In the fourth section we will focus on the way case studies have been appropriated within the industrial networks perspective and the process of de-limiting the boundaries of a case. Finally, we will conclude with some reflections on the interaction between theoretical, methodological and empirical developments in industrial networks research.

What is case research?

The notion of case research is in many ways unclear and diffuse. To confuse matters further, case research is often and unhelpfully conflated with broader methodologies, such as qualitative research (see, e.g., Bonoma, 1985). Furthermore, as observed by Easton (1995, 1998), the notion of case research can be understood from a variety of epistemological positions leading to different appropriations of the methodology. In this section we want to define case research and situate it in the broader context of social science research methods.

The oft-quoted definition of what constitutes a case study is given by Yin (1994, p. 13):

> *A case study is an empirical enquiry that investigates a contemporary phenomenon within its real life context, especially when the boundaries between the phenomenon and context are not clearly evident.*

This definition highlights two important aspects of case research: the first relates to the notion of contemporary versus non-contemporary phenomena, and the second issue hints at the problematic relationship between a phenomenon and its real life context.

As far as the first issue is concerned, Yin (1994) differentiates case studies from case histories by arguing that both deal with entangled situations between phenomenon and context, but history deals with temporally distant rather than contemporary events. Halinen and Tornröos (1995) follow the same approach by distinguishing between historical and follow-up studies. Historical studies deal with the investigation of the past while follow-up studies address phenomena in the "here and now".

In our view the opposition between historical and contemporaneous events is difficult to maintain and requires a more nuanced interpretation. Abbott (2001) contrasts the ontology of cases from a population/analytic and narrative perspective. In a population/analytic perspective, cases are instances in a uniform and largely undifferentiated population. The population/analytic approach requires rigidly delimitable cases, assigns them generic properties and refuses all transformations on the nature of cases. By contrast, a narrative perspective assumes all cases have fuzzy boundaries, takes properties to have case-specific meanings and allows for or even thrives on case transformation as the research process unfolds.

The narrative approach ignores variables when they are deemed unimportant, whereas the population/analytic approach treats all variables as always salient. Narrative approaches follow causal links and attempt to explain events in terms of the causal relevance of factors. This selective attention to what factors are relevant in a given explanation goes hand in hand with an emphasis on contingency and the conjunction of factors acting together in specific circumstances, rather than a set of variables acting independently and continuously.

Contemporary events are always embedded in structures, patterns of activity and resource configurations that "carry history" forward (Stinchcombe, 1968; David, 1994). There is no reason for establishing a tight distinction between contemporary and non-contemporary events if we take a processual approach to the phenomena of interest. History is always encoded in the structures that shape current choices.

The key distinction between case research and case histories lies not in the opposition between contemporary versus non-contemporary events but in the way narratives are organized. Historians usually refrain from transforming complex and intricate stories into more abstract and selective accounts couched in theoretical terms (Roberts, 1996). Social scientists prefer to sacrifice particularistic historical detail and deal with structures and mechanisms abstracted from the specific contexts in which they operate. Pettigrew (1997) argues that the case study goes beyond the case history in attempting to link events and chronologies to analytical frameworks: first, there is a search for patterns in the processes described and, second, case studies attempt to unravel the underlying mechanisms that shape patterning in the events observed.

Case studies present some problems in this regard. As Bennett and George (1997) argue, as a result of case studies following the practice of historians it has inherited a number of tendencies more akin to the historian rather than the social scientist's craft. In particular, as Sayer (2000, p. 143) notes, it is not easy to balance the synchronic or configurative dimensions of narrative with the more traditional episodic or temporal succession aspects. In our view the distinctive characteristic of case studies is that, like historians, case study analysts pay attention to the episodic dimensions of events, but, unlike historians, their focus is on the logical and theory-stamped association of events rather than temporal succession.

The second issue stemming from Yin's definition of a case study relates to the boundary between the phenomenon and the context in which it occurs. Case research is deemed particularly appropriate for instances in which this boundary is unclear or fuzzy. In interaction and industrial networks research the distinction between the phenomenon and the context is problematic and both depend on theory-dependent criteria.

From this perspective the process of conducting case studies is necessarily more open-ended than implied by Yin's definition. Neither the phenomenon nor its context are necessarily known prior to starting the research. Simple problems related to apparently minor changes are often the arbitrary starting points of a research project (e.g., the change of the geometric shape of concrete water-carrying pipes: Holmen, 2001). The task of the analyst is often to progressively construct the context and boundaries of the phenomenon, as theory interacts with method and empirical observations. The research object, its boundaries, context and horizon are thus emergent and unfolding outcomes of the research process. The case study method makes a virtue of these uncertainties as a way to penetrate this obdurate world, rather than seeing it as the default option when a researcher is confronted with distinct but messy and intricate subjects.

Case researchers see cases as complex configurations of events and structures in concrete spatial and temporal contexts, which preserve the character of the phenomenon being studied and which the analyst believes exhibits the operation of some identified theoretical principle (Mitchell, 1983; Ragin, 1997). The boundary around what constitutes the case is malleable and evolves in response to both practical contingencies affecting the research process and the dialogue between theory and empirical evidence (Dubois and Gadde, 2002). If, in general, empirical work benefits from a learning feedback loop between research design, theory and empirical results, in case research the feedback loop often operates within the research process itself as lessons learned earlier on are fed back into subsequent phases of the research (McKeown, 1999).

Case studies thus resonate well with interactions and relationships as basic units of analysis. In networks the chain of consequences following from one action often extend over a series of interconnected relationships and take place over an extended time period. As Abbott (1997, p. 1162) explains, survey-based approaches rely on decontextualization, which allows the production of data sets where contextual effects are reduced to interaction between variables and contextual causation deliberately minimized. Rather than assuming predetermined entities and privileging relationships between variables describing attributes of these entities, a relational mode of thinking suggests the use of flexible methodologies and a process of data gathering and analysis that parallels the connectedness and dynamic processes that are at the heart of industrial networks.

Case research in interaction and industrial networks research

Although this section is not intended as a historic review of interaction and industrial network studies, a brief review of its history, with particular regard to how currently focused phenomena, theoretical frameworks and research methods have evolved, is a useful starting point. A seminal work that inspired many further developments is Jan Johanson's licentiate thesis (Johanson, 1966). Setting out to study how Swedish quality steel was marketed in foreign markets he "discovered" the existence and importance of "business liaisons" between buyers and sellers. These "business liaisons", later referred to as business relationships, were introduced in a chapter of the thesis in the following terms:

> *This chapter differs from the others in this study since it is not based on systematic empirical data. Rather, it is a number of hypotheses based on informal interviews with quality steel producers and their representatives. The background to the chapter was an expectation to be able to discuss the steel producers' choices of different competitive measures based on an analysis of which factors were the most important for the buyers' choice of suppliers. It turned out, however, that the quality steel market – if the market concept applies at all – is differentiated with regard to product features and the users' applications and production to such an extent that it was not possible to arrive at any general comments on the choice of competitive measures* (Johanson, 1966, p. 82).[2]

The discussion started from the notion of rational purchasing behaviour where the theoretically derived assumption that this would imply frequent changes of suppliers was contrasted with arguments in favour of an alternative logic. Important aspects, such as the buyers' knowledge of the suppliers, their experience with the suppliers' performance, the risks associated with changing suppliers and with costs apart from the actual prices paid, were taken as pointing to a different but still rational form of behaviour. In addition, counterpart-specific adjustments in the business liaisons between buyers and sellers were identified as important.

Based on these findings, Johanson called for methods to systematically describe and measure the factors accounting for business liaisons between users and suppliers. Several of the suggested features of these business liaisons were later developed into concepts to describe and measure business relationships. As far as methods are concerned an important aspect of this study was that the "discovery" of business liaisons was enabled by the interaction between the method and phenomenon studied.

[2] Translated from the Swedish original.

The interviews with steel producers and their representatives on foreign markets made it possible to identify the "discovered" phenomenon, although this phenomenon was at odds with what Johanson set out to explain. In addition, explanations as to why the identified business liaisons emerged could be constructed based on interview material. Had Johanson not conducted face-to-face interviews but instead relied on a survey to explore the ways in which Swedish steel producers dealt with foreign markets, he would not have been able to identify and describe the business liaisons in the way he did. Due to the open-ended research design, Johanson could shift the research focus from rational buying criteria and bounded decisions to interaction episodes and relationships. Johanson's thesis is recognized as the starting point for a research programme on business relationships developed by a group of researchers in Uppsala during the 1970s.

During the first IMP (industrial marketing and purchasing) project initiated in 1976 the Uppsala group together with research groups from four other countries made a large case-based survey including about 900 interviews with marketing and purchasing managers about their most important relationships (Håkansson, 1982). The first IMP project was a departure from traditional industrial marketing studies in a number of ways. First, the emphasis was placed on relationships between buyers and sellers in contrast to the traditional literature that tended to focus on single discrete purchases. Second, the need to examine the interaction between buying and selling firms was motivated by the extant view of industrial marketing as the manipulation of the marketing mix variables in order to achieve response from a faceless and passive market. Third, the stability of industrial market structures was stressed in contrast to the conventional view implying an atomistic structure and the assumption that markets consisted of a large number of buyers and sellers that frequently changed counterparts. Fourth, the simultaneous analysis of both the buying and selling sides of relationships was contrasted with the previous separation of industrial marketing and purchasing tasks.

Apart from elaborating the interaction model the first IMP study contributed to establishing business relationships as a legitimate "research object" (Håkansson, 1982). Their existence had been "proven" and a methodological approach to study relationships had been tried out. The theoretical framework, in addition to the operationalization of concepts and their illustration in concrete empirical cases, made the notion of relationships comprehensible; and, in terms of practical research approaches, multiple interviews with a number of people involved in relationships also allowed for insights into their multifaceted and distributed nature. Hitherto, studies of dyadic relationships had often relied on a single perspective and from one side of the dyad only (Phillips, 1981).

Although a standardized approach was taken to enable co-ordinated data collection across different project sites, the analyses of individual cases were also of importance:

The analysis of cases serves two purposes; first, each case can lead to the generation of hypotheses and ideas for subsequent examination of data about other relationships in the data bank. Second, case studies can be chosen which represent relationships encountered in each cell in the matrix[3] and which cover various products and production technologies. This may lead to an improved model (or models) of interaction, which encompasses the spread of situations relevant to the matrix (Håkansson, 1982, pp. 47–48).

The research approach taken by the first IMP project was described as incremental commitment. Researchers shared broad agreement as to the theoretical principles and data collection principles, but at the outset they did not share or indeed seek to share a detailed agreement of principle on all aspects of the research. Work proceeded on the basis of partial agreements and consensus that often developed as the research progressed.

Apart from its undoubted impact on industrial marketing and purchasing studies the first IMP project also turned out to have another important function. It helped to mobilize a number of researchers who, through using similar concepts and methods, developed a shared conceptual framework on the phenomena they wanted to study. Hence, a broad platform was established that allowed further interaction among a growing number of researchers who saw themselves as studying business relationships from an interaction perspective.

Inspired by studies of relationships in social networks, connectedness among relationships was soon recognized as another important phenomena worthy of further study, and the term "industrial networks" soon emerged as a theoretical umbrella for research on business relationships and networks. Again, the case method played an important role in this theoretical move. The last paragraphs in Håkansson (1982, p. 394) prefigured this move from single relationships to networks:

The focus throughout this book has been on relationships between single pairs of companies. One very important idea in our study is that interdependencies between companies are very common in terms of, for example, the development of long lasting relationships. [. . .] The result of this for the whole market system is that it tends to be rather stable. Instead of free moving units within a market we have companies tied together in a close structure and with very little freedom to move.

Håkansson and Snehota (1995, p. 3) recovered this thread by contrasting a business relationship as a self-contained island or as a part of a broader context – a network of connected relationships. In the former case a boundary is arbitrarily drawn around the relationship, and all explanations as to what happens within the relationship must be found within the frame of the relationship

---

[3] The matrix contemplated nine possible combinations of supplier's product technology (raw and processed material, component and parts, and equipment) with the customer's production technology (unit, batch and mass production, and process manufacture).

itself. In the latter case, what happens in each relationship cannot be dissociated from the embeddedness of the focal relationship in other relationships.

Cook and Emerson's (1978, p. 725) definition of exchange networks as "sets of two or more connected exchange relations" where "two exchange relations are connected to the degree that exchange in one relation is contingent upon exchange (or nonexchange) in the other relation" was adopted to develop a network perspective on industrial systems. The concept of connectedness facilitated the move away from dyadic analysis and toward the understanding of the impact of indirect relationships and systemwide effects on single relationships (Easton, 1992; Anderson et al., 1994). Håkansson and Snehota (1995, p. 19) summarized the importance of connectedness effects in these terms: "Generalized connectedness of business relationships implies existence of an aggregated structure, a form of organization we have chosen to qualify as a network."

The network structure thus appears as represented in micro-interaction episodes through the enactment of the constraints and opportunities each actor faces as a result of the sum total of relationships they are engaged in. As Håkansson (1987, p. 210) put it: "The network is the framework within which the interaction takes place but is also the result of the interaction, thus it is affected by the exchanges between the actors." The notion of connectedness of business relationships also implies that dynamic processes are at the heart of the industrial networks approach. As Axelsson and Easton (1992, p. 85) remarked: "... it is only with change that network properties like connectedness and indirect relationships are manifest." Thus, a great deal of empirical work under the industrial networks tradition became concerned with dynamics and change (namely, technological change).

When looking at the current state of the field a number of links back to the roots can be identified: first, *relationships* are still very much at the top of the research agenda (the challenges associated with using relationships as research objects or units of analysis remain and will be discussed later); second, efforts to identify patterns in *industrial network* structures and in change processes continue and are currently dealt with in many different ways; and, third, *interaction* as a major aspect of technical development has been and continues to be the focus in a number of studies.

Two powerful themes emerge from the preceding discussion: (1) the issue of temporality and dynamics in business relationships and networks, and (2) the issue of boundaries for studying interaction and connectedness effects. As far as temporality is concerned the notion of relationship itself is bound up with a conception of temporality and events. A business relationship consists of a serially interdependent pattern of episodes institutionalized in patterns and processes of mutually specialized adaptations. The study of relationships is thus the study of how processes of exchange coalesce around particular patterns and structures. The notion of networks assumes that connectedness effects are typically indirect and delayed and thus only observable over a period of time.

The issue of boundaries is also crucial to understanding interaction and networks. Johanson's seminal study and the IMP Group's first study extended the boundaries of industrial marketing by examining relationships from the buyer and supplier perspectives and looking beyond the narrow confines of marketing and purchasing tasks. A relationship was seen as a complex and intricate pattern of episodes involving multiple players and functional areas rather than an interaction confined to selling and purchasing teams. The network approach takes relationships as the unit of analysis but within a broader context where connectedness among relationships produces important networkwide effects.

The contribution of case studies to the development of the interaction and network approaches is intimately linked to the method's flexibility for dealing with temporal and boundary issues, as we argued in the previous section. Case studies in the interaction and industrial networks tradition have relied on two kinds of theoretical tools. The first category includes tools that may contribute to describe and analyse the phenomenon and its context. Concepts and models from past research conducted within the same tradition as well as complementary concepts drawn from cognate fields helped this task. The use of exchange theory to develop and elaborate the concept of connectedness is one such example. The second category includes the use of alternative theoretical perspectives to examine the same empirical data so that similarities as well as differences can be identified and confronted. The structure–conduct–performance paradigm (Scherer, 1970; Porter, 1980) and transaction cost economics (Williamson, 1996) have provided useful benchmarks against which interpretations of business relationships and interaction patterns in industrial networks can be made (see, e.g., Håkansson and Snehota, 1995, ch. 7).

An illustrative case of case studies in industrial networks

In this section we delve into the details of one of the many doctoral projects conducted within the industrial networks paradigm in recent years. We will use this project as an illustrative and exemplary case to discuss the methodological principles that have evolved in interaction between theory and empirical observation, as well as in interaction among researchers within the field. While the body of theory underpinning the industrial networks approach has been addressed in other chapters of this book, in this section we will discuss how theory has been used as a guide in the process of conducting case research. This argument is in line with Abbott's (2001, p. 189) notion that any methodology parses the social world in particular ways and, thus, must contain elements of an implicit theory. Hence, we argue that case research within the industrial networks paradigm is strongly influenced by a relational world view. As Easton (1995) remarks, case design in industrial network studies has to take into account inter-organizational connections and is usually based on some form of purposeful and sequential sampling (Patton, 1990).

The illustrative case we selected is based on Elsebeth Holmen's (2001) doctoral dissertation entitled "The development of an egg-shaped concrete pipe for the UK market". The case describes change in an existing structure and the general context of that change in terms of how the constellation of technical resources, such as the components of sewer systems and production equipment, have evolved over time. The context also includes the technical and financial angles of designing sewer systems. The change itself focuses on particular actors, activities and resources in the structure and on their interaction to develop interrelated resources and, thus, to identify and make adjustments necessary for the egg-shaped pipes to fit into various contexts.

The research question guiding the study of how the egg-shaped pipes were developed was (Holmen, 2001, p. 101):

How is the development of a new product, which is carried out in co-operation among a number of organisations, embedded in the resource-related context in which it occurs and of which it becomes a part?

The phenomenon of interest is thus product development in an inter-organizational setting. The key concept guiding the research is *embeddedness*, as defined by Granovetter (1992, p. 33), referring to "... the fact that economic action and outcomes, like all social actions and outcomes, are affected by actors' dyadic (pairwise) relations and by the structure of the overall network of relations." The resource dimension of the industrial network model is emphasized, and embeddedness is related to other concepts, such as resource heterogeneity, resource collections, ties and constellations, versatility, flexibility and idiosyncrasy. In addition, resource fixity is introduced as a useful concept when analysing product development using these conceptual lenses.

The background to the context in which the development of egg-shaped pipes takes place is described as a resource constellation that has evolved over time. The description of the resource constellation is general, in the sense that it does not include reference to specific firms, relationships among them or even how the resources were divided among different firms. Instead, the emphasis is on the various technical solutions that have evolved over time. The description relies heavily on theory, and the concept of embeddedness, although not explicitly used, underpins all aspects of the description.[4] The elements of the general resource constellation, such as the materials used, the components of the sewer systems and the production equipment by which components are produced and used, are consequently described as interrelated to other parts including specific

[4] Ragin (2001, p. 70) observes: "While many case study researchers keep their theories hidden or implicit, the entire enterprise is sheer chaos without some form of theoretical guidance."

ties among resources and resource features. For example, concrete pipes are described in the following terms (Holmen, p. 28):

> *Concrete pipes are one of the main components of a sewer. Different types of concrete pipes exist; however, here we shall only consider one type of concrete pipes, the spigot and the socket type of pipe. Such a pipe has two ends, a spigot end and a socket end. The main requirements for a concrete pipe are tightness, durability and strength. Furthermore, the concrete pipe should only absorb very small amounts of water. The ability of a concrete pipe to fulfil these requirements depends partly on the actual shape of the pipe, the concrete from which it is made, and the process by which the concrete has been compacted.*

The way of describing each one of the components of the technical system creates links to other parts of the resource constellation. The features of the concrete pipes – shape, absorption capacity, tightness, durability and strength – are related to a variety of other components, such as joints, the concrete and its components, and to the production techniques available. Finally, the variety of technological solutions and design practices are described.

In addition to providing a picture of the technical structure in which product development is taking place, the contextual description also addresses how this structure has evolved over time. The history of the shape of concrete pipes provides the background and reason for the change in focus (i.e., from circular to egg-shaped sections). Egg-shaped, or ovoid, pipes were originally designed by the Victorians in the 19th century. At that time they were made of brick, which allowed for any shape of pipe section. The egg-shaped pipe with the narrower part at the bottom provides the maximum rate of flow when there is little liquid moving through. This in turn makes the flow sufficient for the sewers to be self-cleansing. However, brick sewers were expensive, and in the years after World War I precast concrete pipes were developed as these could be produced and laid in the ground more cheaply. The only section shape possible by this production technique, however, was circular. The historical account also links to the description of the development of various production techniques and to some economic aspects of their use.

Through this description of the structural and historical context in which product development is taking place, the notion of embeddedness is built into the case description and the case turns into an illustration of the concept. Hence, context description lays the platform for the description of the development process both theoretically and empirically. Context description is thus not simply a "neutral background" to the actual change but is strongly informed by a theoretical perspective. The notion of embeddedness, illustrated by the context description, makes it clear that any change, in this resource constellation, where the features of individual components have been systematically related to each other over time, cannot be made in isolation and that any change will require a large number of other, related changes.

Evidently, this way of describing the context to the focal change is very different from a generic and neutral description of an industry or market, which may have been regarded as the norm within other paradigms. Instead, the technical context, although described in rather broad terms, provides a useful starting point for analysing embeddedness. As Pettigrew (1997, p. 341) argues, a context is not just a stimulus environment it is also "... a nested arrangement of structures and processes where the subjective interpretations of actors perceiving, learning and remembering help shape process."

Every context description thus needs to be specifically related to some empirical unit of analysis. The unit of analysis in Holmen's case is but one among several products developed and manufactured by a particular company. This way of focusing on something "small" in its wider context is a theoretically relevant and empirically useful way of drawing a boundary around the case and developing the analysis. By placing a clearly defined product at the centre of analysis the identification of the structures and processes in which the development of the egg-shaped pipes were embedded was made possible.

Four companies are described as the main actors in the development process:

1. Yorkshire Water Plc which through its subsidiary is responsible for the clean water and sewerage system in Yorkshire, UK. Like other sewerage companies, it experienced problems with siltation and blockage resulting in high operating costs. Its suppliers include the contractors who install the pipelines in which the sewage and surface water runs.
2. ARC Pipes is the largest UK-based producer of concrete pipes and ancillary concrete products. ARC Pipes sells mostly to contractors, but contractors do not normally design the schemes for which they tender; these are normally designed by consulting engineers or by privatized utilities, such as Yorkshire Water. Different factories tend to supply different areas due to the high transportation costs of bulky and heavy concrete pipes. Due to this factor and the existence of country-specific norms and standards most producers of concrete pipes tend to sell in their own countries only.
3. Pedershaab A/S is a Danish manufacturer of concrete pipes and associated equipment. The most important type of equipment relates to moulds and concrete pipe machinery (namely, machines based on vibration-hydraulic technology). The exact configuration of a machine is customer-specific. However, Pedershaab's machines are based on a standard platform and adapted to specific purposes through modular combinations. Pedershaab has sales subsidiaries in a number of countries, including the UK, but technical development takes place primarily in Denmark.
4. Forsheda AB is a Swedish manufacturer of elastometric products for sealing, protection and vibration-absorbing purposes. One of Forsheda's four divisions manufactures sealing systems for concrete and plastic pipe water drainage systems and exports approximately 95% of its sales.

The main part of the analysis of the case is a systematic mapping of the "total" resource constellation and the different kinds of impact the focal product development effort has on related resource elements. When discussing the findings of the study, Holmen returns to the theoretical assumptions of embeddedness and the research question on how the development of the new product was embedded in the resource context (Box 11.1):

Box 11.1

The case study findings reflect that the development of the new product was indeed affected by the resource-related context in which it occurred and of which it became a part. Firstly, the general idea for the new product *arose in relation to* some of the *existing* resources and products across the different, partially tied, resource collections of the firms involved in the development. Secondly, the idea for the new product was *progressively transformed* into a 'concrete' new product by being related to a small but increasing amount of resources and products from the resource collections of the different involved firms. Thereby, the properties of the new product *arose* in relation to some of the (properties of some of the) resources and products in the related resource collections of the firms involved in the development of the new product. Thereby, a context was created in which the new product could function. In order to create such a context, the involved firms searched their respective, but partially tied resource collections for resources and products, which might form part of the context of the new product and enable and support its provision as well as its use. Some combinations of resources and products, which could form part of a context for the new product without being changed or used in a new way, were identified. Furthermore, other resources and products, which were considered possible to use in case they or their use was changed in relation to the new product, were identified. In addition, even if the context for the new product could rely heavily on existing resources and products in existing or changed forms, some additional resources and products had to be created in order to enable the new product and its context to function as a whole. In summary, the development of the new product was embedded in (the development of) a resource-related context:

- by the idea for the new product initially arising in relation to a small number of existing resources and products, in the resource collections of different firms – the particular existing resources and products in question not having been considered in relation to each other in this particular way before;
- by the new product being progressively substantiated in relation to a larger number of existing resources and products in the resource collections as these resources and products are considered and tried out in relation to

each other in order to support the provision and use of the new product – the new product thereby being embedded in the existing resources and products and the relations among these;
- by the progressively substantiated new product concurrently affecting, in different ways, the resources and products supporting the provision and use of the new product – the new product thereby giving rise to different types of changes of existing resources and products and development and/or acquisition of new resources or (non-focal) products, which thereby become embedded in the new product – these changes of the existing resources and products, and the new resources and (non-focal) products, in turn, enabling the new product to become embedded in the resource collections of the different firms involved.

From Holmen (2001, pp. 279–280, emphasis in original).

Thereafter, a typology of resources in relation to change is suggested (Box 11.2):

Box 11.2

In the thesis it is suggested that the resource-related context, in which the development of the new product occurred and of which it became a part, can be conceptualised as a *new product related provision and use resource structure*. Furthermore, it is suggested that this structure can be divided into two parts by means of a *change boundary*. *Inside* the change boundary, four types of resources and products can be identified: (1) *existing resources and products* which were *used* in *new combination and use routines*; (2) *existing resources* which were *modified* and *used* in *new combination and use routines*; (3) *existing resources and products* which were *acquired* from counterparts, but which were *new for the acquiring firm* and were *used* in *new combination and use routines*; and (4) *resources and products* which were *new for both the creating and/or using firm(s)*, and which were *used* in *new combination and use routines*. *Outside* the change boundary, one type of resources and products can be identified: (5) *existing resources and products*, which were *used* in *existing combination and use routines*.

From Holmen (2001, p. 280, emphasis in original).

Emphasizing the unique character of the product development process studied, Holmen goes on to discuss how the results of the case study can be generalized or transferred to other situations. In the next section we will extract some implications from our discussion of Holmen's illustrative case.

The process of "casing" in industrial network studies

In this section we will attempt to extract some lessons concerning the use of case research in industrial network studies. Industrial network studies tend to start with some theoretically and/or empirically inspired ideas. In the process an empirical unit of analysis typically occupies centre stage in the analysis, which implies departing from some kind of arbitrarily chosen centre. In Holmen's case the starting points were an interest in co-operative product development across firm boundaries and easy access to a key actor in the above story, Pedershaab A/S; this does not imply that the effects of these choices are indifferent to the unfolding of the study, but that the consequences of early choices cannot be known prior to the conduct of the study. This, in turn, implies a dynamic relationship between the research question and the boundaries of the study since these typically co-evolve in the course of the research.

In more traditional uses of the case study method, both the research questions and the delimitation of the case can be dealt with as separate issues and addressed in sequence. The answer to the research question (i.e., whether it evolves during the study or is set from the start) is taken as the end point, and defining the boundary of the case is the means to achieve that end (Yin, 1994). In studies of industrial networks the boundaries of the case and the research question can rather be seen as mutually constitutive or as two sides of the same coin: it is not possible to arrive at one without the other.

Using the industrial network model as a theoretical platform implies that the dimensions/components/items of the network(s) are assumed to be interdependent and/or interacting; this means (1) that they cannot be studied in their totality and (2) that there are no natural, pre-fixed boundaries given by independence among components of the system. Rather, the nature of the assumed interdependencies is always the subject of further scrutiny and probing.

In Holmen's case, resource structure interdependencies in the development of the new product created the boundary for the case. The development of the new product was contextualized as a new product-related provision and use resource structure. This resource structure was further subdivided by means of a change boundary. Within the change boundary, four different combinations of resources and products, which were either new or used in new combinations and use routines, were identified. Outside this boundary, existing resources and products that contributed to the development, but were only used in existing combinations and use routines, were also taken into account for their contribution to the new product development (Holmen, 2001, p. 280). The boundaries of the case are thus set in the process of doing the research and rest on the theoretical assumptions of the study concerning patterns of resource interdependencies across firms.

As far as temporal boundaries are concerned, Holmen's study exemplifies the practical difficulties of separating contemporaneous from historical events.

Holmen's initial objective was to study a co-operative product development process in real time. In reality, there was no ongoing process that could fit comfortably the time frame of the research process itself. In the end, Holmen opted to study the egg-shaped concrete pipes case that unfolded in the period 1991–1993. The initial contact with Pedershaab A/B took place in 1995. The case reported in the previous section unfolded between 1991 and 1993. The study was thus largely retrospective, relying on the relatively fresh memories of the participants in the product development process. However, the focal development process could not be understood without uncovering the history of the resource structures in which it was embedded. In the end the case study covered a much longer time frame than 1991–1993, even though the degree of detail and "thick" description was considerably less for the pre-1991 period.

The process of carrying out industrial network studies thus mirrors to a large extent the phenomena studied. Cases evolve as patterned configurations in interaction with processes taking place in the empirical world and what happens to the researcher's theoretical notions and assumptions during the course of the research (Ragin, 2000). Ragin (1992, p. 218) refers to this process as "casing":

> ... *making something into a case or "casing" it can bring operational closure to some problematic relationship between ideas and evidence, between theory and data. Casing, viewed as a methodological step, can occur at any phase of the research process, but occurs especially at the beginning and at the end. Usually, a problematic relation between theory and data is involved when a case is declared.*

Casing thus calls for iterative theoretical and empirical choices, including reconsideration of the focus of the case study (not least regarding "what it is" in relation to other elements) as it changes during the study. Thus, the interplay between theory and the empirical world and their interaction laid the grounds for the evolution of the case as a unit. The process of "casing", as Ragin (1997, p. 32) remarks, may be the primary and most important finding of the investigation. The boundary of the study may be relatively malleable throughout the investigation and will not be fixed until the analysis is completed and written up. As Ragin (1992, p. 6) remarked: "What *it* is a case *of* will coalesce gradually, sometimes catalytically, and the final realization of the case's nature may be the most important part of the interaction between ideas and evidence" (emphasis in original).

Departing from the chosen centre, both the study and thus the boundaries of the case typically develop by analysing items/elements connected to the centre. Important theoretical tools in this process are such concepts as interdependence, links, ties, bonds, etc., depending on the particular empirical phenomenon and focal dimensions of the theoretical model. Dubois and Gadde (2002) have argued that the systematic combining or continuing interaction between theory and the empirical world is the main feature of these studies. One important reason for this approach is expressed by Weick's (1995, p. 15) observation on the impossibility of theory-independent observation: "People make sense of things by seeing a world in which they have already imposed what they believe." That is, theory needs be understood by empirical insights, while at the same time empirical insights can only emerge through theory. Hence, although theoretical assumptions guide every part of any study, theoretical ideas and frameworks are not static and rarely emerge unscathed from the research process:

> *Theoretical ideas are general and imprecise; they are also dynamic and ever-changing. They change through time, reacting to and back on the larger society and historical experience* (Ragin, 1992, pp. 220–221).

Basic theoretical assumptions are used as guidance in case studies to know what to look for in the empirical world, but they are also developed and articulated through empirical insights. Hence, we may argue that confirmatory research is to some extent always involved in the conduct of case studies, since without some form of theoretical guidance a case for research can never be constructed in the first place. As Wieviorka (1992, p. 160) put it: "It does not suffice to observe a social phenomenon, historical events, or set of behaviours and declare them to be 'cases'. If you want to talk about a 'case' you need the means of interpreting or placing it in a context."

We may also claim that not only is theory developed through case studies but our representations of and consequently ability to act on the empirical world are also developed through case studies. Our interaction with respondents raises questions, notions and links they may not have explored and packages their accounts into a different and more complex narrative, as illustrated by Johanson's (1966) seminal study. Sayer (2000) introduces a useful distinction between lay and academic narratives, both focusing on the same object domain. Social scientists confront a world that is already imbued with meaning attributed to it by social actors. The task of social science is to mediate and transcend these universes of meaning with its theoretical schemes. Case studies of industrial networks face the problem of working with lay accounts as its raw, empirical material and having to construct more complex narratives that can relate causes invoked by lay accounts with other causes that are remote, indirect, unintended or mediated by non-human factors (e.g., resource ties).

Theoretical concepts are as much tools used in the process of doing case studies as are empirical "data". Ragin (1992, p. 218) notes that: "... we often use empirical evidence to articulate theories, to flesh them out, to ascertain their spatiotemporal limits and establish their scope conditions (Walker and Cohen, 1985). In short, ideas and evidence are mutually dependent; we transform evidence into results with the aid of ideas, and we make sense of theoretical ideas and elaborate them by linking them to empirical evidence. Cases figure prominently in both of these relationships."

To conduct research following this logic a conceptual "toolbox" is typically used in the process. In addition to the concepts developed and used within the industrial network approach this also includes borrowing concepts from other schools of thought as well as developing fresh concepts. For instance, Holmen (2001) not only based her study on the industrial networks approach she also drew inspiration from works in the history and sociology of technology. Concepts within the industrial network approach that were deemed insufficiently developed for the purpose of analysing empirical material, such as resource structures, were augmented by borrowing from other schools of thought and new insights were generated as a result.

In short, case studies provide excellent opportunities to confront theory with empirical data in an evolving fashion in which the ultimate aim is to account for all the relevant features of the case through a particular framework. As Ragin (1997) observed, cases often deviate from common patterns, but these deviations, rather than being dismissed as error terms, inspire researchers to identify the factors that account for non-conforming cases even when these factors fall outside the initial frameworks they brought to the study. When theoretical notions prove inadequate to capture the essence of the case, they are elaborated on, revised or discarded. In the process, what is salient or irrelevant empirical evidence is also revised and reconfigured (Ragin, 1992).

Conclusions

The purpose of this chapter has been to reflect on how one method, case research, has been employed in industrial marketing studies (namely, interaction and industrial network studies). Our starting point was that a methodology, such as case research, should be seen as a tool that gets appropriated and transformed within the context of a research paradigm. The approach taken in this chapter is congruent with both Pettigrew's (1997) and Abbott's (2001) injunctions for the need to align theories, explanations, methods and research programmes in ways that make them resonate with and support each other.

We draw three main conclusions from the previous discussion. Contrary to methodological advice that regards the case method as essentially dependent on a linear process connecting research questions with the boundaries of the study (see, e.g., Miles and Huberman, 1994), we regard the main strength of the method as the deferral of these decisions. In other words, cases are made through a convoluted process of systematic iteration and combination of empirical evidence, theoretical frameworks and persistent reframing of what it is we are studying. Interactions between ideas and empirical evidence result in the progressive refinement of the nature and boundaries of the case and, in the process, reframe and transform these relationships.

Whereas this may be regarded as a highly unsatisfactory state of affairs, even from the standpoint of other orientations within case research, we would argue that it is precisely this quality of the method that makes it resonate so closely with industrial network studies. Empirical network studies, as we attempted to show through Holmen's illustrative case, often depart from rather hazy beginnings with loosely formulated concepts or ideas. What constitutes the phenomenon of interest and its boundaries is often the outcome of the study rather than a decision that can be firmed up prior to conducting the study.

The second conclusion we offer relates to the evolving interpretation of cases. As Dubois and Gadde (2002) argue, the interpretations of a case depend on the temporal boundary that is set around the case as well as the timing of the inter-pretation. Because cases have to be treated and analysed as singular and homogeneous entities, or configurations, their insertion into longer chains of events leads to a reformulation of their findings and interpretations (Ragin, 2000). The same event inserted into a longer or shorter chain of events could be interpreted rather differently; this is no surprise to the historian, more attuned to the craft of emplotting events into larger historical pictures, but it is a problem often ignored by social scientists, even among those embracing a processual orientation.

Lastly, what constitutes the best interpretative framework for a particular case or set of cases is decided not by lone researchers but by the community of researchers working with a particular paradigm. As we have demonstrated through the example discussed, single case studies are often performed in the context of ongoing research programmes. Case selection, in particular, should not be seen as an isolated and individual decision, but often influenced by the range of cases and frameworks that have emanated from the research programme a particular researcher identifies with. In a sense a databank of existing cases conducted broadly within the same research programme constitutes a body of evidence in support of a theoretical approach, as well as a source for comparisons and further developments. The value of such a corpus is that it may be revisited to provide material for new interpretations, testing of refinements and extensions to theoretical frameworks.

References

Abbott, A. (1997). Of time and space: The contemporary relevance of the Chicago School. *Social Forces*, **75**(4): 1149–1182.

Abbott, A. (2001). *Time Matters: On Theory and Method*. Chicago: University of Chicago Press.

Anderson, J.C., Håkansson, H. and Johanson, J. (1994). Dyadic business relationships within a business network context. *Journal of Marketing*, **58**(4): 1–15.

Axelsson, B. and Easton, G. (eds) (1992). *Industrial Networks: A New View of Reality*. London: Routledge.

Bennett, A. and George, A. (1997). Research design tasks in case study methods. Paper given at *The MacArthur Foundation Workshop on Case Study Methods, Harvard University*.

Bonoma, T.V. (1985). Case research in marketing: Opportunities, problems and a process. *Journal of Marketing Research*, **22**(May): 199–208.

Cook, K.S. and Emerson, R.M. (1978). Power, equity and commitment in exchange networks. *American Sociological Review*, **43**(5): 712–739.

David, P.A. (1994). Why are institutions the "carriers of history"? Path dependence and the evolution of conventions, organizations and institutions. *Structural Change and Economic Dynamics*, **5**(2): 205–220.

Dubois, A. and Gadde, L.E. (2002). Systematic combining: An abductive approach to case research. *Journal of Business Research*, **55**(7): 553–560.

Easton, G. (1992). Industrial networks: A review. In: B. Axelsson and G. Easton (eds), *Industrial Networks: A New View of Reality* (pp. 1–27). London: Routledge.

Easton, G. (1995). Methodology and industrial networks. In: K. Möller and D.T. Wilson (eds), *Business Marketing: An Interaction and Network Perspective* (pp. 411–492). Norwell, MA: Kluwer.

Easton, G. (1998). Case research as a methodology for industrial networks: A realist apologia. In: P. Naudé and P. Turnbull (eds), *Network Dynamics in International Marketing* (pp. 73–87). Oxford, UK: Pergamon Press.

Granovetter, M. (1992). Problems of explanation in economic sociology. In: N. Nohria and R.G. Eccles (eds), *Networks and Organizations: Structure, Form and Action* (pp. 25–56). Boston: Harvard Business School Press.

Håkansson, H. (ed.) (1982). *International Marketing and Purchasing of Industrial Goods: An Interaction Approach*. Chichester, UK: John Wiley & Sons.

Håkansson, H. (ed.) (1987). Strategic implications. *Industrial Technological Development: A Network Approach*. London: Croom-Helm.

Håkansson, H. and Snehota, I. (eds) (1995). *Developing Relationships in Business Networks*. London: Routledge.

Halinen, A. and Tornröos, J-A. (1995). The meaning of time in the study of industrial buyer–supplier relationships. In: K. Möller and D.T. Wilson (eds), *Business Marketing: An Interaction and Network Perspective* (pp. 493–529). Norwell, MA: Kluwer.

Hallén, L., Johanson, J. and Seyed-Mohammed, N. (1991). Interfirm adaptation in business relationships. *Journal of Marketing*, **55**(2): 29–37.

Holmen, E. (2001). Notes on the conceptualization of resource-related embeddedness of interorganisational product development. Unpublished PhD dissertation, University of Southern Denmark.

Johanson, J. (1966). *Svenskt kvallitetsstål på utländska marknader* [*Swedish Special Steel on Foreign Markets*] (Dissertation mimeo, translated from the Swedish original). University of Uppsala, Department of Business Administration.

McKeown, T.J. (1999). Case studies and the statistical worldview. *International Organization*, **53**(1): 161–190.

Miles, M.B. and Huberman, A.M. (1994). *Qualitative Data Analysis: An Expanded Sourcebook*. Thousand Oaks, CA: Sage Publications.

Mitchell, J.C. (1983). Case and situation analysis. *Sociological Review*, **31**(2): 187–211.

Patton, M.Q. (1990). *Qualitative Evaluation and Research Methods*. Thousand Oaks, CA: Sage Publications.

Pettigrew, A. (1997). What is processual analysis? *Scandinavian Journal of Management*, **13**(4): 337–348.

Phillips, L.W. (1981). Assessing measurement error in key informant reports: A methodological note on organizational analysis in marketing. *Journal of Marketing Research*, **18**(4): 395–416.

Porter, M.E. (1980). *Competitive Strategy. Techniques for Analyzing Industries and Competitors*. New York: Free Press.

Ragin, C.C. (1992). "Casing" and the process of social inquiry. In: CC. Ragin and H.S. Becker (eds), *What is a Case? Exploring the Foundations of Social Inquiry* (pp. 217–226). Cambridge, UK: Cambridge University Press.

Ragin, C.C. (1997). Turning the tables: How case-oriented research challenges variable-oriented research. In: G. Brochmann, F. Engelstad, R. Kalleberg, A. Leira and L. Mjøset (eds), *Methodological Issues in Comparative Social Science* (Vol. 16, pp. 27–42). Greenwich, CT: JAI Press.

Ragin, C.C. (2000). *Fuzzy Set Social Science*. Chicago: University of Chicago Press.

Roberts, C. (1996). *The Logic of Historical Explanation*. University Park, PA: Pennsylvania State University Press.

Sayer, A. (2000). *Realism and Social Science*. London: Sage Publications.

Scherer, F.M. (1970). *Industrial Market Structure and Economic Performance*. Chicago: Rand McNally.

Stinchcombe, A.L. (1968). *Constructing Social Theories*. San Francisco: Harcourt, Brace & World.

Walker, H. and Cohen, B. (1985). Scope conditions: Imperatives for evaluating theories. *American Sociological Review*, **50**: 288–301.

Weick, K.E. (1995). *Sensemaking in Organizations*. Thousand Oaks, CA: Sage Publications.

Wieviorka, M. (1992). Case studies: History or sociology? In: C.C. Ragin and H.S. Becker (eds), *What is a Case? Exploring the Foundations of Social Inquiry* (pp. 159–172). Cambridge, UK: Cambridge University Press.

Williamson, O.E. (1996). *The Mechanisms of Governance*. New York: Oxford University Press.

Yin, R.K. (1994). *Case Study Research: Design and Methods* (2nd edn). Newbury Park, CA: Sage Publications.

Toward a new understanding of marketing: Gaps and opportunities

Sigurd Villads Troye and Roy Howell

12

Introduction

Marketing research has been subject to criticism from members of the discipline and from persons outside the discipline. The critical issues that have been raised can be classified into four different domains: first, marketing researchers have been criticized for their selection of phenomena to address (it has been argued that too much attention has been devoted to certain phenomena, while others have been ignored); a related second criticism holds that marketing research is managerially irrelevant, somehow fails to provide support and does not give direction to decision makers; third, marketing researchers have been accused of developing and applying ontological and theoretical frameworks that do not satisfactorily account for the phenomena being addressed; and, fourth, marketing research has been reproached for using research approaches and methods that do not properly challenge theories being put to test or do not provide an adequate description of the subject matter.

We posit that the content of each of these domains of criticism to some extent reflects the developments in other domains and give some examples of how these influences occur. Three of these domains correspond closely to Brinberg and McGrath's (1988) notion of the substantive domain, the conceptual domain and the methodological domain.

The substantive domain, according to Brinberg and McGrath (1988, p. 25), contains "the phenomena, processes, or focal problems of interest" and comprises aspects of reality with which we are concerned. The conceptual domain consists of the "ideas, concepts, and their relations as well as the philosophical assumptions underlying them." It contains theories and models of how states and events in the substantive domain are interrelated as well as fundamental ontological assumptions about reality, such as "modernism" versus "post-modernism" (Firat and Venkatesh, 1995). The methodological domain "contains the methods, designs, and research strategies used to examine concepts and phenomena" and covers on one side specific sampling, design, measurement and analytical approaches and fundamental epistemological positions on the other.

The "managerial or decision domain" can be considered to be a subset of the phenomena referred to in the substantive domain, since the phenomena it contains are the decision makers' choices and decision strategies. We have chosen to treat it as being distinct from the other domains in order to emphasize that marketing practice may not be fully determined by developments in the other domains and vice versa: what managers and other decision makers do that affects the marketplace may not be fully absorbed by the theories that are developed and phenomena that are focused on as part of the discipline's substantive domain.

The purpose of this chapter is twofold. The first goal is to provide a framework that can help provide a systematic inventory of alleged shortcomings in the marketing discipline. In order to illustrate this framework we will give a review of some recent criticisms that have been raised, although it is obvious that such a review cannot be exhaustive. The second goal reflects the premise of this chapter that, in order to meet the challenges and fill the gaps implied by the criticisms, there is a need to understand the dynamics of knowledge generation in a discipline, such as marketing. Using the Brinberg and McGrath (1988) framework discussed above, we discuss the interplay among the domains in the progress of scientific advancement in marketing.

Criteria for evaluating the adequacy of marketing research

While a long array of scientific "criteria" have been suggested in the philosophy of science literature, we follow Larry Laudan (Laudan, 1977, 1989) who uses the term "adequacy" to evaluate research traditions: "We are essentially asking here how effective theories within the research tradition are at solving problems" (Laudan, 1989, p. 375). "Problems" can be puzzles of understanding (e.g., whether theories at hand help us understand and predict the phenomena we are concerned with). The ability of theories to solve problems can however also be tied to managerial issues: Can theories adequately prescribe managerial action? A theory (e.g., attitude theory) that does well in terms of accounting for individual behaviour (e.g., brand choice) may thus not provide a sufficient basis for managerial decisions (e.g., with respect to positioning or advertising). The adequacy requirement can be extended to other aspects of a paradigm, or discipline, which we will return to in closer detail below.

Theoretical adequacy of a discipline can be obtained at the cost of the inadequacies of its substantive domain in the sense that researchers may be reproached for solving the "wrong" problems (i.e., for not attending to phenomena which from some normative perspective they should be concerned with). At the same time it is conceivable that a discipline, regardless of the adequacy of its theoretical foundation and span of attention, may not be equipped with a methodology that adequately helps us capture developments in the substantive domain and allows us to test and refine existing theories.[1]

The criticisms against marketing can be grouped as indicated above in three different categories that correspond to three general criteria for judging marketing as an academic field: attentional, theoretical and methodological adequacy.

Attentional adequacy

The first issue addresses whether *the scope or attention of marketing research is adequate*. Does marketing research address phenomena on which attention should be focused? One requirement is that empirical research should (at least) capture the phenomena suggested by our theories; otherwise, marketing could be considered as an abstract exercise limited to armchair reasoning. Whereas such a criticism might be justifiable in the early period of marketing and still may apply to certain isolated fields in marketing, we do not believe this in general is a valid criticism. Most theories introduced in marketing are put to empirical tests with little delay.

Another requirement is that marketing researchers should also be equipped to capture phenomena that may not follow from extant theories or theoretical frameworks, but that nevertheless may impinge on important marketing aspects. Such phenomena as the Internet, cellular phones, just-in-time manufacturing methods and so on do not follow from our theoretical perspectives, but they still need to be considered and incorporated in order to allow an understanding of how marketing processes evolve. Inclusion of new phenomena can challenge existing theories, can make us more aware of their limitations and provide the basis for amending them. For example, the development of the Internet and e-marketing challenged the existing theories of attention, advertising effects and market information, as well as methods for measuring advertising reach, frequency and effectiveness.

Marketing as a management field will, however, not only be judged for its descriptive and predictive power but also for its ability to provide managerially relevant information, tools and conceptual guidelines. A third requirement, therefore, is that the attentional field of marketing researchers should at least cover phenomena considered important for marketing decisions (see Bass and Wind, 1995).

It appears reasonable that these different attentional fields may not entirely overlap. Malhotra et al. (1999, p. 178) point out that a certain gap exists between academic and commercial market research and that this gap ought to

---

[1] Similarly, Kuhn (1989, p. 357) briefly mentions five criteria for adequacy: (1) accuracy (i.e., consequences deducible from a theory should be in demonstrated agreement with the results of existing experiments and observations), (2) consistency, (3) scope, (4) simplicity and (5) fruitfulness (of new research findings).

be bridged. Such a gap can exist for several reasons. One potential reason for this is that commercial market researchers are not aware of the advancement of tools used by academics. It is, however, also conceivable that the information needs perceived by practitioners call for methods and approaches other than the ones utilized in academic research.

Marketing researchers may to some extent be concerned with issues that are not considered important or relevant by practitioners who from their side may use concepts and procedures that appear inappropriate by academics. Marketing researchers for their part may be occupied with phenomena that are uninteresting from the point of view of more theoretically oriented colleagues. The constituencies of marketing are however not restricted to marketers but also include consumer welfare organizations, legislators and bureaucrats (cf., Hirschman, 1991, p. 4; Wells, 1993). Marketing research has thus also been criticized for not addressing the critical aspects of marketing practice. Consequently, the discipline does not provide sufficient information for regulation of undesired marketing practice. Hirschman (1991), citing homelessness, drug addiction, credit card abuse and alcoholism, asks, "How much more could we accomplish if we turn even a portion of our talents toward ameliorating the dark side of consumer behavior?" (p. 4).

Theoretical adequacy

The second issue is whether marketing research is *theoretically adequate*. In other words, do the theories we develop and apply in fact explain and predict the phenomena they address? For example, does attitude theory account for behaviour and can satisfaction models predict loyalty? Do the theories we use help us attend to phenomena in need of explanation or do the theories we employ cause us to ignore important issues? A third issue is whether our theoretical frameworks lend themselves to empirical testing or whether they somehow are too complex (e.g., criticisms of the Howard and Sheth model) or too imprecise to allow testing. A fourth aspect relates to the normative–descriptive dimension (Hunt, 1991). Whereas marketing theories may be adequate in the sense of providing reasonable explanation and precise predictions, they may not be considered particularly useful from a practitioner's point of view.

Methodological adequacy

The third criterion focuses *on the methodological adequacy of the discipline*. Does, for example, the structure of available methods match the sophistication of the theoretical models we put to test? Prior to the advent of structural equation modelling there was a mismatch between the complexities of consumer behaviour models, such as the Howard and Sheth (1969) model, and such techniques as multiple regression and MANOVA that were available for "testing"

Table 12.1—Criteria for judging the adequacy of marketing research

Concern	Criteria
Attentional adequacy and decision relevance	1. Our attention should allow us to address and register events, states and processes entailed in our theories. 2. Our attention should allow us to address and register events and states and pertain to marketing phenomena even when they are not implied by our theories. 3. Our attention should cover phenomena that are considered important by decision makers or that might change their decisions, tactics and strategies.
Theoretical adequacy	1. Do theories allow explanation and prediction of the phenomena they address? 2. Theories should allow us to attend to and understand phenomena worth explaining and predicting. 3. Theories should improve decision making. 4. Theories should lend themselves to empirical tests.
Methodological adequacy	1. The methods we apply should allow us to test complex explanatory models. 2. Methods should allow us to address and describe new phenomena worth addressing. 3. Methods should provide managerially relevant information.

such theories (see, e.g., Farley and Ring, 1970; Lehman et al., 1974) that might have hampered further development of complex models.

In addition, the methodological toolbox should ideally be flexible and sensitive enough to allow us to detect phenomena and events not accounted for or emphasized in current theories. A third subcriterion is whether our methodological approaches help improve decision making. Do satisfaction surveys offer prescriptive advice to managers? Does conjoint analysis aid in the new product development process? Do positioning studies inform the choice of a marketing mix?

A summary of the criteria for addressing the adequacy of research in marketing is presented in Table 12.1.

Types of criticism against marketing

Criticisms of marketing are abundant; this is not surprising, because any new contribution by necessity points to a gap in our understanding or to an inadequacy as its *raison d'être*. We need look no further than the 1999 millennium issue of the *Journal of the Academy of Marketing Science* or the 1999 special issue of the *Journal of Marketing* for a plethora of criticisms of the current state of the marketing discipline. Table 12.2 provides an incomplete list of recent criticisms. The list of things marketing needs to consider (phenomena addressed) is lengthy, including calls for more research in a variety of areas and issues and suggestions that too much attention has been paid to other phenomena (presumably at the expense of devoting attention to other, more relevant or important phenomena).

As noted in Table 12.2 the relevance of marketing research has also been questioned. In a recent discussion of the "relevance and rigor" debate, Varadarajan (2003, p. 369) "... questions and concerns regarding the relevance of scholarly research in marketing persist." Similarly, specific issues regarding the theoretical and methodological adequacy of research in marketing are also detailed in Table 12.2. It is interesting to note that of the criticisms in Table 12.2 few claim that marketing is blatantly wrong, but that it is too narrow in some respects.

In sum, it appears that marketing is criticized more for what it does *not* do than for what it does.

The interaction of the four domains

Our thesis is that the four domains – Brinberg and McGrath's substantive, theoretical and methodological domains along with the managerial domain – interact to bring about changes in the nature of marketing as an academic discipline; this does not imply that the interdependence of the four domains necessarily is due to "causal" influences between the various domains. The use of qualitative, "Verstehen"-like approaches will typically be implied by a given ontological stance (e.g., postmodernism) in very much the same manner that experimental approaches may be dictated by a behaviourist or operationist point of departure in the theoretical domain. Our choice in one domain may thus not be "caused" by our choices in other domains, but will frequently follow as a logical consequence. Fundamental assumptions about how consumers "are" (as an aspect of the theoretical domain) will typically condition our approach to describe them (as an aspect of the methodological domain).

As shown in Figure 12.1, we suggest that each domain influences and, in turn, is influenced by each of the other domains. For example, we suggest that advances in the methodological domain affect developments in the theoretic domain and, conversely, that theory development informs and affects our methods. Thus, each of the 6 numbered paths in Figure 12.1 represents 2 relationships (1 each way between pairs of constructs, giving a true total of 12). In addition, we acknowledge the impact of environmental changes on the substantive domain, giving a total of 13 "paths" for development and change in the marketing discipline. It is these interrelationships (not the existence of the domains

Table 12.2—Types of criticisms raised against marketing research

Type of criticism	Reference/Example
Attentional inadequacy Does the phenomena addressed coincide with what should be within the boundaries of the discipline's subject matter?	• Too much attention on free-standing domestic companies (Kinnear, 1999). • Shortage of studies addressing cross-functional processes, decision-making mechanisms, organizational structures and cross-functional business teams (Deshpande, 1999). • Over-focus on dealers in dyadic relationships (Malhotra et al., 1999). • Marketing research has left it to other disciplines, such as organizational ecology and evolutionary economics, to pursue questions of market dynamics and diversity (Montgomery, 1995; Day and Montgomery, 1999). • Fixation with brand as the unit of analysis in marketing strategy (Varadarajan and Jayachandran, 1999). • Most choice models in marketing assume that the fundamental unit of analysis is the brand. In practice, however, many more of the decisions occur at the level of the stock-keeping unit (SKU) (Malhotra et al., 1999, p. 165). • Lack of competitive focus in marketing strategy (Varadarajan and Jayachandran, 1999). • Lack of international orientation in marketing strategy (Varadarajan and Jayachandran, 1999). • Lack of focus on tacit collusion in marketing strategy (Varadarajan and Jayachandran, 1999). • Limited focus on strategy-making processes and what mental maps guide strategy formulation processes (Varadarajan and Jayachandran, 1999). • Little focus on forces driving product failures (Malhotra et al., 1999, p. 168). • Lack of focus on consumers' participation in production processes and artificial separation of production and consumption (Firat and Venkatesh, 1995). • Consumer behaviour viewed as response behaviour (not goal-directed behaviour) in which purchase is only one element (e.g., Bagozzi and Dholakia, 1999). • Little interest in poverty, misery and violence (Firat and Venkatesh, 1995). • Lack of focus on symbolic aspects of consumption. • Application of Bourdieu's theory of cultural capital has been applied to explain consumption of objects and not (as it should) to understand consumption practices (Holt, 1998). • Too much focus on individual salespeople at the expense of sales-teams (Malhotra et al., 1999, p. 170).

continued

Table 12.2—(*cont.*)

Type of criticism	Reference/Example
Managerial irrelevance Does the research provide support and direction to decisions that affect marketing phenomena?	• Marketing research deals too much with tactical, rather than strategic problems (Deshpande, 1999). • Executives need guidance that is not provided by marketing researchers with respect to cross-border, cross-disciplinary issues (Kinnear, 1999).
Theoretical inadequacy Does the theoretical framework adequately describe and predict the phenomena it purports to account for?	• Lack of empirical evidence that satisfaction accounts for repurchase behaviour (Mittal and Kamakura, 2001). • Lack of theoretical base for marketing strategy (Varadarajan and Jayachandran, 1999). • Researchers erroneously assume that alliances are formed by individual firms that evaluate alternative courses of action and fail to acknowledge that actions of firms are embedded in social contexts (Varadarajan and Jayachandran, 1999). • Marketing research must be grounded in theory. Theory enables us to meaningfully interpret and integrate the findings with previous research. Plausible theories of how consumers actively and passively search for information have not received due attention and, hence, our understanding of this phenomenon is lacking (Malhotra et al., 1999, p. 177). • Attitude research. • Personality research. • We have theories that account for the behaviour of humans, not of products and markets.
Methodological inadequacy Does the methodological approach allow a proper test of the theories and an adequate description of the phenomena that are investigated?	• Use of student samples. • Use of homogeneous samples (e.g., Oliver and Sarbo, 1988). • Lack of use of qualitative research (Gummesson, 2001). • Scarcity of empirical studies in marketing strategy (Varadarajan and Jayachandran, 1999). • Techniques that marketing researchers apply are too adaptive and not sufficiently proactive for evaluating investments in future technologies (Achrol and Kotler, 1999). • Marketing will need stronger support by anecdotes, rather than fully developed studies (Kinnear, 1999). • "The New World" views are supported by anecdotes, rather than fully developed studies (Kinnear, 1999). • Malhotra (1988) cautions researchers as to LISREL's analytical appropriateness (Malhotra et al., 1999, p. 168). • Unjustified use of estimation methods in regression analysis (Malhotra et al., 1999, p. 175). • Few longitudinal studies (Malhotra et al., 1999, p. 168).

Table 12.2—(*cont.*)

Type of criticism	Reference/Example
	• Few examples of using multiple samples for assessing external validity (Malhotra et al., 1999, p. 168).
	• Regrettably, integrating technology-based advancements in measurements to natural settings remains elusive (Malhotra et al., 1999, p. 162).
	• Over-reliance on laboratory experiments to study effects of brand extensions (Malhotra et al., 1999, p. 164).
	• Over-reliance on cross-sectional data (Malhotra, 1988; Malhotra et al., 1999, p. 165).
	• Over-reliance on non-experimental field data to examine causal relationships (Malhotra et al., 1999, p. 170).
	• Due to underutilization of existing theory, our understanding of several substantive areas is limited, despite numerous studies (Malhotra et al., 1999, p. 177).
	• Need for development of procedures for visual presentation of data, so that marketing research may be more clearly communicated, especially to managers (Holbrook, 1997; Novak, 1995; Malhotra et al., 1999, p. 175).

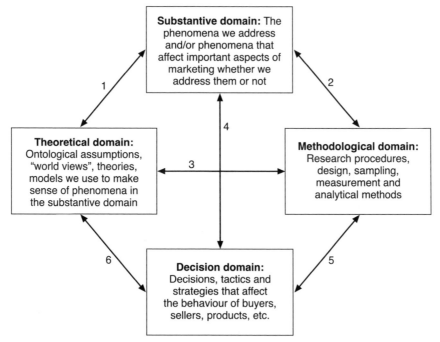

Figure 12.1—Conceptualization of a discipline as consisting of four interrelated domains.

themselves) that are key. We will briefly discuss each in turn and attempt to provide examples.

Relationship 1

We can view Relationship 1 from an idealist (or relativist) perspective (in which theories constitute the phenomena) and from a realist perspective where phenomena cause theories to emerge. Manfred Bruhn (2003), in line with a realist perspective on the link between theories and phenomena, suggests that the development of relationship marketing occurred in response to changes in the marketplace in the 1970s and 1980s: "Changes in the economic and competitive framework in the past few years have led to a new focus in marketing. For instance, today's marketers are faced with a marketplace which is enormously more complex, while in earlier stages marketing focused rather on mass marketing principles and 'making the sale'" (p. 1). Similarly, "quality", "attitudes" and "satisfaction" probably existed in a real sense even before the theories addressing these concepts were developed. From a realist perspective, the observation of a robust positive association between market share and profitability also called for explanation (see Varadarajan and Jayachandran, 1999, p. 134) and gave rise to four different types of explanation: the quality explanation, the market power explanation, the efficiency explanation and the third-factor explanation.

These are examples of theory building in marketing which starts with observation. However, we view the substantive phenomena that we investigate through the lens of extant theories and conceptualizations. Wilkie and Moore (1999, p. 123), citing Sirgy et al. (1982), suggest, "economists defined issues to fit their research forms, as did psychologists, sociologists, ecologists, and political scientists." According to Gigerenzer (1991), cognitive phenomena were suppressed as research topics in psychology in the early 20th century due to the allied forces of behaviourism and operationism. In their criticism of the literature that addresses the "groupthink phenomenon", Aldag and Fuller (1993) claim that the groupthink model suggested by Janis (1971) has functioned as a heuristic device that conditions researchers to restrict their attention to negative decision outcomes (failures), to look for a limited set of explanatory variables and to serve as a biased tool for interpreting research findings.

Marketers are not immune from this type of criticism (see Wilkie and Moore, 1999, p. 139). More than 20 years ago, Oliver (1980, p. 207) made the observation that models borrowed from communications theory, social comparison theory and facet research had been "enlightening but epistemologically inefficient explanations of satisfaction perceptions." The substantive areas we choose to investigate are often the ones where theories exist, definitions have been agreed on and research approaches have been established. Speaking to this difficulty of doing research in a "new" domain, Kinnear (1999, p. 113) states, "At the most elementary level, it is almost impossible to do high quality research that builds the state of knowledge without a set of agreed upon definitions. The emperor indeed may have no clothes, but because there is no definition of what clothes are, no one will know." Until we have the vocabulary and a guiding theory, new phenomena in the substantive domain may not receive adequate attention (while more developed areas of research may be investigated beyond the point of diminishing returns).

Similarly, much research in marketing has been "predictor-oriented" – a theory or construct (often borrowed from another discipline) investigated to see where in marketing it might apply or what marketing phenomena it might explain (cf., James et al., 1982). The starting point is an interesting theory or construct, not a phenomenon to be explained. We have all seen articles of the form, "An interesting theory X has been developed in discipline Y. This study describes theory X in the context of marketing phenomenon Z." The theory drives the choice of subject matter.

While the availability of theory may affect our choice of which phenomena to investigate, the "normal science" view is that phenomena are observed and theories are developed to explain them. "We have observed phenomenon Z. How can we predict it?" As new phenomena are observed in the substantive domain, calls for new research (and new theories) are issued. As noted previously, the marketing discipline is often criticized on its choice of phenomena for investigation: "Marketing research does not reflect the top research problems facing the marketing discipline" (Deshpande, 1999, p. 95). "In a world with few boundaries among functions, channels, cultures, and countries; with networks of companies and e-commerce facilitating consumer and distribution relationships, and with new modes of supply chain and distribution channel dynamics, the challenges for excellence in scholarship abound. The old mode of research that focuses on a functional marketing issue in a free-standing domestic company simply does not deal meaningfully with the critical issues of the new world of marketing" (Kinnear, 1999, p. 113). For a further discussion of phenomena in need of investigation see Day and Montgomery (1999).

Relationship 2

We suggest that research tools restrict and condition the phenomena to which we pay attention and, conversely, that we develop tools and methods in response to the need to investigate particular phenomena; that is, theory drives and influences developments in the methodological domain, and, perhaps not as obviously, developments in the methodological domain allow for new theorizing in the domain of theory. These relationships are discussed below.

Ideally, the substantive phenomena we need to address would drive the development of tools and methods needed to address them. Indeed, the need to determine advertising effects leads to the development of split cable consumer scanner panels, the need to model choice behaviour leads to the development of the multinomial logit model, the need to assess brand loyalty/switching behaviour leads to the collection and analysis of scanner data, etc. However, it can be argued that the availability of research tools and methods affects the choice of substantive issues to which we devote our attention, both positively (we investigate areas where we have appropriate tools and methods) and negatively (we avoid addressing otherwise important phenomena when available tools and methods are inadequate).

Empirical tools, such as exploratory techniques like cluster analyses and common factor analysis, can help us see "phenomena" and patterns we were not aware of – with or without theories. Cross-national, cross-cultural research has been given too little attention because of the difficulties associated with such research. Research in the "network" and "relationship" marketing areas has been sparse, given the importance of the topic, perhaps because of the lack of easily employed methods for their study. Many of the criticisms of marketing's "attentional" inadequacies in Table 12.1 can be traced to difficulties in conducting research in some areas, often due to underdeveloped, difficult or non-existent methodologies rather than a lack of awareness or a sense of their importance. The other side of the coin is that we tend to investigate areas where we have well-developed methods and tools. Like the drunk under a street lamp searching for his missing keys, we look in well-lit areas.

Relationship 3

We posit an interplay between the theoretical domain and the methodological domain. The "traditional" sequence would have it that tools and methods are developed in response to the demands of the theories we need to investigate. Theories suggest data necessary for their testing, along with methods for their assessment. Examples are abundant and will be familiar to most readers. For example, Kelly's repertory grid seems to be a method derived directly from the associated theory, and the IDB (information display board) as a research tool follows directly from theories of consumer information processing. Moreover, theoretical models can also serve as interpretive schemata or tools that condition the way we extract information from data, blurring the distinction between theory on one side and analysis on the other (see Aldag and Fuller, 1993).

A less obvious relationship seems to be the extent to which our tools and methods affect our theories. Gigerenzer (1991) documents and provides examples of this relationship, the most compelling being how theories of the brain and cognitive processing are inspired by analytical methods (such as ANOVA, factor analysis, hypothesis testing, etc.) and the computer (inputs, outputs, encoding, decoding, memory allocation, bits and bytes, multiprocessing, CPU, short-term storage, long-term storage, signal-to-noise ratio, etc.) resulting in the conception of mind as an intuitive statistician or as a "human computer". Indeed, "brain-as-computer" has become such a well-established metaphor that it is difficult to imagine how the brain was conceived of prior to the advent of the computer and its associated concepts and terminology. Similarly, as researchers became trained in statistics, theories (in psychology, in particular) came to incorporate statistical elements (the "brain-as-intuitive-statistician" – e.g., the work of Kahneman and Tversky, 1979).

The field of structural equation modelling (SEM) was developed out of the need to test complex theories containing latent constructs, yet it seems apparent that the SEM approach to theory testing has affected theorizing in marketing. Prior to the 1980s few marketing theories were multivariate, with multiple endogenous variables. In recent years many marketing theories have been expressed in the form of a "boxes-and-arrows" diagram. Mediated relationships are explicitly theorized, and relatively complex theories have become the norm. However, until very recently, moderated relationships (interaction terms) have been difficult to model in traditional SEM software (e.g., LISREL). As a result, few theories have postulated interactions and moderated relationships.

This is in direct contrast with theories in areas where the experimental tradition, using ANOVA as the primary analysis tool, has held sway. In those areas, interaction hypotheses (easily dealt with in ANOVA)[2] are abundant and theories containing multiple dependent variables and mediated relationships are scarce.

In marketing, it can be argued that our theories of market segmentation are informed by the structure and logic of cluster analysis, that our theories of "product" both inform and are informed by the structure of conjoint analysis and that our theories of positioning are closely interwoven with the maps produced by popular multidimensional scaling algorithms.

Relationship 4

This relationship deals with the interplay between the substantive domain and the domain of managerial decisions. It is easy to see that changes in the substantive domain affect the decisions managers need to make. The rapid growth of the Internet calls for many decisions on the part of the manager that would not have been necessary without this technology. The availability of CRM (customer relationship management) systems likewise necessitates new decisions. Should an investment be made? How should the system be implemented? In general, changes in the substantive domain are the primary driving force behind the scope and configuration of the managerial decision process.

It may also be the case that the decision domain affects the substantive domain. Managers do not simply react to the environment but, instead, are often proactive in changing it, through their advertising messages, lobbying efforts in the legal and

---

[2] It is also conceivable that the ease with which interaction effects are tested in most ANOVA programs makes it tempting to formulate hypothesis involving the interaction term and to provide a theoretical rationale for it, even in situations where there may be no a priori ground to assume such effects.

political environment or through the introduction of new technology. Similarly, the decisions managers make can have an impact on the phenomena in the substantive domain. Managers' collective decisions to, for example, use email as a direct marketing tool have brought about public policy concerns regarding the impact of "spam" and methods to control it. Managers' decisions to promote, for example, cigarettes to young people raise issues that need to be addressed in the substantive domain.

Relationship 5

In a fashion similar to Relationships 1 and 2, methods and managerial decisions also seem to be interrelated. The development of conjoint analysis was at least in part driven by product developers' need for a research tool to aid in the product design decision. Although applied in many fields, substantial work in the area of cluster analysis resulted from managers' needs to make segmentation decisions. Managers have to make decisions, and tools (along with theories) that inform those decisions have been and are being developed.

At the same time, we posit that the availability of research tools, such as ServQual, satisfaction scales, conjoint analysis and MDS, influence the way managers think and act. Managers are explicitly addressing some decision areas due to the availability of tools for their investigation. The availability (or absence) of tools affects the form (if not the content) of managerial decisions. We suggest that managers' information needs drive the development of tools and methods, while, simultaneously, managers' perceptions of their decisions and, thus, their information needs are affected by the tools and methods at their disposal.

Relationship 6

Theories offer managers a mechanism for construing their environment. Attitude theory, attribution theory, satisfaction theory, relationship marketing, transaction cost theory, etc. have shaped the mental maps of managers and their theories-in-use. At the same time, managers' questions have guided theorizing in marketing. Much theory in marketing has been developed to answer managers' questions. When managers ask "Why?" theories are developed or amended to answer the question.

The willingness to serve practitioners' theoretical needs has not however necessarily been beneficial for marketing as an academic discipline with respect to theory construction, methodological developments and the content of the substantive domain. The economic interests of the firm can easily explain marketers' natural obsession with those factors and functions that lead to and facilitate a transaction. Marketing scholars on their side appear for a long time to have accepted this rather myopic view which has led to what Vargo and Lusch (forthcoming) label the dominant "goods-centred logic" in marketing where value or utility is viewed as embedded in a tangible good as opposed to an emerging "service-centred logic" that acknowledges the role of the customer in the value creation process.

In service-centred logic, offerings simply facilitate value creation and the ultimate values from a customer perspective are co-created in concert with the customer. Service-centred-logic meanwhile calls for conceptualization of the buyer as an actor rather than a responder and suggests a more phenomenological, experiential view of consumption (Holbrook and Hirschman, 1982). This shift in world view has obvious implications for theory construction and methodological developments.

Relationship 6 may well warrant further investigation. For example, what do we know about the theories underlying marketing practitioners' decisions? It would be beneficial to make systematic comparisons of Argyris and Schön's (1974) "theories in use" (i.e., those theories that appear to guide marketing practice), "espoused theories" (i.e., theories that practitioners may accept, but not necessarily use) and "scientific theories" (i.e., theories developed by marketing academics).

Since research-based journals may not be fully comprehensible for non-academic audiences it is hoped that textbooks could play an important role of disseminating research findings and theories to students and practitioners outside the research community. However, recent cases (Armstrong and Schultz, 1993; Rothfeld, 2000) suggest that we cannot be sure this is happening as textbooks have been demonstrated to "institutionalize theoretical approaches from previous years" (Rotfeld, 2000) which can lead to "(t)he dogmatic retention of unsupported and outdated theories, as well as the implicit endorsement and propagation of these in journal articles." Armstrong and Schultz (1993) found 566 normative statements pertaining to pricing, communications, and product or distribution decisions that were not supported by empirical evidence. With an increasing amount of research and an accompanying need to summarize research findings, the risk of oversimplifying and misrepresenting research may become ever larger.

Conclusions

Gaps will most likely occur if the discipline gets too "compartmentalized" and specialized. In other words, if theoreticians only theorize, if market research institutes only carry out market research and market surveillance, if methodologists only develop methods and if practitioners only make decisions, then the desired "natural flow" between the various domains will not take place.

Suggestions

Many of the criticisms of marketing scholarship fall under our Relationship 1: the linkage between the realms of theory and the substantive domain. Perhaps abductive research (where peculiarities and puzzles are observed and lead to the search for theories and explanatory models) presents a possible partial remedy. The work of Kahnemann and Tversky on decision making is perhaps an example of observed anomalies resulting in a rich behavioural theory. Theories in this paradigm become tools to extract information from reality.

Along with abductive research, marketing knowledge could similarly be advanced through greater incorporation of *theory triangulation* – bringing alter-native theories to bear on the job of explaining a given puzzle. Testing "theory *A* versus theory *B*" can be much more productive and informative than testing "theory *A* versus the (usually weak) null hypothesis". Paul Meehl (1990) points out the lack of progress made in psychology and attributes many of the problems to testing against a weak null hypothesis (i.e., no relationship, no difference) wherein large sample sizes work "in favour" of the theory. He suggests the exam-ination of competing theories as a preferred practice.

Another recommendation is to use an expanded set of methodologies to capture the richness and complexity of a given phenomenon, as suggested by Aldag and Fuller (1993) in their criticism of the groupthink tradition.

We believe marketing would benefit *from multidisciplinary projects* addressing different phenomena, using different theories, but using the same research context (to avoid narrow-minded "contextless" research). One example is a project on tourism at the Norwegian School of Economics and Business Administration sponsored by the Royal Ministry of Industries. In this project the topics pursued ranged from guest (customer) satisfaction, service quality, organizational culture and economic performance measures, like capacity utilization, profit margins and ROI. By using the same hotels and allowing different researchers to use a number of alternative theoretical perspectives, like satisfaction theory, quality management, organization behaviour and industrial economics, a comprehensive, multidisciplin-ary, yet context-specific understanding of the interplay between these different areas was possible (see Troye and Øgaard, 1999).

A challenge is to establish *better ways to align marketing practice and marketing research*. This challenge raises two issues: first, how can marketing research gain from better insight into marketing practice and vice versa? and, second, how can practice benefit from marketing as an academic discipline? The first issue was addressed by Wilson and Ghingold (1980) who suggested that theories could be built from practice, using what they referred to as a "theory-in-use approach" in which an attempt is made to extract the theories that are being used by practitioners: "Thus, the theory-in-use approach calls for the study of the methods that the common man, the marketing practitioner, [employs] in attempting to construct reliable and valid statements about the world . . . beyond the methods posited by scientific/academic investigators" (Wilson and Ghingold, 1980, p. 237).

The second issue – how marketing practice can make better use of marketing research – deals partly with how to *popularize theories, research findings and methods* in order to bridge many of the gaps involving the managerial domain. The findings reported by Rotfeld (2000) and Armstrong and Schultz (1993), cited earlier, suggest that care should be taken to avoid the "textbook effect" – distorting theories and findings while ignoring valid and potentially useful research contributions. *Industry–academic research teams and projects* is one option that can alleviate the practitioner–academic communication gap: by allowing such teams to be cross-disciplinary, knowledge transfer between industry and academic institutions and between various disciplines would be facilitated and should lead to cross-fertilization.

References

Achrol, R.S. and Kotler, P. (1999). Marketing in the network economy. *Journal of Marketing*, **63**(Special issue): 146–163.

Achrol, R.S. and Stern, L.W. (1988). Environmental determinants of decision making uncertainty in marketing channels. *Journal of Marketing Research*, **25**(February): 36–50.

Aldag, R.J. and Fuller, S.R. (1993). Beyond fiasco: A reappraisal of the groupthink phenomenon and a new model of group decisions processes. *Psychological Bulletin*, **113**(3): 533–552.

Armstrong, J.S. and Schultz, R. (1993). Principles involving marketing policies: An empirical assessment. *Marketing Letters*, **4**(3): 253–265.

Argyris, C. and Schön, D. (1974). *Theory in Practice*. San Fransisco: Jossey-Bass.

Bagozzi, R.P. and Dholakia, U. (1999). Goal setting and goal striving in consumer behavior. *Journal of Marketing*, **63**(Special issue): 19–32.

Bass, F. and Wind, Y. (1995). Special issue on empirical generalizations in marketing. *Marketing Science*, **14**(3): 1–236.

Brinberg, D. and McGrath, J.E. (1988). *Validity and the Research Process*. Newbury Park, CA: Sage Publications.

Bruhn, M. (2003). *Relationship Marketing: Management of Customer Relationships*. London: Prentice Hall.

Day, G.S. and Montgomery, D.B. (1999). Charting new directions for marketing. *Journal of Marketing*, **63**(Special issue): 3–13.

Deshpande, R. (1999). Introduction: "Foreseeing" marketing. *Journal of Marketing*, **63**(Special issue): 164–167.

Farley, J.U. and Ring, L.W. (1970). An empirical test of the Howard–Sheth model of buyer behavior. *Journal of Marketing Research*, **7**(November): 427–438.

Firat, A.F. and Venkatesh, A. (1995). Liberatory postmodernism and the reenchantment of consumption. *Journal of Consumer Research*, **22**(December): 239–268.

Gigerenzer, G. (1991). From tools to theories: A heuristic of discovery in cognitive psychology. *Psychological Review*, **98**(2): 1–14.

Gummesson, E. (2001). Are current research approaches leading us astray? *Marketing Theory*, **1**(1): 27–48.

Hirschman, E.C. (1991). Secular mortality and the dark side of consumer behavior. In: R. Holman and M. Soloman (eds), *Advances in Consumer Research* (Vol. 18, pp. 145–156). Provo, UT: Association for Consumer Research.

Holbrook, M.B. (1997). Visual representation of data: Stereographic visual displays and the three-dimensional communication of findings in marketing research. *Journal of Marketing Research*, **34**(November): 526–536.

Holbrook, M.B. and Hirschman, E.C. (1982). The experiential aspects of consumption: Consumer fantasies, feelings, and fun. *Journal of Consumer Research*, **9**(September): 132–140.

Holt, D.B. (1998). Does cultural capital structure American consumption? *Journal of Consumer Research*, **25**(June): 1–25.

Howard, J.A. and Sheth, J.N. (1969). *The Theory of Buyer Behavior*. New York: John Wiley & Sons.

Hunt, S.D. (1991). *Modern Marketing Theory: Critical Issues in the Philosophy of Marketing Science*. Cincinnati, OH: South-Western Publishing.

James, L.R., Mulaik, S.A. and Brett, J.M. (1982). *Causal Analysis*. Beverly Hills, CA, Sage Publications.

Janis, I. (1971). Groupthink. *Psychology Today*, **5**(November): 43–46 and 74–76.

Kahneman, D. and Tversky, A. (1979). Prospect theory: An analysis of decisions under risk. *Econometrica*, **47**: 313–327.

Kinnear, T.C. (1999). Introduction: A perspective on how firms relate to their markets. *Journal of Marketing*, **63**(Special issue): 112–114.

Kuhn, T. (1989). Objectivity, value judgment, and theory choice. In: B.A. Brody and R.E. Grandy (eds), *Readings in the Philosophy of Science*. Englewood Cliffs, NJ: Prentice Hall.

Laudan, L. (1977). *Progress and Its Problems*. Berkeley, CA: University of California Press.

Laudan, L. (1989). From theories to research traditions. In: B.A. Brody and R.E. Grandy (eds), *Readings in the Philosophy of Science* (pp. 368–378). Englewood Cliffs, NJ: Prentice Hall.

Lehman, D.R., O'Brien, T.V., Farley, J. and Howard, J. (1974). Some empirical contributions to buyer behavior theory. *Journal of Consumer Research*, **1**(December): 48–55.

Malhotra, N. (1988). Self-concept and product choice: An integrated perspective. *Journal of Economic Psychology*, **9**(1): 1–28.

Malhotra, N., Peterson, M. and Kleiser, S.B. (1999). Marketing research: A state-of-the-art review and directions for the twenty-first century. *Journal of the Academy of Marketing Science*, **27**(Spring): 160–183.

Meehl, P.E. (1990). Appraising and amending theories: The strategy of Lakatosian defense and two principles that warrant it. *Psychological Inquiry*, **1**(2): 108–141.

Mittal, V. and Kamakura, W. (2001). Satisfaction, repurchase intent, and purchase behavior: Investigating the moderating role of customer characteristics. *Journal of Marketing Research*, **38**(1), February: 131–142.

Montgomery, C.A. (1995). *Resource-based and Evolutionary Theories of the Firm*. Norwell, MA: Kluwer.

Novak, T.P. (1995) MANOVAMAP: Graphical representation of MANOVA in marketing research. *Journal of Marketing Research*, **32**(August): 357–374.

Oliver, R.L. (1980). Theoretical bases of consumer satisfaction research: Review, critique, and future direction. In: C.W. Lamb and P.M. Dunne (eds), *Theoretical Developments in Marketing* (pp. 206–210). Chicago: American Marketing Association.

Oliver, R.L. (1999). Whence consumer loyalty. *Journal of Marketing*, **63**(Special issue): 33–44.

Oliver, R.L. and DeSarbo, W.F. (1988). Response determinants in satisfaction judgements. *Journal of Consumer Research*, **14**(March): 495–507.

Rotfeld, H.J. (2000). The textbook effect: Conventional wisdom, myth, and error in marketing. *Journal of Marketing*, **64**(2).

Sirgy, M. Joseph, A., Samli, C. and Meadow, H.L. (1982). The interface between quality of life and marketing: A theoretical framework. *Journal of Marketing & Public Policy*, **1**(1): 69–84.

Troye, S.V. and Øgaard, T. (1999). The many effects of service: An empirical study of service and product quality in the hospitality industry. In: B. Edvardsson and A. Gustafsson (eds), *Nordic School of Quality Management* (pp. 362–392). Lund, Sweden: Studentlitteratur.

Varadarajan, P.R. (2003). From the editor: Musings on relevance and rigor of scholarly research in marketing. *Journal of the Academy of Marketing Science*, **31**(Fall): 368–376.

Varadarajan, P.R. and Jayachandran, S. (1999). Marketing strategy: An assessment of the state of the field and outlook. *Journal of the Academy of Marketing Science*, **27**(Spring): 120–143.

Vargo, S.L. and Lusch, R.F. (2004). Evolving the new dominant logic for marketing. *Journal of Marketing*, **68**(1): 1–17.

Wells, W.D. (1993). Discovery-oriented consumer research. *Journal of Consumer Research*, **19**(March): 489–504.

Wilkie, W.L. and Moore, E.S. (1999). Marketing's contribution to society. *Journal of Marketing*, **63**(Special issue), 198–218.

Wilkie, W.L. and Moore, E.S. (2003). Scholarly research in marketing: Exploring the "four eras" of thought development. *Journal of Public Policy and Marketing*, **22**(2): 116–146.

Wilson, D.T and Ghingold, M. (1980). Building theory from practice: A theory-in-use approach. In: C.W. Lamb and P.M. Dunne (eds), *Theoretical Developments in Marketing* (pp. 236–239). Chicago: American Marketing Association.

Conclusions: Reinterpreting the four Ps

13

Håkan Håkansson and Alexandra Waluszewski

If we compare the number of issues and themes covered by the current state of the art in marketing with those in the mid-20th century, the development must be considered as overwhelming. Since the "four Ps" model was launched in the 1960s, marketing has been transformed from a rather restricted and practice-oriented set of models to an established research field resting on a solid theoretical ground. With the elegant, strict and simple traditional economic assumptions behind it, marketing unfolds into a branch of economic theory appropriate for analytical issues and for producing practical managerial guidelines. The only severe problem seems to be, as was articulated in Chapter 1, the misfit between this elaborate research tool and the empirical area where it is supposed to be used. Or, to quote one of the most well-known aphorisms Mark Twain is credited with: "If the only tool you have is a hammer, you tend to approach every problem as if it were a nail."

The chapters of this book emphasize that the empirical issues of marketing are far from being so simple and straightforward that they can all be classified as "nails". Although the articles cover a wide area of issues and suggestions for how to solve them, they all pay attention to an important peculiarity of marketing: they suggest that marketing is about active counterparties' creation of an exchange of resources, when those features are never fully known. It is an issue that by definition is characterized by the presence of dynamics and interdependencies. Thus, the common message brought forward by the chapters is the urgent need for new analytical tools specifically devoted to these circumstances.

The aim of this final chapter is *not* to deliver such a tool kit, but to take some first steps on this journey by identifying some important characteristics of marketing to capture and investigate. The natural starting point for such endeavours is the marketing mix model. It is difficult to find any model that has influenced our thinking about marketing as much as the "four Ps" in the various editions Kotler's *Marketing Management* – a work once applauded as "one of the 50 top business books of all time" by the *Financial Times*. By starting out from the marketing mix model and its underlying assumptions, it is possible to identify some development paths that we need to take if we want to catch some of the main peculiarities of market exchange: that both producing and using business actors consciously struggles with creating exchange interfaces where the activated resources are treated as heterogeneous.

What's missing in the "four Ps"?

The elegant "four Ps", or marketing mix, model, presented by Rasmussen (1955), McCarthy (1960) and Kotler (1967), grew out of economic theory and embedded some of its key assumptions in the marketing analysis tool. From the outset the "four Ps" model was a resource allocation model, resting on the assumption that the relevant resources involved in the exchange process, including the products, are homogeneous. As was described in Chapter 1, when a resource is assumed to be homogeneous its economic value becomes independent of how and with which other resources it is combined. With this underlying assumption in the setting the allocation problem first shows up as an issue of how much to allocate to marketing in total. The next issue is to decide how much to allocate to each of the different means – which in the marketing mix model are the "four Ps": product, price, place and promotion. In order to work, the model has to add another important assumption: that there is a specific linear curve dependency that includes the decreasing marginal return between the resources put into a mean and the outcome. In other words, each mean must be assumed to have a specific influence on the outcome. The latter can then be formulated in different dimensions.

Without the homogeneity and one-directed dependence assumptions the model could not provide the marketing actor with the possibility of finding an optimal solution between means and outcome, of finding an optimal amount of resources to spend on marketing or an optimal division of these resources between the means (or customer segments, products or geographical markets). The homogeneity and one-directed dependence assumptions are also prerequisites to estimating the trade-off in terms of curves. Since these assumptions are shared with traditional economic theory, these analytical tools fit nicely with each other.

However, if there is something in the increasing amount of empirical observations of market conditions characterized by exchange of heterogeneous resources and interacted interdependencies, we cannot deny that there is a need for something more substantial than further complicating traditional economic assumptions. If, as we discussed in Chapter 1, a basic characteristic of business life is the interaction concerning creation of supply and use of heterogeneous resources, and if these processes create fallout in terms of relationships and embedding of resource features over the borders of companies, there is a severe need for a new theoretical point of reference. Since the early 1970s IMP (industrial marketing and purchasing) researchers and relationship marketing researchers have argued that such characteristics are not exceptions but typical features of business life. What these three decades of deep empirical studies of business exchange, carried out in several different political, geographical and economical contexts, have drawn attention to is that interaction affects both human beings and the resources involved in these processes as well as the economic outcome. These interaction processes concern how to create a supply and use of resources that are not given, and hence their value is dependent on how they can be combined with other resources; this means that market exchange presents itself as a process where the economic actors consider each other as both subjects and objects.

None of these observations are trivial from a theoretical point of view, since they challenge the basic assumptions of traditional economic theory and the two important cornerstones in the marketing mix model: the resource homogeneity and one-directed dependence assumptions. Thus, if we agree with the empirical observations of interaction and how it appears in business life, then we also have to abandon the idea that marketing takes place between autonomous units exchanging homogeneous resources. In other words, we have to change the view of what companies can do in a dramatic way. We can no longer assume that companies are searching for optimal allocations of given resources. With interaction between subjects concerning heterogeneous resources a basic point of reference, we have to regard company life as opportunity-driven: companies will try to develop non-given resources through interaction with active counterparts in order to create economic values.

Furthermore, with this basic point of reference the understanding of how business activities can be captured is also dramatically changed. If we assume that interaction between conscious and active subjects concerning heterogeneous resources occurs in and, presumably, also characterizes business life, then we have to develop research tools able to address the fact that companies are living in a world of movement and change. Or, as Scott (2001, p. 917) puts it: "If structures exist it is because they are continually being created and recreated, and if the world has a meaning, it is because actors are constructing and reconstructing intentions and accounts, and thereby their own and the others' identities." Thus, investigating marketing is trying to capture an empirical world that is not at all given but constructed by the companies involved which are constantly wrestling with the issue of how to combine and activate resources over company and organizational borders. It is like trying to capture a world in motion.

Marketing is dealing with dynamics

To point out that a resource homogeneity assumption needs to be replaced by a resource heterogeneity assumption can at first glance appear rather trivial. But, while the first assumption evokes a static economic world where allocation is the key issue (as in the marketing mix model), the alternative produces the opposite view – exchange deals with dynamic creation of new solutions. Furthermore, as all the chapters have illustrated, these alteration forces tend to express themselves in many ways, something that certainly makes great demands on both the construction and use of analytical tools. If Snehota (Chapter 2) is right, then dynamics is a compulsory feature of exchange. The question is how it will appear and whether we are able to catch its appearance. Blois (Chapter 3) also emphasizes that dynamics is a basic characteristic of exchange. However, he argues that this will transfer specialized markets to situations that are closer to classical market assumptions. In Chapter 4, Easton, who applies a different methodological perspective, presents another interpretation of the effects of market dynamics: increased variety in the exchange process.

The dynamic feature of exchange also comes to the fore when approaching exchange from the perspective of interaction between individual market actors. Håkansson and Prenkert (Chapter 5) reveal how the view of marketing activities interacts with both what researchers are able to see and what marketing actors are able to perform. The authors stress that if marketing actors apply an interactive perspective toward exchange, both the possibilities to create change and direct it in a certain way increase. A similar understanding is expressed by Ford and Ritter (Chapter 6), who draw attention to the deep interaction between actors on both the supply and user side of an exchange interface, including the essential role of this process in product development. In Chapters 7 and 8, Selnes & Johnson and Anderson, respectively, illustrate how the dynamic features of exchange can be utilized in the creation of customer value, while Gadde and Person (Chapter 9) discuss how the purchasing side contributes to the value-creating process.

Almost all the chapters touch on the fact that any ambition to capture the dynamic features of marketing and exchange puts both the analytical tools and the way to use them under pressure. However, when considering marketing from a scientific perspective the close connection between the research tools used and the images of the empirical world they produce becomes obvious. Gripsrud (Chapter 10) shows how a dynamic perspective of marketing calls for a broader perspective on the resources and functions involved in the exchange process. The author illustrates how distribution, which since the introduction of the "four Ps" generally has been regarded as a cost, in an interactive, resource heterogeneity perspective also appears as an important source for creation of benefits. In Chapter 11, Dubois and Araujo emphasize the necessity of incorporating time as an attribute, in order to capture the dynamic features of market exchange. Troye and Howell (Chapter 12) stress the close connection between identified opportunities and the approaches used to produce them. The authors reveal how the analytical tools, the assumptions embedded in them and the methods with which they are used bring forth certain managerial possibilities. What all these authors stress is that the characteristics of the analytical tools used to investigate marketing influences the pictures produced and the opportunities identified by academics as well as managers.

In sum, if we suspect that the resources exchanged in marketing processes are heterogeneous (i.e., their values are dependent on how active counterparts can create combinations that can be embedded in their different business activities), then there is an urgent need to incorporate dynamics in marketing theory. This need is not due to any indication that the general level of change should be higher today than 50 or 100 years ago or that resource heterogeneity should be a new or increasing phenomenon; however, what obviously has changed is the pattern of resources, which have been combined and embedded in highly integrated structures that stretch beyond the borders of companies and organizations. Marketing is no longer an issue that can be dealt with within two or three interfaces between companies with integrated production and use of certain resources. Due to conscious actors' endeavours to develop new technological solutions *and* efficient production structures, increasingly intricate patterns of related resource interfaces are created; these are the result of interaction processes that often stretch over several company and organizational borders, where predecessors of related resources are systematically trying to influence each other. Such interaction processes have both short and long-term effects. They not only create specific, new solutions that can be embedded in the existing structure but also prepare the ground for larger investments and structural changes.

But, if empirical observations of marketing evoke a world of interdependent actors systematically interacting concerning the ways partially unknown resources can be combined in order to create value, why then has the static "four Ps" model shown such fantastic vitality? There must be something more in this vigorous model than its ability to supply market analysts with simple guidelines on how to cope with allocation issues. One explanation behind the vital force of the "four Ps" model is that it clearly identifies four important issues from an empirical perspective. The model draws rings around the exchanged *product* and three related aspects; its *price*, the *place* where it is available and the *promotion* with which it is brought forward. Any interpreter of marketing would most likely agree that these four features are important ingredients in the exchange process, whether viewed from an academic or business perspective. However, what is more interesting is that the "four Ps" appear quite differently when viewing them from an assumption of resource heterogeneity versus homogeneity.

Products – given solutions or open opportunities?

When making empirical observations of exchange the *product* must be regarded as one of the most visible indications of what is going on. In the marketing mix model the product is also credited with the role of being the basic resource involved in the exchange process. Assuming resource homogeneity the product is treated as given but also as being generic in nature. Consequently, the product is seen as the result of a production system of which its features and value are independent. It is regarded as an input in a user system that affects neither its features nor its value. In other words, there is no need to pay close attention to the system that handles the product's supply and use; the focus can instead be concentrated on how the product is composed and presented by the producing company. In comparison with the marketing mix model's other Ps, however, the *product* is supposed to have a distinguished position in the exchange process. The homogeneous and solitary product is given the double role of being a basic parameter determining the borders of the market and a means that, in combination with the other three Ps, has a direct influence on the outcome.

An interactive perspective grounded in assumptions of resource heterogeneity does not detract from the fact that a product can be an important parameter in market conditions and a means in the exchange process. However, it is problematic to reduce the complexity of the product to being no more than this; it is like cutting out a small, static slice of something much bigger, which also includes a wide variety of dynamic aspects. When the features of a resource, such as a product, are not regarded as given, but created in interaction, neither its features nor its value in the exchange process can be determined from the product itself. The same applies from the producing company's perspective. If, as Penrose (1959) puts it, the value of a resource is determined by "the services it yields", both the features and the value of a product are issues of how it is combined with other resources and of how the results of these combinations are actively embedded in the structures related to the supply and user sides, respectively.

Thus, in this perspective the product is much more than a given unit, which the supply and user structures are automatically adapting to (free of cost); instead, the product appears as a carrier of both opportunities and restrictions, and therefore tensions. Its features and value are created in interaction processes that can involve technical resources (such as the use of internal and external distribution and production facilities) as well as internal and external social resources (such as the skills of human beings) embedded in business units and business relationships. It is impossible to find an optimal solution to how to combine a product and other related resources when they are characterized by heterogeneity. However, by actively relating resource combinations on the supply and user side to the product, several of these resources, including the product, can be developed. This process is far from automatic or cost-free, but can lead to a conscious, directed development of related resources; this increases their value in certain combinations and decreases the likelihood of value creation in other combinations. This implies that a product will always be exposed to suggestions of change from actors engaged in handling interfaces where it is combined with other resources on both its supply and user side. Whenever changed or just activated in another way the product will also create tension in both direct and indirect related interfaces. In other words, embedding a product into supply and user interfaces means embedding a source of dynamics into them.

The empirical pictures produced using an investigation tool resting on a resource heterogeneity assumption also emphasize that the exchange of a product is not something that takes place in isolation, but in a context full of restrictions *and* possibilities. In the chapters of this book we have seen how the features and the value of a product can be developed by engaging the producing company to interact with purchasing functions of the using side, the technological development functions of several direct or indirect related companies and the different functions of independent intermediaries, such as distributors. Since the product has to fit into all these structures it is exposed to a wide variety of complementary or contradictory demands; this means that the product never has the same role in the different structures it is related to, due to its supply and use. Consequently, a product's features and value are always a result of compromises between different requests.

From this perspective the marketing mix model's reduction of the product to a given, basic parameter of the boundaries of the market appears as rather unfair, something that is illustrated by Selnes and Johnson (Chapter 7) and Easton (Chapter 4). Although it is possible and probable that some actors choose to see the product as a given, it can simultaneously be treated as a variable by other actors, with the possibility of being developed due to how it is combined with other resources. The peculiarity that the product's role in the exchange process is affected by the way it is viewed by academic or business actors is highlighted by Håkansson and Prenkert (Chapter 5). In three out of the four identified models of exchange, aspects other than products were credited with important contributions to this process. Products were certainly involved in all these three perspectives; but rather than dominating the exchange process they were subordinate to other aspects.

When searching for new tools for marketing analysis a key aspect seems to be the need to catch the dynamic features of a product (i.e., the opportunities, restrictions and tensions it carries with it or is exposed to). It must be possible to identify the interfaces between a focal product and other resources related to its supply and use and what is happening in them; this means that the research tool has to allow the investigation of the role of the product both as an individual resource and as part of a larger system. This is similar to what was articulated in the innovation literature (e.g., von Hippel, 1998), in studies of technological development (e.g., Rosenberg, 1994; Hughes, 1998; van de Ven et al., 1999) and by scholars dealing with technological interdependences (e.g., Stabell and Fjeldstad, 1998). Such models would allow the study of both how the product is viewed and the effect of this view: as long as the product is treated as a given, subordinate to other technical or social resources and, thus, handled as an outcome of and compromise between other interaction processes. Alternatively, the product is given a more dynamic role in the exchange process, forcing the development of both itself and other technical and social resources that are directly and indirectly related to its supply and use. In other words, we need a marketing analysis tool that allows for the investigation of both restrictions and opportunities when heterogeneous resources and the business actors' conscious work with them are included in the product exchange process.

Price – the only element that does not produce costs?

When considering how pricing is approached in the marketing mix model, once again the heritage from economic theory becomes clear. Due to the resource homogeneity assumption, it is solely through its price that a product can contribute to creating revenue. Or, as Kotler (1991, p. 474) puts it: "Price is the only element in the marketing mix that produces revenue; the other elements produce costs." According to traditional economic theory, however, price is something a company need not worry about. The price of a product is independent of any individual user's preferences and of the way in which the product is combined with other resources. Price is given by the interplay between supply and demand. Whenever there is a pure market situation a company cannot affect the price and has to be a price-taker. In the marketing mix model, however, companies are supposed to be able to modify the price in order to create an optimal mix between market share, revenue and profit. Thus, it is generally assumed that business actors are working in a market characterized by monopolistic competition.

From an interactive resource heterogeneity perspective, however, price no longer appears to be the only element that produces revenue. Any resource, be it a product, a production facility, a business unit or a business relationship, can be used both to reduce costs and create benefits. Furthermore, the possibility of increasing the value of a product by changing the way it is combined with other resources on both its supply and user sides implies that price is not necessarily driven by the market, but can be one of several factors affected by resource interaction; this means that price can always be influenced by directly or indirectly related business actors. That price can be affected by active counterparts' engagement in resource interaction is illustrated by Anderson (Chapter 8) and Gadde and Persson (Chapter 9). These authors reveal a phenomenon that is also familiar to accounting theory scholars: how companies actively build physical and social resource combinations with the aim of influencing not only costs but also the value of these resources and, thereby, also the price.

A second key aspect when searching for new tools for marketing analysis seems to be the need to grasp the dynamic features of price (i.e., how actively confronting resources can affect it). Instead of being driven by the intersection of the demand and supply curves the price of a product or any other resource appears as a function of how it is embedded in the structure of its producer and user side; this implies, for example, that a structure in which business actors are consciously directing and combining resources in relation to each other (i.e., a network-like structure) can create a lower price for a certain product compared with a structure behaving in accordance with traditional market exchange. Thus, a marketing analysis tool has to allow for investigation of how price is created by business actors engaged in developing resource combinations; for example, how price is an integral part of the way in which physical resources (products and production facilities) and social resources (business units and business relationships) are combined within and over company and organizational borders.

Place – a cost for connecting supply with demand or a source for value creation?

In the marketing mix model the place issue is equal to handling a distribution channel that brings the given product to its potential users, and the main task is to link an existing supply to an existing demand. Or, to use the wording of Kotler (1991, p. 70), it is the "various activities the company undertakes to make the product easily accessible and available to target customers." Since the distribution channel is a cost and a means that can create a certain outcome, attention is directed to how best to balance it by choosing between different kinds of internal or external channel solutions and creating a suitable mix between it, price and promotion of the product. In accordance with its heritage from traditional economic theory, in the marketing mix model's interpretation the chosen channel is regarded as having no influence on the resources distributed through it. As was underlined earlier by Ford and Ritter (Chapter 6) and Gripsrud (Chapter 10), this is also a view that characterizes the state of the art of the research area that explicitly focuses on place issues. Although distribution scholars have opened up the perspective to include, for example, questions about reducing uncertainty and handling power dependency, the place issue is still dealt with as a "how-to-handle-distance" problem as a creator of costs and not of benefits.

The place issue deals with much more than the question about connecting a given supply to a given demand, as has been articulated by scholars engaged in cluster and industrial district research. Although these research traditions represent a rather wide variety of approaches, emphasizing the role of competition as well as co-operation, they share the common understanding that place is not only a cost driver but also includes features that can create benefits. These benefits are mainly seen in the learning processes that can occur within special places, within districts or clusters where the traditional, anonymous market exchange due to proximity has been replaced by interaction and relationships. The localization of related industries within clusters facilitates knowledge spillover. Thus, according to industrial district and cluster scholars, these islands of dense relationships in an otherwise traditional market appear as important sources of knowledge, useful in product development and value creation.

An interactive perspective resting on a resource heterogeneity assumption agrees with the understanding that the place issue is much richer than simply being the cost of bringing the product from the producer to the user. However, place-related qualities are not limited to special geographical areas where the traditional market exchange is played out in favour of relationships. Whether or not there is any geographical proximity between the parties engaged in the exchange process, the activated resources are characterized by place-related features. Any resource – a product, a production facility, a business unit or business relationship – can include place-related features; these can be both costs and benefits, depending on how resources are combined. This understanding has important consequences for the way in which functions are viewed which in a traditional perspective are treated as being solely a cost and a means, such as the distribution channel. Like any resource involved in the exchange process, these resource combinations appear as important sources for the development of new features of resources and, thus, for the creation of economic benefits.

Consequently, since the resources involved in the market exchange process involve different functions of different companies and organizations in different locations, creating an economic value of place can be regarded as an issue of identifying and developing new combinations. How can the features of a product, some production facilities including a distribution channel, some business units and business relationships be combined in new ways to create economic benefits? From this perspective a company's or a group of companies' creation of economic benefits can also be a result of their skill in transferring and transforming physical and social resources, available elsewhere, because of their ability to take advantage of locally available resources. Place appears to be a heterogeneous phenomenon, created by each company at each place, because of its way of combining local and distant resources. Thus, place must be approached as a dependent variable – something a company can reduce to a cost issue or actively try to utilize in the exchange process.

A third key aspect when searching for new marketing analysis tools seems to be the need to catch the dynamic features of a place (i.e., how place-related features interact with the resources that are activated in the exchange process). Such a research tool has to allow for the investigation of place as an object of analysis in itself. In other words, how can it be used consciously by business actors in order to reduce costs and create benefits?

Promotion – a cost for one-way communication or a double-sided value creation process?

The promotion issue is in the marketing model's interpretation a question of how to send a message about a given product to potential users. Promotion, according to Kotler (1991, p. 49), is "the various activities that a company undertakes to communicate the product's merits and persuade target customers to buy them." Like the price and place elements, promotion is not supposed to have any effect on the features of the products involved nor is the promotion endeavour considered to have any influence on the structure that is related to the production and use of promoted products. Assuming resource homogeneity, promotion appears to be an issue of how to create an optimal mix of communication tools in order to get a product's message from the producer to the user. Although feedback is ascribed an important role in this process, its content is mainly considered as evidence of how well the company has succeeded in communicating a certain message.

If a resource homogeneity assumption ascribes to the product a distinguished position in market exchange, then a resource heterogeneity assumption gives the promotion or communication element an extraordinary role in these processes. From the latter perspective, promotion appears to be much more than a directed means which in response to a certain cost can be used to send a message about a product from a given supply to a given demand. First, promotion or communication is assumed to be a double-sided process (i.e., it is approached as interaction). This interaction is not restricted to just a focal exchange interface, it can also involve predecessors of directly and indirectly related resources. Thus, interaction takes place within companies, over the borders of companies and over the borders of visible relationships.

Second, interaction creates fallout in terms of features of both the physical and social resources involved. This process is far from the assumption of the one-directed communication described above. Instead, it is a process whereby direct and indirect resources are confronted and recombined, thus creating new features of physical resources, such as products and production facilities, and/or social resources, such as business units and business relationships. Since these resources are developed in interaction a directed and co-ordinated development pattern is created that stretches over the borders of companies and organizations. Communication in terms of interaction is considered as a fundamental mechanism in the market exchange process. It is a process that:

1. Constructs the structure behind an exchange interface. It is through interaction that a certain resource combination (a product and the structures behind its production and use) is created.
2. Holds together the structure behind an exchange interface. It is through interaction that the structures responsible for the production and use of a certain resource combination are co-ordinated, adapted and made more efficient.
3. Develops the structure behind an exchange interface. It is through interaction that the resources related to the production and use of a certain resource combination are confronted and recombined (i.e., that new features and economic values are created).

Hence, in a resource heterogeneity perspective, interaction appears to be crucial for the transformation of physical and social elements to resources with an economic value. Interaction has a double role in this process: it is essential both in the creation of economic resources and in the creation of market exchange. Crediting interaction with such an importance (instead of reducing it to a one-directed promotion issue) implies that the issue of creating active communication between business actors should be at the top of the marketing agenda, something that was illustrated by Troye and Howell (Chapter 12) and Ford and Ritter (Chapter 6). As soon as knowledge about the resource involved in exchange is incomplete, business actors' active and conscious engagement in resource interaction appears to be an essential element in the value creation process and to be an infinite source of dynamics; this stresses the importance of considering the role and features of social resources. Both business units and business relationships can be more or less consciously adapted to identify and handle interactive issues. An interesting complication concerns how to interact with predecessors of indirectly related resource interfaces (i.e., those that are not available through existing business relationships).

A fourth key aspect when searching for new marketing analysis tools seems to be the need to catch the dynamic features of promotion and communication (i.e., the role of interaction and the effects on both economic resources and the market exchange process).

Thus, it has to allow the investigation of interaction in business actors' handling of the interface between physical and social resources. We need a research tool that facilitates the investigation of how interaction shapes and directs features of physical and social resources and how this influences their economic value.

Four distinctly different Ps – which can all contribute to the creation of benefits

To summarize, when considering the four Ps from an interactive, resource heterogeneity perspective, the empirical issues they represent still appear to be extremely important characteristics in the market exchange process. What also becomes clear is how distinctly different the "four Ps" present themselves from a resource heterogeneity perspective. If the "four Ps", viewed from the latter perspective, have any genuine commonality it is that they are all carriers of opportunities and restrictions and, thus, are important sources of dynamics. However, they appear to have a completely different logic and, consequently, there is a need for different models or tools to analyse them. However, it is possible to find a logic wherein they relate to each other.

Two "Ps" appear to be essential in the creation of economic resources and market exchange

Promotion, or rather *interaction*, appears as the elixir of life in the market exchange process. It is promotion in terms of interaction concerning the features and abilities of resources that gives rise to the creation of economic value and market exchange.

Place appears to be the elixir of life in the value creation process. It is through identifying and combining features of resources at different locations that are related through the market exchange process (i.e., products and production facilities including distribution channels) in business units and business relationships that new economic value can be created.

Two "Ps" appear to be embedded in the logic of promotion and place

Price appears to be the outcome of the structure that has been created in the promotion and place processes. It is through relating the structures responsible for production and use of a certain resource combination that price is created. Through such processes price can even become lower than in a situation where there is a pure market solution.

Product also appears to be the outcome of the structure that has been created in the promotion and place processes. The product is created through the structures that are responsible for its production and use, which consequently are of utmost importance in the product development process. However, to solely focus on products seems too narrow a perspective. Another physical resource of great importance in the product creation process is the production facility. Furthermore, social resources, such as business units and business relationships, are also of great importance in this process.

References

Hughes, T. (1998). *Rescuing Prometheus: Four Monumental Projects that Changed the Modern World*. New York.

Kotler, P. (1967). *Marketing Management: Analysis, Planning, and Control*. Englewood Cliffs, NJ: Prentice Hall.

Kotler, P. (1991). *Marketing Management: Analysis, Planning, Implementation and Control* (7th edn). Englewood Cliffs, NJ: Prentice Hall.

McCarthy, J.E. (1960). *Basic Marketing: A Managerial Approach*. Homewood, IL: Richard D. Irwin.

Penrose, E.T. (1959) *The Theory of the Growth of the Firm*. Oxford, UK: Basil Blackwell.

Rasmussen, A. (1955). *Pristeori eller parameterteori*. København: Copenhagen School of Business [in Danish].

Rosenberg, N. (1994). *Exploring the Black Box: Technology Economics and History*. Cambridge, UK: Cambridge University Press.

Scott, R.W. (2001). Organizations overview. In: N.J. Smelser and P.B. Baltes (eds), *International Encyclopedia of the Social and Behavioral Sciences* (Vol. 16, pp. 910–917) Amsterdam: Pergamon.

Stabell, C. and Fjeldstad, Ø. (1998). Configuring value for competitive advantage: On chains, shops and networks. *Strategic Management Journal,* **19**: 413–437.

Van de Ven, A., Polley, D., Garud, R. and Venkataraman, S. (1999). *The Innovation Journey.* Oxford, UK: Oxford University Press.

Von Hippel, E. (1998). Economics of product development by users: The impact of "sticky" local information. *Management Science,* **44**(5): 629–644.

Wilk, R.R. (1996). *Economics and Cultures. Foundation of Economic Anthropology.* Oxford, UK: Westview Press.

Index